FREE Test Taking Tips Video/DVD Offer

To better serve you, we created videos covering test taking tips that we want to give you for FREE. **These videos cover world-class tips that will help you succeed on your test.**

We just ask that you send us feedback about this product. Please let us know what you thought about it—whether good, bad, or indifferent.

To get your **FREE videos**, you can use the QR code below or email freevideos@studyguideteam.com with "Free Videos" in the subject line and the following information in the body of the email:

   a. The title of your product

   b. Your product rating on a scale of 1-5, with 5 being the highest

   c. Your feedback about the product

If you have any questions or concerns, please don't hesitate to contact us at info@studyguideteam.com.

Thank you!

ATI TEAS 7 Math Workbook
TEAS Test Prep with Practice Problems

Joshua Rueda

Copyright © 2022 by TPB Publishing

All rights reserved. No part of this publication may be reproduced, distributed, or transmitted in any form or by any means, including photocopying, recording, or other electronic or mechanical methods, without the prior written permission of the publisher, except in the case of brief quotations embodied in critical reviews and certain other noncommercial uses permitted by copyright law.

Written and edited by TPB Publishing.

TPB Publishing is not associated with or endorsed by any official testing organization. TPB Publishing is a publisher of unofficial educational products. All test and organization names are trademarks of their respective owners. Content in this book is included for utilitarian purposes only and does not constitute an endorsement by TPB Publishing of any particular point of view.

Interested in buying more than 10 copies of our product? Contact us about bulk discounts:
bulkorders@studyguideteam.com

ISBN 13: 9781637753569
ISBN 10: 163775356X

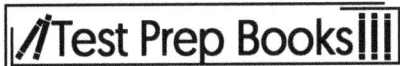

Table of Contents

Quick Overview 1

Test-Taking Strategies 2

FREE Videos/DVD OFFER 6

Introduction for the TEAS 7 7

Study Prep Plan 10

Reference Sheet 12

Numbers and Operations 13

    Numbers 13

    Place Value 17

    Fractions 28

    Decimals 51

    Percentages 59

    Arithmetic Operations 66

    Estimation and Rounding 88

    Translating Phrases and Sentences 93

Patterns, Relationships, and Algebraic Reasoning 99

    Creating Patterns 99

    Comparing and Ordering Rational Numbers 104

    Solving Equations in One Variable 107

    Solving Real-World Problems with Rational Numbers 113

    Solving Real-World Problems with Proportions 135

    Solving Real-World Problems with Ratios 144

Geometry 153

Calculating Geometric Quantities 153

Measurement and Data *186*

Interpreting Information from Tables, Graphs, and Charts 186

Explaining the Relationship Between Two Variables 206

Evaluating Information Using Statistics 211

Converting Between Standard and Metric Systems 216

Index *225*

Quick Overview

As you draw closer to taking your exam, effective preparation becomes more and more important. Thankfully, you have this study guide to help you get ready. Use this guide to help keep your studying on track and refer to it often.

This study guide contains several key sections that will help you be successful on your exam. The guide contains tips for what you should do the night before and the day of the test. Also included are test-taking tips. Knowing the right information is not always enough. Many well-prepared test takers struggle with exams. These tips will help equip you to accurately read, assess, and answer test questions.

A large part of the guide is devoted to showing you what content to expect on the exam and to helping you better understand that content. In this guide are practice test questions so that you can see how well you have grasped the content. Then, answer explanations are provided so that you can understand why you missed certain questions.

Don't try to cram the night before you take your exam. This is not a wise strategy for a few reasons. First, your retention of the information will be low. Your time would be better used by reviewing information you already know rather than trying to learn a lot of new information. Second, you will likely become stressed as you try to gain a large amount of knowledge in a short amount of time. Third, you will be depriving yourself of sleep. So be sure to go to bed at a reasonable time the night before. Being well-rested helps you focus and remain calm.

Be sure to eat a substantial breakfast the morning of the exam. If you are taking the exam in the afternoon, be sure to have a good lunch as well. Being hungry is distracting and can make it difficult to focus. You have hopefully spent lots of time preparing for the exam. Don't let an empty stomach get in the way of success!

When travelling to the testing center, leave earlier than needed. That way, you have a buffer in case you experience any delays. This will help you remain calm and will keep you from missing your appointment time at the testing center.

Be sure to pace yourself during the exam. Don't try to rush through the exam. There is no need to risk performing poorly on the exam just so you can leave the testing center early. Allow yourself to use all of the allotted time if needed.

Remain positive while taking the exam even if you feel like you are performing poorly. Thinking about the content you should have mastered will not help you perform better on the exam.

Once the exam is complete, take some time to relax. Even if you feel that you need to take the exam again, you will be well served by some down time before you begin studying again. It's often easier to convince yourself to study if you know that it will come with a reward!

Test-Taking Strategies

1. Predicting the Answer

When you feel confident in your preparation for a multiple-choice test, try predicting the answer before reading the answer choices. This is especially useful on questions that test objective factual knowledge. By predicting the answer before reading the available choices, you eliminate the possibility that you will be distracted or led astray by an incorrect answer choice. You will feel more confident in your selection if you read the question, predict the answer, and then find your prediction among the answer choices. After using this strategy, be sure to still read all of the answer choices carefully and completely. If you feel unprepared, you should not attempt to predict the answers. This would be a waste of time and an opportunity for your mind to wander in the wrong direction.

2. Reading the Whole Question

Too often, test takers scan a multiple-choice question, recognize a few familiar words, and immediately jump to the answer choices. Test authors are aware of this common impatience, and they will sometimes prey upon it. For instance, a test author might subtly turn the question into a negative, or he or she might redirect the focus of the question right at the end. The only way to avoid falling into these traps is to read the entirety of the question carefully before reading the answer choices.

3. Looking for Wrong Answers

Long and complicated multiple-choice questions can be intimidating. One way to simplify a difficult multiple-choice question is to eliminate all of the answer choices that are clearly wrong. In most sets of answers, there will be at least one selection that can be dismissed right away. If the test is administered on paper, the test taker could draw a line through it to indicate that it may be ignored; otherwise, the test taker will have to perform this operation mentally or on scratch paper. In either case, once the obviously incorrect answers have been eliminated, the remaining choices may be considered. Sometimes identifying the clearly wrong answers will give the test taker some information about the correct answer. For instance, if one of the remaining answer choices is a direct opposite of one of the eliminated answer choices, it may well be the correct answer. The opposite of obviously wrong is obviously right! Of course, this is not always the case. Some answers are obviously incorrect simply because they are irrelevant to the question being asked. Still, identifying and eliminating some incorrect answer choices is a good way to simplify a multiple-choice question.

4. Don't Overanalyze

Anxious test takers often overanalyze questions. When you are nervous, your brain will often run wild, causing you to make associations and discover clues that don't actually exist. If you feel that this may be a problem for you, do whatever you can to slow down during the test. Try taking a deep breath or counting to ten. As you read and consider the question, restrict yourself to the particular words used by the author. Avoid thought tangents about what the author *really* meant, or what he or she was *trying* to say. The only things that matter on a multiple-choice test are the words that are actually in the question. You must avoid reading too much into a multiple-choice question, or supposing that the writer meant something other than what he or she wrote.

5. No Need for Panic

It is wise to learn as many strategies as possible before taking a multiple-choice test, but it is likely that you will come across a few questions for which you simply don't know the answer. In this situation, avoid panicking. Because most multiple-choice tests include dozens of questions, the relative value of a single wrong answer is small. As much as possible, you should compartmentalize each question on a multiple-choice test. In other words, you should not allow your feelings about one question to affect your success on the others. When you find a question that you either don't understand or don't know how to answer, just take a deep breath and do your best. Read the entire question slowly and carefully. Try rephrasing the question a couple of different ways. Then, read all of the answer choices carefully. After eliminating obviously wrong answers, make a selection and move on to the next question.

6. Confusing Answer Choices

When working on a difficult multiple-choice question, there may be a tendency to focus on the answer choices that are the easiest to understand. Many people, whether consciously or not, gravitate to the answer choices that require the least concentration, knowledge, and memory. This is a mistake. When you come across an answer choice that is confusing, you should give it extra attention. A question might be confusing because you do not know the subject matter to which it refers. If this is the case, don't eliminate the answer before you have affirmatively settled on another. When you come across an answer choice of this type, set it aside as you look at the remaining choices. If you can confidently assert that one of the other choices is correct, you can leave the confusing answer aside. Otherwise, you will need to take a moment to try to better understand the confusing answer choice. Rephrasing is one way to tease out the sense of a confusing answer choice.

7. Your First Instinct

Many people struggle with multiple-choice tests because they overthink the questions. If you have studied sufficiently for the test, you should be prepared to trust your first instinct once you have carefully and completely read the question and all of the answer choices. There is a great deal of research suggesting that the mind can come to the correct conclusion very quickly once it has obtained all of the relevant information. At times, it may seem to you as if your intuition is working faster even than your reasoning mind. This may in fact be true. The knowledge you obtain while studying may be retrieved from your subconscious before you have a chance to work out the associations that support it. Verify your instinct by working out the reasons that it should be trusted.

8. Key Words

Many test takers struggle with multiple-choice questions because they have poor reading comprehension skills. Quickly reading and understanding a multiple-choice question requires a mixture of skill and experience. To help with this, try jotting down a few key words and phrases on a piece of scrap paper. Doing this concentrates the process of reading and forces the mind to weigh the relative importance of the question's parts. In selecting words and phrases to write down, the test taker thinks about the question more deeply and carefully. This is especially true for multiple-choice questions that are preceded by a long prompt.

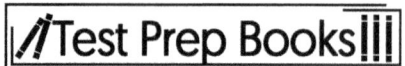

Test-Taking Strategies

9. Subtle Negatives

One of the oldest tricks in the multiple-choice test writer's book is to subtly reverse the meaning of a question with a word like *not* or *except*. If you are not paying attention to each word in the question, you can easily be led astray by this trick. For instance, a common question format is, "Which of the following is…?" Obviously, if the question instead is, "Which of the following is not…?," then the answer will be quite different. Even worse, the test makers are aware of the potential for this mistake and will include one answer choice that would be correct if the question were not negated or reversed. A test taker who misses the reversal will find what he or she believes to be a correct answer and will be so confident that he or she will fail to reread the question and discover the original error. The only way to avoid this is to practice a wide variety of multiple-choice questions and to pay close attention to each and every word.

10. Reading Every Answer Choice

It may seem obvious, but you should always read every one of the answer choices! Too many test takers fall into the habit of scanning the question and assuming that they understand the question because they recognize a few key words. From there, they pick the first answer choice that answers the question they believe they have read. Test takers who read all of the answer choices might discover that one of the latter answer choices is actually *more* correct. Moreover, reading all of the answer choices can remind you of facts related to the question that can help you arrive at the correct answer. Sometimes, a misstatement or incorrect detail in one of the latter answer choices will trigger your memory of the subject and will enable you to find the right answer. Failing to read all of the answer choices is like not reading all of the items on a restaurant menu: you might miss out on the perfect choice.

11. Spot the Hedges

One of the keys to success on multiple-choice tests is paying close attention to every word. This is never truer than with words like almost, most, some, and sometimes. These words are called "hedges" because they indicate that a statement is not totally true or not true in every place and time. An absolute statement will contain no hedges, but in many subjects, the answers are not always straightforward or absolute. There are always exceptions to the rules in these subjects. For this reason, you should favor those multiple-choice questions that contain hedging language. The presence of qualifying words indicates that the author is taking special care with his or her words, which is certainly important when composing the right answer. After all, there are many ways to be wrong, but there is only one way to be right! For this reason, it is wise to avoid answers that are absolute when taking a multiple-choice test. An absolute answer is one that says things are either all one way or all another. They often include words like *every*, *always*, *best*, and *never*. If you are taking a multiple-choice test in a subject that doesn't lend itself to absolute answers, be on your guard if you see any of these words.

12. Long Answers

In many subject areas, the answers are not simple. As already mentioned, the right answer often requires hedges. Another common feature of the answers to a complex or subjective question are qualifying clauses, which are groups of words that subtly modify the meaning of the sentence. If the question or answer choice describes a rule to which there are exceptions or the subject matter is complicated, ambiguous, or confusing, the correct answer will require many words in order to be expressed clearly and accurately. In essence, you should not be deterred by answer choices that seem

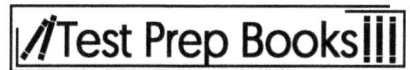

excessively long. Oftentimes, the author of the text will not be able to write the correct answer without offering some qualifications and modifications. Your job is to read the answer choices thoroughly and completely and to select the one that most accurately and precisely answers the question.

13. Restating to Understand

Sometimes, a question on a multiple-choice test is difficult not because of what it asks but because of how it is written. If this is the case, restate the question or answer choice in different words. This process serves a couple of important purposes. First, it forces you to concentrate on the core of the question. In order to rephrase the question accurately, you have to understand it well. Rephrasing the question will concentrate your mind on the key words and ideas. Second, it will present the information to your mind in a fresh way. This process may trigger your memory and render some useful scrap of information picked up while studying.

14. True Statements

Sometimes an answer choice will be true in itself, but it does not answer the question. This is one of the main reasons why it is essential to read the question carefully and completely before proceeding to the answer choices. Too often, test takers skip ahead to the answer choices and look for true statements. Having found one of these, they are content to select it without reference to the question above. Obviously, this provides an easy way for test makers to play tricks. The savvy test taker will always read the entire question before turning to the answer choices. Then, having settled on a correct answer choice, he or she will refer to the original question and ensure that the selected answer is relevant. The mistake of choosing a correct-but-irrelevant answer choice is especially common on questions related to specific pieces of objective knowledge. A prepared test taker will have a wealth of factual knowledge at his or her disposal, and should not be careless in its application.

15. No Patterns

One of the more dangerous ideas that circulates about multiple-choice tests is that the correct answers tend to fall into patterns. These erroneous ideas range from a belief that B and C are the most common right answers, to the idea that an unprepared test-taker should answer "A-B-A-C-A-D-A-B-A." It cannot be emphasized enough that pattern-seeking of this type is exactly the WRONG way to approach a multiple-choice test. To begin with, it is highly unlikely that the test maker will plot the correct answers according to some predetermined pattern. The questions are scrambled and delivered in a random order. Furthermore, even if the test maker was following a pattern in the assignation of correct answers, there is no reason why the test taker would know which pattern he or she was using. Any attempt to discern a pattern in the answer choices is a waste of time and a distraction from the real work of taking the test. A test taker would be much better served by extra preparation before the test than by reliance on a pattern in the answers.

FREE Videos/DVD OFFER

Doing well on your exam requires both knowing the test content and understanding how to use that knowledge to do well on the test. We offer completely FREE test taking tip videos. **These videos cover world-class tips that you can use to succeed on your test.**

To get your **FREE videos**, you can use the QR code below or email freevideos@studyguideteam.com with "Free Videos" in the subject line and the following information in the body of the email:

    a. The title of your product

    b. Your product rating on a scale of 1-5, with 5 being the highest

    c. Your feedback about the product

If you have any questions or concerns, please don't hesitate to contact us at info@studyguideteam.com.

Thanks again!

Introduction for the TEAS 7

Background of the ATI TEAS

The Test of Essential Academic Skills (TEAS) is a standardized test created and distributed by Assessment Technologies Institute (ATI) to examine the test taker's aptitude for skillsets fundamental to a career in nursing. As such, the TEAS is used by nursing schools and allied health schools in the United States and Canada as a chief criterion for admission. The TEAS is currently in its seventh iteration.

The TEAS 7 is a nationwide test, and there is no variation in the difficulty of content among the versions given from state to state; the content of the TEAS is a standard measure for entry-level skills and abilities for nursing applicants. However, the required minimum TEAS scores can vary widely between schools and programs. Because the TEAS is used for admission to nursing and allied health programs, the majority of TEAS takers are high school diploma or GED graduates pursuing a career in nursing or are applicants to programs requiring prerequisite academic coursework. These applicants can range in background from sophomore-level collegiates to professionals looking to change careers into a healthcare field.

Test Administration

The TEAS 7 may be administered by a PSI testing center or a nursing or allied health school. The testing schedule is chosen by each individual facility, and the regularity of testing can vary from major metropolitan areas (where it may be offered multiple times per week in several locations) to sparsely populated towns (where it may be offered once per month every hundred miles). The test will also be proctored to ensure that testing protocols are enforced. Test takers can register at atitesting.com or directly through the school to which they wish to apply, as most nursing schools offer the test on-campus periodically throughout the year. The cost to take the TEAS 7 is set by the local administrator.

Students may retake the TEAS 7, but most schools have limitations regarding the number of days students must wait between attempts or the number of attempts students may make in a given period. For instance, many schools will accept the higher score of two attempts within a twelve-month period but will not consider a third attempt until twelve months has lapsed since the first attempt. Disability accommodations are generally available and can be arranged by contacting the local test administration site.

Test Format

The TEAS 7 is comprised of 150 questions. The questions are divided between four subject areas: Reading, Mathematics, Science, and English & Language Usage. There will also be 20 unscored "pretest"

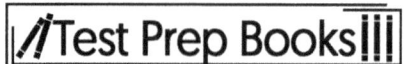

questions on the exam that ATI is beta testing. You will not know which questions these are, so give your best effort on every question.

Subject Area	Scored Questions	Unscored Questions	Total Questions
Reading	39	6	45
Mathematics	34	4	38
Science	44	6	50
English & Language Usage	33	4	37
Total	150	20	170

A certain amount of time is allotted for each section as seen below:

Subject Area	Minutes
Reading	55
Mathematics	57
Science	60
English & Language Usage	37
Total	209 (3 hours & 39 minutes)

Once a test taker begins a subject area, the timer will start. When the timer expires, the test taker may stretch, go to the bathroom, or otherwise relax before the timer begins for the next section. The TEAS 7 is offered in both a pencil-and-paper version and a computerized version, depending on the preference of the local test administrator. TEAS 7 test takers are not permitted to use cell phones, but four-function calculators are now permitted on the TEAS 7.

Alternate Item Types

In addition to multiple choice questions with four answer choices, the TEAS 7 includes four "alternate items types":

- Multiple-select
- Supply answer
- Ordering
- Hot spot

Multiple-Select

Multiple-select items, also referred to as *select all that apply*, are like multiple choice questions except that there may be multiple correct answers. Select every correct answer that you see. Keep in mind that there may just be one correct answer.

Supply Answer

Supply Answer items are fill-in-the blank questions. Rather than choosing from a list of choices, you must enter a number into the blank.

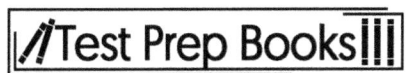

Introduction for the TEAS 7

<u>Ordering</u>

For these item types, you will be given a list that needs to be put in the correct order. This may involve ranking a list from greatest to least based on some criteria or putting steps in order.

<u>Hot Spot</u>

For these item types, you will be given an image, and you must select a certain area of that image. For example, you may be given a diagram of the digestive system and be asked to select the stomach.

Scoring

Shortly after the examination, test takers will receive several different numbered scores with their TEAS 7 results, including scores on all the various sections and subsections. This includes the national and state-level percentile rankings that a test taker has achieved. This rank is equal to the percentage of test takers from nationwide samples that scored equal to or lower than the test taker. Higher percentiles indicate more correct answers and fewer people who scored higher than the given test taker. However, although this may be of interest to the test taker, schools do not use this score as a basis for acceptance decisions.

Instead, schools typically look at the Composite Individual Total Score. The composite score is a good determination of the test taker's performance and is calculated by averaging the test taker's performance from each section of the test. The national average composite score generally lies between 65% correct and 75% correct. Many schools have a minimum required score in this range, but each school and program chooses their own minimum standards; more prestigious schools require higher minimum scores and vice versa. Besides meeting minimum requirements, TEAS scores can display the competitiveness of the applicant just like previous GPAs and extracurricular activities, though this too varies from school to school.

Recent Developments

TEAS 7 is the successor the to the TEAS 6. In January 2022, ATI announced that the transition from the 6th edition to the 7th edition would take place in June of 2022. The TEAS 7 is similar in difficulty, but with slight differences in emphasis placed on various subjects.

Study Prep Plan

1 **Schedule** - Use one of our study schedules below or come up with one of your own.

2 **Relax** - Test anxiety can hurt even the best students. There are many ways to reduce stress. Find the one that works best for you.

3 **Execute** - Once you have a good plan in place, be sure to stick to it.

One Week Study Schedule

Day	Topic
Day 1	Numbers and Operations
Day 2	Decimals
Day 3	Estimation and Rounding
Day 4	Solving Equations in One Variable
Day 5	Solving Real-World Problems with Ratios
Day 6	Measurement and Data
Day 7	Take Your Exam!

Two Week Study Schedule

Day	Topic	Day	Topic
Day 1	Numbers and Operations	Day 8	Solving Real-World Problems with...
Day 2	Fractions	Day 9	Solving Real-World Problems with Ratios
Day 3	Decimals	Day 10	Geometry
Day 4	Arithmetic Operations	Day 11	Properties of Circles
Day 5	Estimation and Round...	Day 12	Measurement and Data
Day 6	Patterns, Relationships, and Algebraic Reasoning	Day 13	Evaluating Information Using Statistics
Day 7	Solving Real-World Problems with Ration...	Day 14	Take Your Exam!

Study Prep Plan

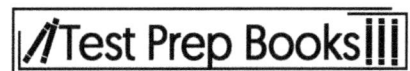

One Month Study Schedule					
Day 1	Numbers and Operations	Day 11	Estimation and Rounding	Day 21	Geometry
Day 2	Place Value	Day 12	Translating Phrases and Sentences	Day 22	Classifying Three-Dimensional...
Day 3	Fractions	Day 13	Patterns, Relationships, and Algebraic...	Day 23	Finding Perimeter and Area
Day 4	Composing and Decomposing Fractions	Day 14	Comparing and Ordering Rational Numbers	Day 24	Finding Volume and Surface Area
Day 5	Multiplying and Dividing Fractions	Day 15	Solving Equations in One Variable	Day 25	Measurement and Data
Day 6	Decimals	Day 16	Solving Real-World Problems with Ration...	Day 26	Solving Problems Using Categorical Data
Day 7	Percentages	Day 17	Solving Linear Inequalities	Day 27	Explaining the Relationship Between...
Day 8	Arithmetic Operations	Day 18	Building and Evaluating Functions	Day 28	Evaluating Information Using Statistics
Day 9	Understanding the Relationship Between Multiplication...	Day 19	Solving Real-World Problems with Proportions	Day 29	Converting Between Standard and Metric Systems
Day 10	Interpreting Remainders	Day 20	Solving Real-World Problems with Ratios	Day 30	Take Your Exam!

Build your own prep plan by visiting:

testprepbooks.com/prep

Reference Sheet

Symbol	Phrase
+	added to, increased by, sum of, more than
-	decreased by, difference between, less than, take away
×	multiplied by, 3 (4, 5 . . .) times as large, product of
÷	divided by, quotient of, half (third, etc.) of
=	is, the same as, results in, as much as
x, t, n, etc.	a variable which is an unknown value or quantity
<	is under, is below, smaller than, beneath
>	is above, is over, bigger than, exceeds
≤	no more than, at most, maximum; less than or equal to
≥	no less than, at least, minimum; greater than or equal to
√	square root of, exponent divided by 2

Geometry	Description
$P = 2l + 2w$	for perimeter of a rectangle
$P = 4 \times s$	for perimeter of a square
$P = a + b + c$	for perimeter of a triangle
$A = \frac{1}{2} \times b \times h = \frac{bh}{2}$	for area of a triangle
$A = b \times h$	for area of a parallelogram
$A = \frac{1}{2} \times h(b_1 + b_2)$	for area of a trapezoid
$A = \frac{1}{2} \times a \times P$	for area of a regular polygon
$C = 2 \times \pi \times r$	for circumference (perimeter) of a circle
$A = \pi \times r^2$	for area of a circle
$c^2 = a^2 + b^2; c = \sqrt{a^2 + b^2}$	for finding the hypotenuse of a right triangle
$SA = 2xy + 2yz + 2xz$	for finding surface area
$V = \frac{1}{3}xyh$	for finding volume of a rectangular pyramid
$V = \frac{4}{3}\pi r^3; \frac{1}{3}\pi r^2 h; \pi r^2 h$	for volume of a sphere; a cone; and a cylinder

Radical Expressions	Description
$\sqrt[n]{a} = a^{\frac{1}{n}}; \sqrt[n]{a^m} = (\sqrt[n]{a})^m = a^{\frac{m}{n}}$	a is the radicand, n is the index, m is the exponent
$\sqrt{x^2} = (x^2)^{\frac{1}{2}} = x$	to convert square root to exponent
$a^m \times a^n = a^{m+n}$	multiplying radicands with exponents
$(a^m)^n = a^{m \times n}$	multiplying exponents
$(a \times b)^m = a^m \times b^m$	parentheses with exponents

Property	Addition	Multiplication
Commutative	$a + b = b + a$	$a \times b = b \times a$
Associative	$(a + b) + c = a + (b + c)$	$(a \times b) \times c = a \times (b \times c)$
Identity	$a + 0 = a; 0 + a = a$	$a \times 1 = a; 1 \times a = a$
Inverse	$a + (-a) = 0$	$a \times \frac{1}{a} = 1; a \neq 0$
Distributive		$a(b + c) = ab + ac$

Data	Description
Mean	equal to the total of the values of a data set, divided by the number of elements in the data set
Median	middle value in an odd number of ordered values of a data set, or the mean of the two middle values in an even number of ordered values in a data set
Mode	the value that appears most often
Range	the difference between the highest and the lowest values in the set

Graphing	Description
(x, y)	ordered pair, plot points in a graph
$y = mx + b$	slope-intercept form; m represents the slope of the line and b represents the y-intercept
$f(x)$	read as f of x, which means it is a function of x
(x_2, y_2) and (x_2, y_2)	two ordered pairs used to determine the slope of a line
$m = \frac{y_2 - y_1}{x_2 - x_1}$	to find the slope of the line, m, for ordered pairs
$Ax + By = C$	standard form of an equation, also for solving a system of equations through the elimination method
$M = (\frac{x_1 + x_2}{2}, \frac{y_1 + y_2}{2})$	for finding the midpoint of an ordered pair
$y = ax^2 + bx + c$	quadratic function for a parabola
$y = a(x - h)^2 + k$	quadratic function for a parabola with vertex
$y = ab^x; y = a \times b^x$	function for exponential curve
$y = ax^2 + bx + c$	standard form of a quadratic function
$x = \frac{-b}{2a}$	for finding axis of symmetry in a parabola; given quadratic formula in standard form
$f = \sqrt{\frac{\Sigma(x - \bar{x})^2}{n - 1}}$	function for standard deviation of the sample; where $\bar{x}$ = sample mean and n = sample size

Proportions and Percentage	Description
$\frac{\text{gallons}}{\text{cost}} = \frac{\text{gallons}}{\text{cost}}; \frac{7 \text{ gallons}}{\$14.70} = \frac{x}{\$20}$	written as equal ratios with a variable representing the missing quantity
$\frac{y_1}{x_1} = \frac{y_2}{x_2}$	for direct proportions
$(y_1)(x_1) = (y_2)(x_2)$	for indirect proportions
$\frac{\text{change}}{\text{original value}} \times 100 = \text{percent change}$	for finding percentage change in value
$\frac{\text{new quantity} - \text{old quantity}}{\text{old quantity}} \times 100$	for calculating the increase or decrease in percentage

Numbers and Operations

Numbers

Classifying Whole Numbers, Integers, and Rational Numbers

Definitions

Whole numbers describe a set of numbers that does not contain any fractions or decimals. The set of whole numbers includes zero. For example, 0, 1, 2, 3, 4, 189, and 293 are all whole numbers.

Integers describe whole numbers and their negative counterparts. (Zero does not have a negative counterpart here. Instead, zero is its own negative.) Negative whole numbers such as -1, -2, -3, -4, and -5 are considered negative integers, and positive whole numbers such as 1, 2, 3, 4, and 5 are considered positive integers. For example, -1, -2, -3, -4, -5, 0, 1, 2, 3, 4, and 5 are all integers.

Even numbers describe any number that can be divided by 2 evenly, meaning the answer has no decimal or remainder portion. It does not matter whether the number is positive or negative. For example, 2, 4, 9082, -2, -16, and -504 are all considered even numbers, because they can be divided by 2, without a remainder or decimal.

Odd numbers describe any number that does not divide evenly by 2. For example, 1, 21, 541, 3003, -9, -63, and -1257 are all considered odd numbers, because they cannot be divided by 2 without a remainder or a decimal.

Prime numbers describe a number that is only evenly divisible, resulting in no remainder or decimal, by 1 and itself. For example, 2, 3, 7, 13, and 113 are all considered prime numbers because they can only be evenly divided by 1 and itself.

Composite numbers describe a positive integer that is formed by multiplying two smaller integers together. Composite numbers can be divided evenly by numbers other than 1 or itself. For example, 9, 24, 45, 66, 2348, and 10002 are all considered composite numbers because they are the result of multiplying two smaller integers together.

Real numbers describe both rational numbers and irrational numbers.

Rational numbers describe any number that can be expressed as a fraction, with a non-zero denominator. Since any integer can be written with 1 in the denominator without changing its value, all integers are considered rational numbers. Every rational number has a decimal expression that terminates or repeats. That is, any rational number either will have a countable number of nonzero digits or will end with an ellipsis or a bar (3.6666... or $3.\bar{6}$) to depict repeating decimal digits. For example, 12, -3.54, $110.\overline{256}$, $\frac{-35}{10}$, and $4.\bar{7}$ are all rational numbers.

Irrational numbers are numbers which cannot be written as a finite decimal. Pi (π) is considered to be an irrational number because its decimal portion is unending or a non-repeating decimal. The most common irrational number is π, which has an endless and non-repeating decimal, but there are other well-known irrational numbers like e and $\sqrt{2}$.

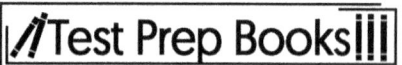

Examples

Example 1: How is the number 7 classified?

7 is a whole number because it does not contain any fractions or decimals. Like all whole numbers it is also an integer. It is an odd number because it cannot be evenly divided by 2. It is a prime number because it can only be divided by 1 and itself. All integers are rational numbers and all rational numbers are real numbers, so 7 is also a rational number and a real number. Of the terms outlined above, 7 could be classified as a whole number, integer, odd number, prime number, real number, and rational number.

Practice Questions

1. How is the number -4 classified?
    a. Real, rational, integer, whole
    b. Real, irrational, integer
    c. Real, rational, integer
    d. Real, irrational

2. Which of the following is the definition of a prime number?
    a. A number that factors only into itself and 1
    b. A number greater than one that factors only into itself and 1
    c. A number less than 10
    d. A number divisible by 10

3. Which of the following is a composite number?
    a. 113
    b. 7
    c. 64
    d. 59

Understanding Absolute Value

Both positive and negative numbers are valued according to their distance from 0. Look at this number line for +3 and -3:

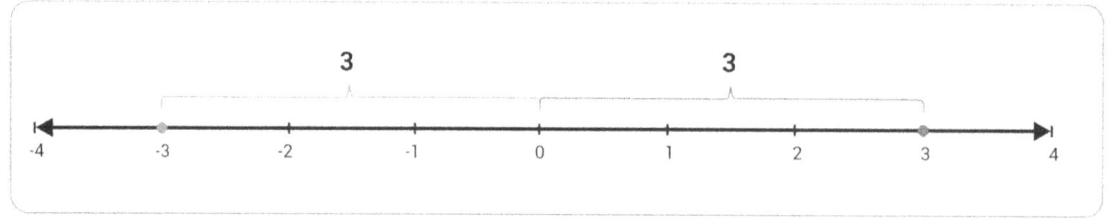

Both 3 and -3 are three spaces from 0. The distance from 0 is called its absolute value. Thus, both -3 and 3 have an absolute value of 3 since they're both three spaces away from 0.

An absolute number is written by placing | | around the number. So, |3| and |−3| both equal 3, as that's their common absolute value.

**Numbers and Operations
Numbers**

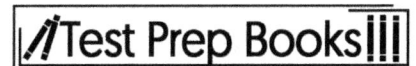

Examples

Example 1: What is the absolute value of -693?

The absolute value of -693 (also written as |-693|) is 693, because -693 is 693 spaces away from 0. The absolute value of 693 would also be 693, because it is also 693 spaces away from zero.

Practice Questions

1. What is the absolute value of 24?
    a. -24
    b. 1
    c. 48
    d. 24

2. What is the absolute value of -100?
    a. -100
    b. 100
    c. 1
    d. -1

Factorization

Factors are the numbers multiplied to achieve a product. Thus, every product in a multiplication equation has, at minimum, two factors. For the sake of most discussions, assume that factors are positive integers.

To find a number's factors, start with 1 and the number itself. Then divide the number by 2, 3, 4, and so on, seeing if any divisors can divide the number without a remainder, keeping a list of those that do. Stop upon reaching either the number itself or another factor.

Prime factorization involves an additional step after breaking a number down to its factors: breaking down the factors until they are all prime numbers.

A **common factor** is a factor shared by two numbers.

The **greatest common factor** is the largest number among the shared, common factors.

The **least common multiple** is the smallest number that's a multiple of two numbers. If two numbers share no factors besides 1 in common, then their least common multiple will be simply their product. If two numbers have common factors, then their least common multiple will be their product divided by their greatest common factor. This can be visualized by the formula $LCM = \frac{x \times y}{GCF}$, where x and y are some integers and **LCM** and **GCF** are their least common multiple and greatest common factor, respectively.

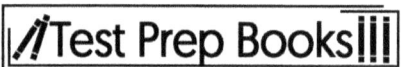

Examples

Example 1: What are all the factors of 45?

For the factors of 45, start with 1 and 45. Then try to divide 45 by 2, which fails. Now divide 45 by 3. The answer is 15, so 3 and 15 are now factors. Dividing by 4 doesn't work, and dividing by 5 leaves 9. Lastly, dividing 45 by 6, 7, and 8 all don't work. The next integer to try is 9, but this is already known to be a factor, so the factorization is complete. The factors of 45 are 1, 3, 5, 9, 15, and 45.

Example 2: What are the prime factors of 129?

Break 129 down into its prime factors. First, the factors are 3 and 43. Both 3 and 43 are prime numbers, so we're done. But if 43 was not a prime number, then it would also need to be factorized until all of the factors are expressed as prime numbers.

Example 3: What are the common factors of 45 and 30?

To find the common factors of 45 and 30, find the factors for each number. The factors of 45 are: 1, 3, 5, 9, 15, and 45. The factors of 30 are: 1, 2, 3, 5, 6, 10, 15, and 30. The common factors are 1, 3, 5, and 15.

Practice Questions

1. What are all the factors of 12?
    a. 12, 24, 36
    b. 1, 2, 4, 6, 12
    c. 12, 24, 36, 48
    d. 1, 2, 3, 4, 6, 12

2. What is the greatest common factor of 45 and 30?
    a. 1
    b. 5
    c. 15
    d. 45

3. What is the least common multiple of 4 and 9?
    a. 36
    b. 13
    c. 9
    d. 45

Numbers and Operations
Place Value

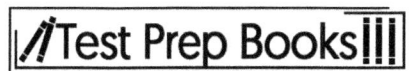

Answer Explanations

Classifying Whole Numbers, Integers, and Rational Numbers

1. C: The number negative four is classified as a real number because it exists and is not imaginary. It is rational because it does not have a decimal that never ends. It is an integer because it does not have a fractional component. The next classification would be whole numbers, for which negative four does not qualify because it is negative. Choice *D* is wrong because -4 is not considered an irrational number because it does not have a never-ending decimal component.

2. B: A number is prime because its only factors are itself and 1. Positive numbers (greater than one) can be prime numbers.

3. C: 64 is a composite number because it can be divided evenly by numbers other than 1 or 64; as one example, $8 \times 8 = 64$. 113, 7, and 59 are all prime numbers.

Understanding Absolute Value

1. D: The absolute value of 24 (also written as |24|) is 24, because 24 is 24 spaces away from 0. The absolute value of -24 would also be 24, because it is also 24 spaces away from zero.

2. B: The absolute value of -100 (also written as |-100|) is 100, because -100 is 100 spaces away from 0. The absolute value of 100 would also be 100, because it is also 100 spaces away from zero.

Factorization

1. D: The full list of factors of 12 would be 1, 2, 3, 4, 6, and 12. A given number divides evenly by each of its factors to produce an integer (no decimals). The number 5, 7, 8, 9, 10, 11 (and their opposites) do not divide evenly into 12. Therefore, these numbers are not factors.

2. C: From the factors of 45 and 30, the common factors are 1, 3, 5, and 15. Thus, 15 is the greatest common factor, as it's the largest number.

3. A: To find the least common multiple of 4 and 9, find multiples of each number until you find the lowest multiple that they share. The multiples of 4 are 4, 8, 12, 16, 20, 24, 28, 32, 36, and so on. For 9, the multiples are 9, 18, 27, 36, 45, 54, etc. Thus, the least common multiple of 4 and 9 is 36, the lowest number where 4 and 9 share multiples.

Place Value

Base-10 Place Value System

Numbers are counted in groups of 10. That number, 10, is the same throughout the set of whole numbers. This is referred to as working within a **base-10 system**. In this system, the numbers from zero to 9 can be used to represent any number. The foundation for doing this involves **place value**. Numbers are written side by side to show the amount in each place value. In accordance with the base-10 numeration system, the value of a digit increases by a factor of ten each place it moves to the left.

Consider the number 7. Moving the digit one place to the left (70), increases its value by a factor of 10 ($7 \times 10 = 70$). Moving the digit two places to the left (700) increases its value by a factor of 10 twice

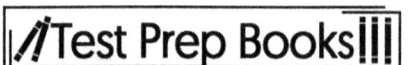

(7 × 10 × 10 = 700). Moving the digit three places to the left (7,000) increases its value by a factor of 10 three times (7 × 10 × 10 × 10 = 7,000), and so on.

Conversely, the value of a digit decreases by a factor of ten each place it moves to the right. (Note that multiplying by $\frac{1}{10}$ is equivalent to dividing by 10).

Consider the number 40. Moving the digit one place to the right (4) decreases its value by a factor of 10 (40 ÷ 10 = 4). Moving the digit two places to the right (0.4), decreases its value by a factor of 10 twice (40 ÷ 10 ÷ 10 = 0.4) or (40 × $\frac{1}{10}$ × $\frac{1}{10}$ = 0.4). Moving the digit three places to the right (0.04) decreases its value by a factor of 10 three times (40 ÷ 10 ÷ 10 ÷ 10 = 0.04) or (40 × $\frac{1}{10}$ × $\frac{1}{10}$ × $\frac{1}{10}$ = 0.04), and so on.

Examples

Example 1: A number has a 7 in the ten-thousandths place, an 8 in the tenths place, a 4 in the tens place, a 9 in the ones place, a 3 in the thousandths place, and a 9 in the thousands place. The other place values contain zeros. What is the number?

The place values in order from left to right are the following: thousands, hundreds, tens, ones, tenths, hundredths, thousandths, and ten-thousandths. 9 is in the thousands place, 0 is in the hundreds place, 4 is in the tens place, and 9 is in the ones place. Then, a decimal point is inserted. After the decimal, an 8 is in the tenths place, a zero is in the hundredths place, a 3 is in the thousandths place, and a 7 is in the ten-thousandths place. The corresponding number is 9,049.8037.

Practice Questions

1. Which of the following is equivalent to the value of the digit 3 in the number 792.134?
    a. 3 × 10
    b. 3 × 100
    c. $\frac{3}{10}$
    d. $\frac{3}{100}$

2. One digit in the following number is in **bold**, and the other is underlined: 3<u>6</u>,**6**01.
Which of the following statement about the underlined digit is true?
    a. Its value is $\frac{1}{10}$ the value of the bold digit.
    b. Its value is 10 times the value of the bold digit.
    c. Its value is 100 times the value of the bold digit.
    d. Its value is 60 times the value of the bold digit.

3. Consider the following decimal, 34.15689721. In which place value does the 2 reside?
    a. Hundred-thousandths
    b. Billionths
    c. Millionths
    d. Ten-millionths

Numbers and Operations
Place Value

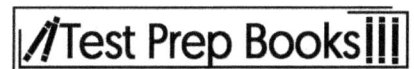

4. Which of the following is equivalent to the digit 7 in the number 371,982.204?
   a. 7 × 10,000
   b. 7 × 100,000
   c. 7 ÷ 10,000
   d. 7 ÷ 100,000

Representing Decimals to the Hundredths

The **decimal place** denotes how far to the right of the decimal point a numeral is. The first digit to the right of the decimal point is in the tenths place. The next is the hundredths. The third is the thousandths. For example, 3.142 has a 1 in the tenths place, a 4 in the hundredths place, and a 2 in the thousandths place.

The **decimal point** is a period used to separate the *ones* place from the *tenths* place when writing out a number as a decimal.

A **decimal number** is a number written out with a decimal point instead of as a fraction, for example, 1.25 instead of $\frac{5}{4}$. Depending on the situation, it can sometimes be easier to work with fractions and sometimes easier to work with decimal numbers.

A number less than one contains only digits in some decimal places. For example, 0.53 is less than one. A **mixed number** is a number greater than one that also contains digits in some decimal places. For example, 3.43 is a mixed number. Adding a zero to the right of a decimal does not change the value of the number. For example, 2.75 is the same as 2.750. However, 2.75 is the more accepted representation of the number. Also, zeros are usually placed in the ones column in any value less than one. For example, 0.65 is the same as .65, but 0.65 is more widely used.

In order to read or write a decimal, the decimal point is ignored. The number is read as a whole number, and then the place value unit is stated in which the last digit falls. For example, 0.089 is read as eighty-nine thousandths. The number 0.1345 is read as one thousand, three hundred forty-five ten thousandths.

In mixed numbers, the word "and" is used to represent the decimal point. The number 2.56 is read as two and fifty-six hundredths.

A decimal number is **terminating** if it stops at some point. It is called **repeating** if it never stops, but repeats a pattern over and over. It is important to note that every rational number can be written as a terminating decimal or as a repeating decimal.

To precisely understand a number being represented on a number line, the first step is to identify how the number line is divided up. When utilizing a number line to represent decimal portions of numbers, it is helpful to label the divisions, or insert additional divisions, as needed.

Examples

Example 1: How would the number 4.986 be read?

This mixed number would be read as four and nine-hundred eighty-six thousandths. The four is before the decimal. After the decimal are three numbers, meaning they extend into the thousandths.

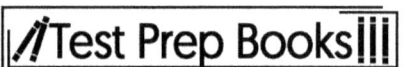

Numbers and Operations
Place Value

Example 2: What number, to the nearest hundredths place is marked by the point on the following number line?

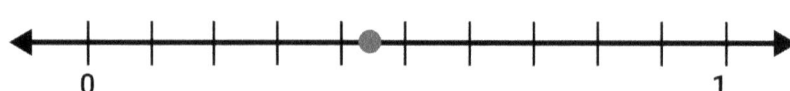

First, figure out how the number line is divided up. In this case, it has ten sections, so it is divided into tenths. To use this number line with the divisions, label the divisions as follows:

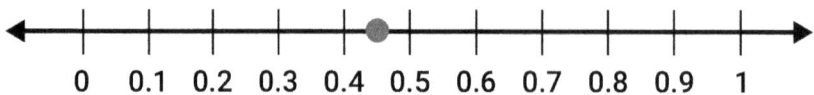

Because the dot is placed equally between 0.4 and 0.5, it is at 0.45.

Practice Questions

1. What is the value, to the nearest tenths place, of the point indicated on the following number line?

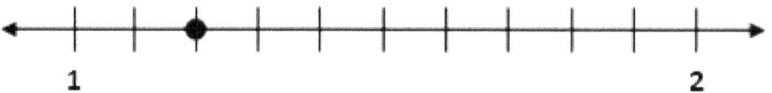

   a. 0.2
   b. 1.4
   c. 1.2
   d. 2.2

2. Which represents the number 0.65 on a number line?

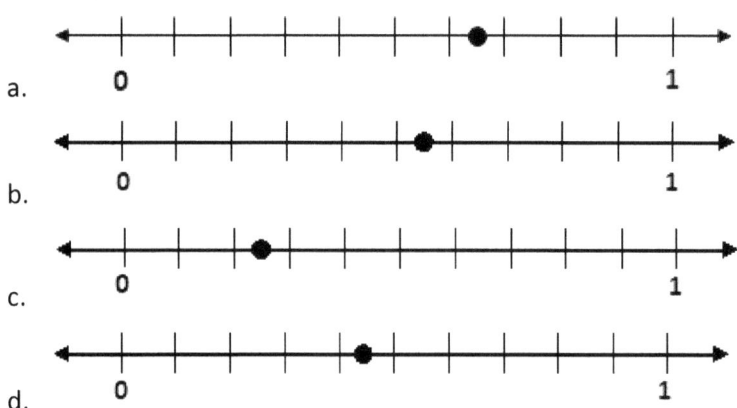

3. Round 245.89742 to the nearest hundredth.
   a. 200
   b. 245.897
   c. 245.89
   d. 245.90

Numbers and Operations
Place Value

4. A customer gave a cashier nine $10 bills, seven $1 bills, 8 dimes, and 6 pennies. How much money did the customer give the cashier?
    a. $11.68
    b. $97.86
    c. $17.86
    d. $91.68

5. Which of the following is equivalent to 0.56?
    a. $56 \div 10$
    b. $56 \div 1000$
    c. $56 \div 100$
    d. 56×100

Composing and Decomposing Numbers

Composing and decomposing numbers aids in conceptualizing what each digit of a multi-digit number represents. The standard, or typical, form in which numbers are written consists of a series of digits representing a given value based on their place value. Consider the number 592.7. This number is composed of 5 hundreds, 9 tens, 2 ones, and 7 tenths.

Composing a number requires adding the given numbers for each place value and writing the numbers in standard form. For example, composing 4 thousands, 5 hundreds, 2 tens, and 8 ones consists of adding as follows: $4,000 + 500 + 20 + 8$, to produce 4,528 (standard form).

Decomposing a number requires taking a number written in standard form and breaking it apart into the sum of each place value. For example, the number 8,317 is decomposed by breaking it into the sum of 4 values (for each of the 4 digits): 8 thousands, 3 hundreds, 1 tens, and 7 ones. The decomposed or "expanded" form of 8,317 is $8,000 + 300 + 10 + 7$.

A place value chart can be used to show the place value for each digit of a large number. For example, given the number 65,084, start from the far-right column on the chart and fill in one number per box.

Hundred thousands	Ten thousands	Thousands	Hundreds	Tens	Ones
	6	5	0	8	4

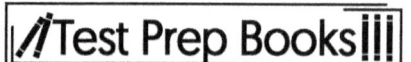

Another method involves decomposing a large number into its individual parts. Fill in the leading number and then place zeros in the other boxes. To decompose the number 134,802, you could do the following.

```
+  1  0  0,  0  0  0
+     3  0,  0  0  0
+         4,  0  0  0
+              8  0  0
+                 0  0
+                    2
```

This could be written as:

$$100,000 + 30,000 + 4,000 + 800 + 2$$

This represents the total value of each digit.

Examples

Example 1: Determine the correct way to state the following value: 56,764,345.

56 is in the millions place, 764 is in the thousands place, and 345 is in the hundreds place. Therefore, the number 56,764,345 can be written as fifty-six million, seven hundred sixty-four thousand, three hundred forty-five.

Example 2: Decompose the following number: 5,431,312.

The five is in the millions place, which represents 5,000,000. The 4 is in the hundred-thousands place, which is equal to 400,000. The first 3 is in the ten-thousands place, which adds 30,000. The first 1 is in the thousands place, which is equal to 1,000. The next three is in the hundreds place (300), the next 1 is in the tens place (10), and the 2 is in the ones place (2). Therefore, the correct decomposition is $5,000,000 + 400,000 + 30,000 + 1,000 + 300 + 10 + 2$.

Practice Questions

1. Which of the following represents one hundred eighty-two million, thirty-six thousand, four hundred twenty-one and three hundred fifty-six thousandths?
    a. 182,036,421.356
    b. 182,036,421.0356
    c. 182,000,036,421.0356
    d. 182,000,036,421.356

2. Which is the correct decomposition of the number 36,901?
    a. $36,000 + 901$
    b. $3,000 + 600 + 90 + 1$
    c. $30,000 + 6,000 + 900 + 1$
    d. $30,000 + 6,000 + 900 + 10$

Numbers and Operations
Place Value

3. Determine the correct way to state the following value: 3.4567.
    a. Three and four thousand, five hundred sixty-seven thousandths
    b. Three and four thousand, five hundred sixty-seven hundredths
    c. Three and four thousand, five hundred sixty-seven ten-thousandths
    d. Three and four thousand, five hundred sixty-seven millionths

4. Decompose the following decimal: 0.050412.
    a. 0.5 + 0.04 + 0.001 + 0.0002
    b. 0.05 + 0.0004 + 0.00001 + 0.000002
    c. 0.05 + 0.004 + 0.0001 + 0.00002
    d. 0.5 + 0.0004 + 0.00001 + 0.000002

5. Determine the correct way to decompose the following dollar amount: $4,503,720.09.
    a. $4,000,000 + $500,000 + $3,000 + $700 + $20 + $0.09
    b. $4,000,000 + $50,000 + $3,000 + $700 + $20 + $0.9
    c. $400,000 + $50,000 + $3,000 + $700 + $20 + $0.09
    d. $4,000,000 + $500,000 + $3,000 + $700 + $20 + $0.9

Representing Numbers on a Number Line

A **number line** typically consists of integers (…3, 2, 1, 0, -1, -2, -3…), and is used to visually represent the value of a rational number. Each rational number has a distinct position on the line determined by comparing its value with the displayed values on the line.

Example

If plotting -1.5 on the number line below, it is necessary to recognize that the value of -1.5 is .5 less than -1 and .5 greater than -2. Therefore, -1.5 is plotted halfway between -1 and -2.

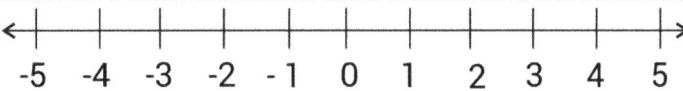

The number system that is used consists of only ten different digits or characters. However, this system is used to represent an infinite number of values. As mentioned, the **place value system** makes this infinite number of values possible. The position in which a digit is written corresponds to a given value. Starting from the decimal point (which is implied, if not physically present), each subsequent place value to the left represents a value greater than the one before it. Conversely, starting from the decimal point, each subsequent place value to the right represents a value less than the one before it.

Practice Questions

1. Of the numbers -1, 17, -13, or -6, which is farthest from 5 on the number line?
    a. -1
    b. 17
    c. -13
    d. -6

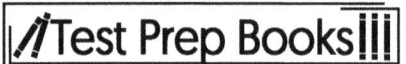

2. Which of the following values lies farthest to the left on a number line?
   a. 0.05
   b. 0.005
   c. 0.5
   d. 0.0005

3. Find the distance between the numbers 7 and -3 on the number line.
   a. 4 units
   b. 10 units
   c. 13 units
   d. 3 units

Using Scientific Notation

Scientific notation is the conversion of extremely small or large numbers into a format that is easier to comprehend and manipulate. It changes the number into three separate parts: a mathematical sign $(+/-)$, a digit term (known as a **significand**), and an exponential term.

$$Scientific\ notation = (+ \text{ or } -)\ significand \times exponential\ term$$

To put a number into scientific notation, one should use the following steps:

- Move the decimal point to after the first non-zero number to find the digit number.
- Count how many places the decimal point was moved in step 1.
- Determine if the exponent is positive or negative.
- Create an exponential term using the information from steps 2 and 3.
- Combine the digit term and exponential term to get scientific notation.

Examples

Example 1: Put 0.0000098 into scientific notation.

To put 0.0000098 into scientific notation, the decimal should be moved so that it lies between the last two numbers: 000009.8. This creates the digit number: 9.8

Next, the number of places that the decimal point moved is determined; to get between the 9 and the 8, the decimal was moved six places to the right. It may be helpful to remember that a decimal moved to the right creates a negative exponent, and a decimal moved to the left creates a positive exponent. Because the decimal was moved six places to the right, the exponent is negative.

Now, the exponential term can be created by using the base 10 (this is always the base in scientific notation) and the number of places moved as the exponent, in this case: 10^{-6}

Finally, the digit term and the exponential term can be combined as a product. Therefore, the scientific notation for the number 0.0000098 is: 9.8×10^{-6}

Numbers and Operations
Place Value

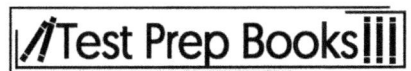

Example 2: Express the number 5.0601×10^{-5} in standard form.

Because the exponent in the scientific notation is equal to -5, the decimal needs to be moved to the left 5 units, adding zeros when necessary. In this case, 4 zeros need to be added to the left of the 5. Therefore, the equivalent value is 0.000050601.

Practice Questions

1. $52.3 \times 10^{-3} =$
    a. 0.00523
    b. 0.0523
    c. 0.523
    d. 523

2. Which of the following correctly displays 8,600,000,000,000 in scientific notation (to two significant figures)?
    a. 8.6×10^{12}
    b. 8.6×10^{-12}
    c. 8.6×10^{11}
    d. 8.60×10^{12}

3. Express the number 8.9031×10^7 in standard form.
    a. 8,903,100
    b 89,031,000
    c. 0.00000089031
    d. 890,310,000

4. Express the number 0.000008123 in scientific notation.
    a. 8.123×10^6
    b. 8.123×10^{-6}
    c. 8.123×10^5
    d. 8.123×10^7

5. The Earth is approximately 384,400,000 meters from the moon. Express this value in scientific notation using three significant figures.
    a. 3.844×10^8 m
    b. 3.84×10^9 m
    c. 3.84×10^{-8} m
    d. 3.84×10^8 m

Answer Explanations

Base-10 Place Value System

1. D: The digit 3 in 792.134 is equivalent to $\frac{3}{100}$. Each digit to the left of the decimal point represents a higher multiple of 10 and each digit to the right of the decimal point represents a quotient of a higher multiple of 10 for the divisor. The first digit to the right of the decimal point is equal to the value ÷ 10. The second digit to the right of the decimal point is equal to the value ÷(10 × 10), or the value ÷ 100.

25

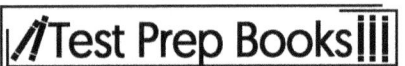

2. B: The underlined digit is the 6 in 6,000. The bold digit is the 6 in 600. Because 6,000 is equal to 6,000 × 10, we know that the underlined 6 has a value that is 10 times that of the bold 6. Additionally, the base-10 system we use helps us determine that the place value increases by a multiple of ten when you go from the right to the left.

3: D: In order, starting from the unit to the right of the decimal point, the following place values exist: tenths, hundredths, thousandths, ten-thousandths, hundred-thousandths, millionths, ten-millionths, and hundred-millionths. The 2 is seven place values to the right, which corresponds to the ten-millionths place.

4. A: The 7 is to the left of the decimal point, and any value to the left represents a power of 10. The 7 is 5 digits over from the left, so it is in the ten-thousands place. This value represents 70,000 or, equivalently, 7 × 10,000, which is Choice A.

Representing Decimals to the Hundredths

1. C: The number line is divided into 10 sections, so each portion represents 0.1. Because the number line begins at 1 and ends at 2, the number in question would be between those two numbers. Since there are only two portions out of ten marked, this represents the number 1.2. All other choices are incorrect due to a misreading of the number line.

2. A: The number line is divided into ten portions, so each mark represents 0.1. Halfway between the sixth and seventh marks would be 0.65. Choice B shows 0.55, Choice C shows 0.25, and Choice D shows 0.45.

3. D: The 7 is in the thousandths place, and the 9 is in the hundredths place. To round to the nearest hundredths place, look at the value in the thousandths place. If it is 5 or above, round the value in the hundredths place up one unit. If it is 4 or less, round down. Since 7 is larger than 5, round up. Adding 1 to the hundredths place results in 245.90.

4. B: The customer has nine $10 bills, which equals $90. A 9 goes in the tens place. The customer also has seven $1 bills, which equals $7. A 7 goes in the ones place. They have eight dimes, which equals $0.80. An 8 goes in the tenths place. Finally, they have six pennies, which equals $0.06. A 6 goes in the hundredths place. The total amount is $97.86.

5. C: The 5 is in the tenths place, and the 6 is in the hundredths place. Therefore, 56 should be divided by one hundred since the rightmost digit is in the hundredths place.

$$0.56 = 56 \div 100$$

Composing and Decomposing Numbers

1. A: 182 is in the millions, 36 is in the thousands, 421 is in the hundreds, and 356 is the decimal.

2. C: This answer has the proper place values for each of the digits: 3 is in the ten-thousands place, 6 is in the thousands place, 9 is in the hundreds place, and 1 is in the ones place. Choice A is not correct because it does not decompose the entire number into all of its place values. Choice B is not correct because the 3, 6, and 9 are decomposed into the wrong place values. Choice D is not correct because it places the 1 in the tens place, not the ones place.

Numbers and Operations
Place Value

3. C: When reading a decimal, locate the digit in the rightmost place value and use that place value for the naming convention. The 7 is in the ten-thousandths place. The decimal is read as the word "and." Therefore, the correct choice is three and four thousand, five hundred sixty-seven ten-thousandths.

4. B: In the number 0.050412, the 5 is in the hundredths place (0.05), the 4 is in the ten-thousandths place (0.0004), the 1 is in the hundred-thousandths place (0.00001), and the 2 is in the millionths place (0.000002). Add these values together to obtain:

$$0.05 + 0.0004 + 0.00001 + 0.000002 = 0.050412$$

5. A: The value $4,503,720.09 can be read as four million, five hundred three thousand, seven hundred twenty dollars and nine cents. Therefore, this can be decomposed as:

$$\$4,000,000 + \$500,000 + \$3,000 + \$700 + \$20 + \$0.09$$

Representing Numbers on a Number Line

1. C: The number line below can be labeled with all 4 given numbers. The number 5 is shown with the open dot. By observing the placement of the dots and their relation to the open dot at 5, the number -1 can be eliminated as an answer because it is the closest. After that, the distance to the other dots can be counted. The distance is shown below with the arcs.

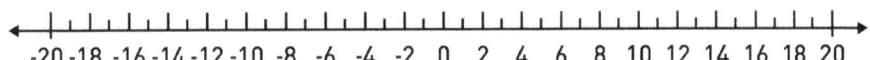

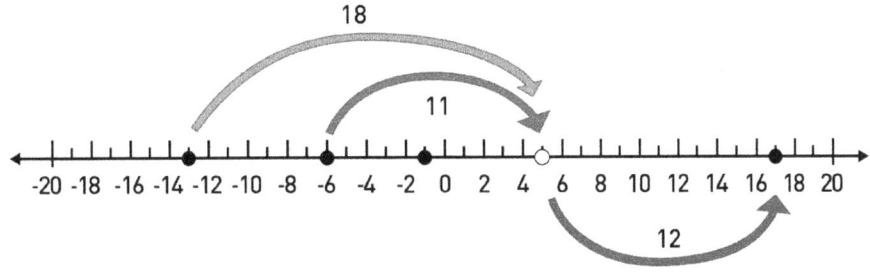

As demonstrated from the arcs showing distance on the number line, the number -13 is furthest from 5 on the number line at a distance of 18.

2. D: The smallest value always lies farthest to the left on the number line. In this example, the values are all positive, so the one that is closest to zero lies farthest to the left. It is true that $0.0005 < 0.005 < 0.05$ 0.5. Therefore, 0.0005 is the smallest, and it lies farthest to the left on a number line.

3. B: The number 7 lies 7 units to the right of 0. The number -3 lies 3 units to the left of 0. Add these values together to determine that there are 10 units in between the values of 7 and -3.

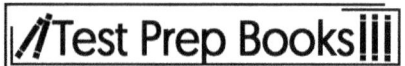

Numbers and Operations
Fractions

Using Scientific Notation

1. B: Multiplying by 10^{-3} means moving the decimal point three places to the left, putting in zeroes as necessary.

2. A: The decimal point for this value is located after the final zero. Because the decimal is moved 12 places to the left in order to get it between the 8 and the 6, then the resulting exponent is positive, so Choice A is the correct answer. Choice B is false because the decimal has been moved in the wrong direction. Choice C is incorrect because the decimal has been moved an incorrect number of times. Choice D is false because this value is written to three significant figures, not two.

$$8{,}600{,}000{,}000{,}000$$
$$\text{12 11 10 9 8 7 6 5 4 3 2 1}$$

3. B: Because the exponent in the scientific notation is equal to 7, the decimal needs to be moved to the right 7 units, adding zeros where necessary. In this case, three zeros need to be added to the right of the 1. Therefore, the equivalent number is 89,031,000.

4. B: The decimal needs to be moved 6 units to the right so that it would be between the first and second nonzero digits (8 and 1). Because the decimal is moved to the right, the exponent in the corresponding scientific notation is negative. Therefore, the correct expression is 8.123×10^{-6}. Note that all zeros before the 8 have been removed.

5. D: To place this amount in scientific notation, the decimal point needs to be moved 8 places to the left. Therefore, the exponent is an 8 in the notation. Choice A is incorrect because four significant figures are used. 3.84×10^8 is the correct response.

Fractions

Understanding the Unit Fraction as One Part of a Whole

A **fraction** is a part of something that is whole. Items such as apples can be cut into parts to help visualize fractions. If an apple is cut into 2 equal parts, each part represents ½ of the apple. If each half is then cut into two parts, the apple now is cut into quarters. Each piece now represents ¼ of the apple. In this example, each part is equal because they all have the same size. Geometric shapes, such as circles and squares, can also be utilized to help visualize the idea of fractions.

For example, a circle can be drawn on the board and divided into 6 equal parts:

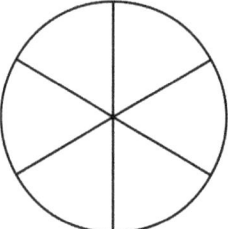

**Numbers and Operations
Fractions**

Shading can be used to represent parts of the circle that can be translated into fractions. The top of the fraction, the **numerator**, can represent how many segments are shaded. The bottom of the fraction, the **denominator**, can represent the number of segments that the circle is broken into. A pie is a good analogy to use in this example. If one piece of the circle is shaded, or one piece of pie is cut out, $\frac{1}{6}$ of the object is being referred to. An apple, a pie, or a circle can be utilized in order to compare simple fractions. For example, showing that $\frac{1}{2}$ is larger than $\frac{1}{4}$ and that $\frac{1}{4}$ is smaller than $\frac{1}{3}$ can be accomplished through shading. A **unit fraction** is a fraction in which the numerator is 1, and the denominator is a positive whole number. It represents one part of a whole—one piece of pie.

As an example, imagine that an apple pie has been baked for a holiday party, and the full pie has eight slices. After the party, there are five slices left. How could the amount of the pie that remains be expressed as a fraction? The numerator is 5 since there are 5 pieces left, and the denominator is 8 since there were eight total slices in the whole pie. Thus, expressed as a fraction, the leftover pie totals $\frac{5}{8}$ of the original amount.

Examples

Example 1: A set of twelve dinner plates is used to serve five guests. Assuming each guest used one plate, how could you represent the number of unused dinner plates as a fraction?

To begin with, find out how many plates were not used. Out of twelve plates, five were used, which leaves seven unused plates. The numerator is 7 since there are 7 unused plates, and the denominator is 12 since there were originally twelve plates available. Expressed as a fraction, the unused plates total $\frac{7}{12}$ of the original amount.

Example 2: What reduced fraction represents the shaded amount shown below?

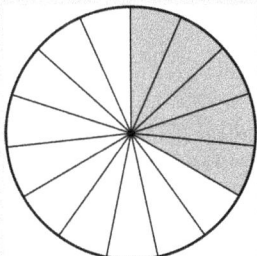

The circle (the whole) is broken up into 15 equal parts, and 5 of them are shaded. The unshaded region is equal to $\frac{10}{15}$, but the shaded region is equal to $\frac{5}{15}$. This can be reduced by dividing both the top and bottom numbers by 5, to find a reduced fraction of $\frac{1}{3}$.

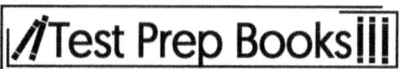

Practice Questions

1. Which fraction represents the greatest part of the whole?
   a. $\frac{1}{4}$
   b. $\frac{1}{3}$
   c. $\frac{1}{5}$
   d. $\frac{1}{2}$

2. A pumpkin pie was split into 8 equal parts and 5 family members ate a slice. Which of the following fractions represents the amount of pie left over?
   a. $\frac{5}{8}$
   b. $\frac{3}{8}$
   c. $\frac{1}{8}$
   d. $\frac{1}{2}$

3. Which of the following amounts is equivalent to $\frac{1}{2}$?
   a. $\frac{4}{6}$
   b. $\frac{3}{9}$
   c. $\frac{5}{10}$
   d. $\frac{1}{3}$

4. A box of cereal is divided into 20 equal parts and placed in snack bags. 7 of the bags were given out to kids, but 2 of those were left uneaten. How much of the original box was left uneaten in total?
   a. $\frac{2}{20}$
   b. $\frac{5}{20}$
   c. $\frac{9}{20}$
   d. $\frac{15}{20}$

Numbers and Operations
Fractions

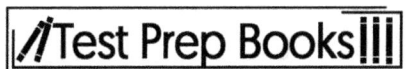

5. There are 21 students in a class. 6 of them wear glasses. What fraction of students do NOT wear glasses?
   a. $\frac{6}{21}$
   b. $\frac{15}{21}$
   c. $\frac{6}{15}$
   d. $\frac{15}{6}$

Proper Fractions, Improper Fractions, and Mixed Numbers

Fractions come in three different varieties: proper fractions, improper fractions, and mixed numbers. **Proper fractions** have a numerator less than the denominator, such as $\frac{3}{8}$, but **improper fractions** have a numerator greater than the denominator, such as $\frac{15}{8}$. **Mixed numbers** combine a whole number with a proper fraction, such as $3\frac{1}{2}$. Any mixed number can be written as an improper fraction by multiplying the integer by the denominator, adding the product to the value of the numerator, and dividing the sum by the original denominator:

$$3\frac{1}{2} = \frac{3 \times 2 + 1}{2} = \frac{7}{2}$$

Whole numbers can also be converted into fractions by placing the whole number as the numerator and making the denominator 1:

$$3 = \frac{3}{1}$$

The bar in a fraction represents division. Therefore $^6/_5$ is the same as $6 \div 5$. In order to rewrite it as a mixed number, division is performed to obtain $6 \div 5 = 1$ R 1. The remainder is then converted into fraction form. The actual remainder becomes the numerator of a fraction, and the divisor becomes the denominator. Therefore 1 R 1 is written as $1\frac{1}{5}$, a mixed number. A mixed number can also decompose into the addition of a whole number and a fraction. Every fraction can be built from a combination of unit fractions. As examples, $1\frac{2}{5} = 1 + \frac{1}{5} + \frac{1}{5}$ and $4\frac{5}{6} = 4 + \frac{1}{6} + \frac{1}{6} + \frac{1}{6} + \frac{1}{6} + \frac{1}{6}$.

Examples

Example 1: Express as a reduced mixed number $\frac{69}{12}$.

Divide 69 by 12. This gives you a result of $5\frac{9}{12}$. Reduce the remainder for the final answer, $5\frac{3}{4}$.

Example 2: Express as an improper fraction $6\frac{4}{5}$.

Multiply the denominator by the whole number portion. Add the numerator and put the total over the original denominator.

$$\frac{(6 \times 5) + 4}{5} = \frac{34}{5}$$

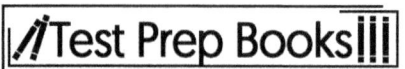

Practice Questions

1. Express $4\frac{11}{12}$ as an improper fraction.
   a. $\frac{48}{12}$
   b. $\frac{59}{12}$
   c. $\frac{44}{12}$
   d. $\frac{15}{12}$

2. Express as a reduced mixed number $\frac{54}{15}$.
   a. $3\frac{3}{5}$
   b. $3\frac{1}{15}$
   c. $3\frac{3}{54}$
   d. $3\frac{1}{54}$

3. Express as an improper fraction $8\frac{3}{7}$.
   a. $\frac{11}{7}$
   b. $\frac{21}{8}$
   c. $\frac{5}{3}$
   d. $\frac{59}{7}$

4. Which of the following is the largest amount?
   a. $\frac{55}{13}$
   b. $4\frac{2}{13}$
   c. $6\frac{1}{13}$
   d. $\frac{65}{13}$

**Numbers and Operations
Fractions**

5. Express $-\frac{117}{15}$ as a mixed number.
   a. $7\frac{13}{15}$
   b. $-1\frac{13}{15}$
   c. $-7\frac{12}{15}$
   d. $-7\frac{12}{15}$

Representing Fractions using Models

If an area model is used to represent a fraction, a fraction can be shown visually by using parts of a whole area or region. Shapes such as rectangles and circles can represent the whole areas. If a mixed number is represented by an area model, the whole number portion is represented by that number of whole areas and the fraction portion is represented by a part of another whole.

As an example, we can use an area model to represent the mixed number $2\frac{1}{2}$.

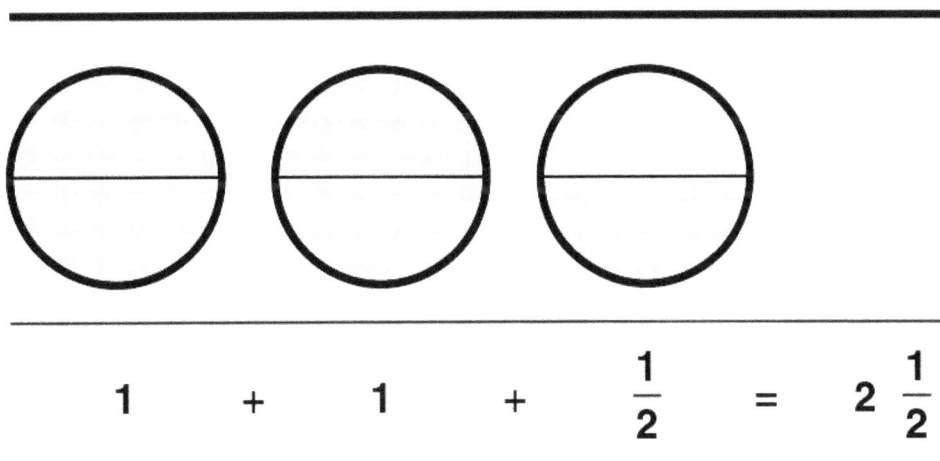

Note that 2 full circles are used to represent the whole number 2, and one half of the third circle is filled in to represent the $\frac{1}{2}$.

Such models can be used to solve word problems involving addition and subtraction of fractions with like denominators.

For example, Let's say a classmate has selected 4 pencils out of a box of 10, and another classmate has selected 3 of the remaining pencils from the box. If you want to visualize the number of pencils each

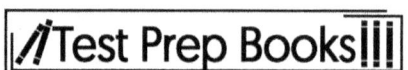

Numbers and Operations
Fractions

classmate took out of the total, and then calculate the fraction of the total they took together, we would utilize the following area model:

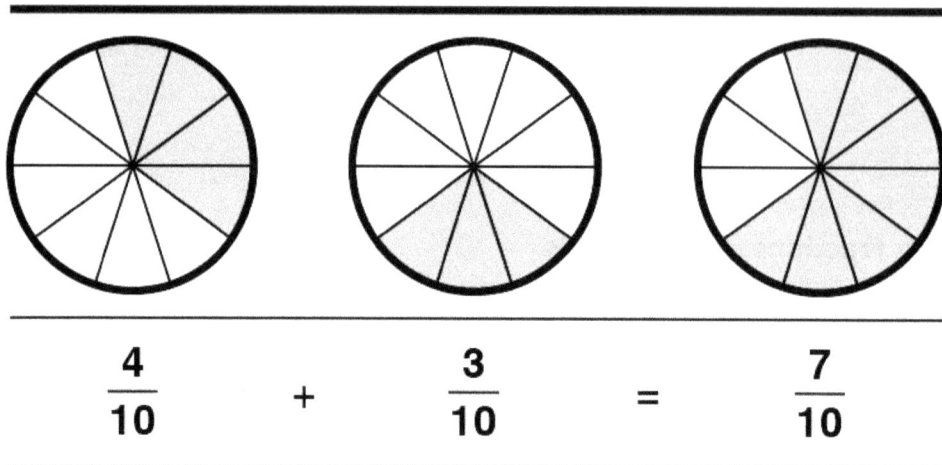

The first circle represents that 4 out of 10, or $\frac{4}{10}$, pencils were selected first, and the second circle represents that 3 out of 10, or $\frac{3}{10}$, were selected second. Adding them together, we have $\frac{4}{10} + \frac{3}{10} = \frac{7}{10}$ pencils. Note that 7 out of 10 pencils were removed from the box, which means 3 pencils (or $\frac{3}{10}$ of the box) remain.

Practice Questions

1. Angie wants to shade $\frac{3}{5}$ of this strip. Which is the correct representation of $\frac{3}{5}$?

a.

b.

c.

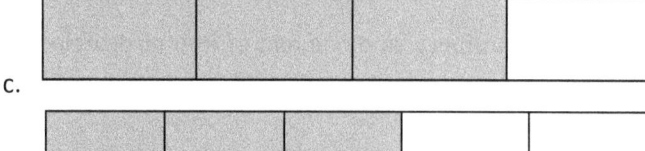

d.

Numbers and Operations
Fractions

2. What equation, involving the addition of two fractions, is represented on the following number line?

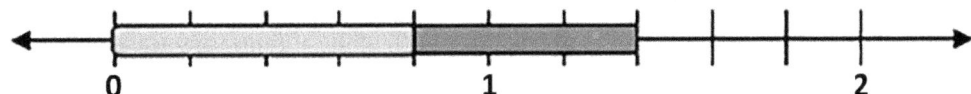

a. $\frac{4}{5} + \frac{3}{5} = \frac{7}{5}$
b. $\frac{4}{5} + \frac{7}{5} = \frac{7}{5}$
c. $\frac{3}{5} + \frac{3}{5} = \frac{6}{5}$
d. $\frac{4}{5} + 1\frac{3}{5} = \frac{7}{5}$

3. Which of the following values is equivalent to the shaded portion of the circles?

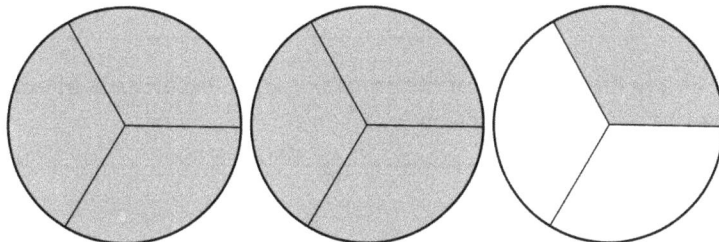

a. $1\frac{1}{3}$
b. $2\frac{1}{3}$
c. $1\frac{2}{3}$
d. $2\frac{2}{3}$

Composing and Decomposing Fractions

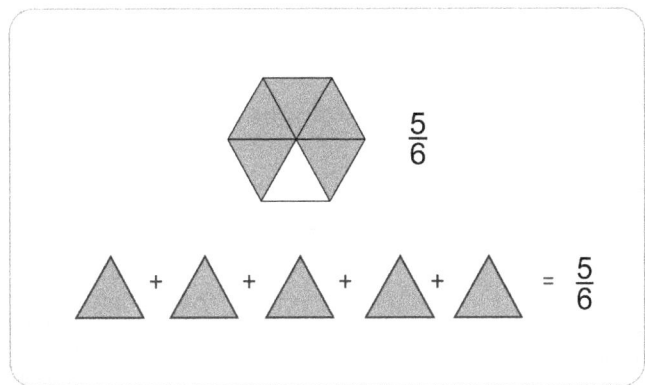

Fractions can be broken apart into sums of fractions with the same denominator.

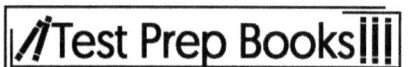

**Numbers and Operations
Fractions**

Example

The fraction $\frac{5}{6}$ can be decomposed into sums of fractions with all denominators equal to 6 and the numerators adding to 5. The fraction $\frac{5}{6}$ is decomposed as:

$$\frac{3}{6}+\frac{2}{6}; \text{ or } \frac{2}{6}+\frac{2}{6}+\frac{1}{6}; \text{ or } \frac{3}{6}+\frac{1}{6}+\frac{1}{6}; \text{ or } \frac{1}{6}+\frac{1}{6}+\frac{1}{6}+\frac{2}{6}; \text{ or } \frac{1}{6}+\frac{1}{6}+\frac{1}{6}+\frac{1}{6}+\frac{1}{6}$$

A unit fraction is a fraction in which the numerator is 1. If decomposing a fraction into unit fractions, the sum will consist of a unit fraction added the number of times equal to the numerator.

Example

$\frac{3}{4}=\frac{1}{4}+\frac{1}{4}+\frac{1}{4}$ (unit fractions $\frac{1}{4}$ added 3 times)

Composing fractions is simply the opposite of decomposing. It is the process of adding fractions with the same denominators to produce a single fraction.

Example

$\frac{3}{7}+\frac{2}{7}=\frac{5}{7}$ and $\frac{1}{5}+\frac{1}{5}+\frac{1}{5}=\frac{3}{5}$

Examples

Example 1: What fraction, over 11, is equivalent to $\frac{1}{11}+\frac{1}{11}+\frac{1}{11}+\frac{1}{11}+\frac{1}{11}+\frac{1}{11}$?

Each individual fraction $\frac{1}{11}$ can be thought of as a piece of a pie broken up into 11 equal parts. There are 6 of these fractions added together, so 6 out of the 11 pieces of the pie are accounted for. In fraction notation this amount can be represented as $\frac{6}{11}$.

Example 2: Determine the missing value in the following expression: $\frac{4}{7}+?=\frac{7}{7}$.

On the lefthand side of the equals sign, the fraction $\frac{4}{7}$ is shown. This is equivalent to a whole being divided into 7 equal parts and 4 of them being accounted for. The right-hand side of the equals sign represents a whole (7 out of 7 equal parts). Therefore, to obtain a whole on the right-hand side, three more equal parts need to be added. This can be represented by the fraction $\frac{3}{7}$.

**Numbers and Operations
Fractions**

Practice Questions

1. Which of the following expressions is equivalent to $\frac{8}{7}$?

    a. $\frac{1}{7}+\frac{1}{7}+\frac{1}{7}+\frac{1}{7}+\frac{1}{7}+\frac{1}{7}+\frac{1}{7}+\frac{1}{7}$

    b. $\frac{1}{8}+\frac{1}{8}+\frac{1}{8}+\frac{1}{8}+\frac{1}{8}+\frac{1}{8}+\frac{1}{8}$

    c. $\frac{1}{7}+\frac{8}{1}$

    d. $\frac{7}{8}+7$

2. Determine which of the following fractions is equivalent to $\frac{1}{5}+\frac{1}{5}+\frac{1}{5}+\frac{1}{5}+\frac{1}{5}+\frac{1}{5}+\frac{1}{5}$.

    a. 1
    b. $\frac{5}{7}$
    c. $1\frac{2}{5}$
    d. $\frac{6}{5}$

3. Determine which of the following is a correct way to decompose the fraction $\frac{8}{9}$.

    a. $\frac{1}{9}+\frac{1}{9}+\frac{1}{9}+\frac{1}{9}+\frac{1}{9}+\frac{1}{9}+\frac{1}{9}$

    b. $\frac{2}{9}+\frac{1}{9}+\frac{6}{9}$

    c. $\frac{3}{9}+\frac{4}{9}+\frac{1}{9}$

    d. $\frac{7}{9}+\frac{2}{9}$

4. Determine which of the following is the missing value in the equation $\frac{2}{5}+\frac{?}{5}+\frac{1}{5}=\frac{5}{5}$.

    a. 5
    b. 3
    c. 1
    d. 2

5. Determine the missing value in the following expression: $\frac{3}{8}+?=\frac{11}{8}$.

    a. $\frac{8}{8}$
    b. $\frac{9}{8}$
    c. $\frac{3}{8}$
    d. $\frac{8}{3}$

Representing Equivalent Fractions

One of the most fundamental concepts of fractions is their ability to be manipulated by multiplication or division. This is possible since $\frac{n}{n} = 1$ for any non-zero integer. As a result, multiplying or dividing by $\frac{n}{n}$ will not alter the original fraction since any number multiplied or divided by 1 doesn't change the value of that number. Fractions of the same value are known as equivalent fractions.

This means $\frac{2}{8}, \frac{25}{100}$, and $\frac{40}{160}$ are equivalent, as they are all equal to $\frac{1}{4}$.

Like fractions, or **equivalent fractions**, are the terms used to describe these fractions that are made up of different numbers but represent the same quantity. For example, the given fractions are $4/_8$ and $3/_6$. If a pie was cut into 8 pieces and 4 pieces were removed, half of the pie would remain. Also, if a pie was split into 6 pieces and 3 pieces were eaten, half of the pie would also remain. Therefore, both of the fractions represent half of a pie. These two fractions are referred to as like fractions. **Unlike fractions** are fractions that are different and do not represent equal quantities. When working with fractions in mathematical expressions, like fractions should be simplified. Both $\frac{4}{8}$ and $\frac{3}{6}$ can be simplified into $\frac{1}{2}$.

Comparing fractions can be completed through the use of a number line. For example, if $\frac{3}{5}$ and $\frac{6}{10}$ need to be compared, each fraction should be plotted on a number line. To plot $\frac{3}{5}$, the area from 0 to 1 should be broken into 5 equal segments, and the fraction represents 3 of them. To plot $\frac{6}{10}$, the area from 0 to 1 should be broken into 10 equal segments, and the fraction represents 6 of them.

It can be seen that $\frac{3}{5} = \frac{6}{10}$:

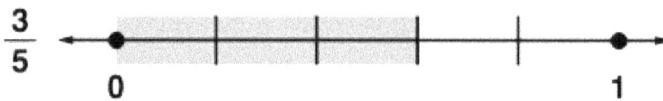

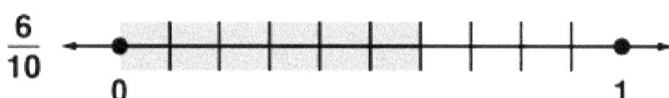

Numbers and Operations
Fractions

Examples

Example 1: Determine the missing value in the following expression: $\frac{4}{7} = \frac{?}{14}$.

If a circle is broken up into 7 equal parts, the image below represents if 4 are shaded in. This image represents the fraction $\frac{4}{7}$.

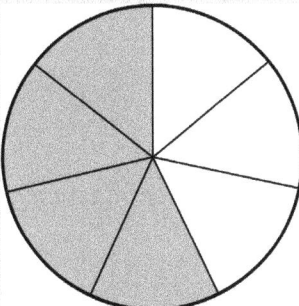

If a circle is broken up into 14 equal parts, the image below represents if 8 are shaded in. One can see that the circle is shaded in the exact same amount as the image seen previously. Therefore, the fractions $\frac{4}{7}$ and $\frac{8}{14}$ are equivalent.

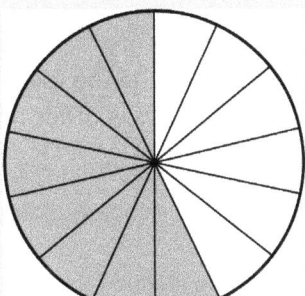

Example 2: Change the fraction $\frac{5}{8}$ into an equivalent fraction with a numerator of 25.

The numerator needs to be multiplied by 5 to become 25. To have an equivalent fraction, the same operation must be done to the denominator. Therefore, the new denominator is $8 \times 5 = 40$. The equivalent fraction is $\frac{25}{40}$.

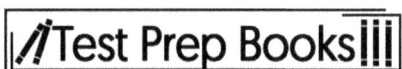

Practice Questions

1. Which fractions are equivalent, or would fill the same portion on a number line?
    a. $\frac{2}{4}$ and $\frac{3}{8}$
    b. $\frac{1}{2}$ and $\frac{4}{8}$
    c. $\frac{3}{6}$ and $\frac{3}{5}$
    d. $\frac{2}{4}$ and $\frac{5}{8}$

2. Given $\frac{2}{5}$, which of the following is NOT an equivalent fraction?
    a. $\frac{16}{40}$
    b. $\frac{8}{20}$
    c. $\frac{4}{10}$
    d. $\frac{6}{10}$

3. To add fractions, denominators must be the same. In the following addition problem, what fraction would the second expression need to be changed into in order to add the fractions together?
$$\frac{1}{8} + \frac{1}{2}$$
    a. $\frac{4}{8}$
    b. $\frac{1}{8}$
    c. $\frac{2}{8}$
    d. $\frac{8}{8}$

4. Given $3\frac{4}{5}$, which of the following is an equivalent fraction?
    a. $\frac{38}{15}$
    b. $\frac{34}{5}$
    c. $\frac{30}{10}$
    d. $\frac{38}{10}$

**Numbers and Operations
Fractions**

5. Write $\frac{96}{80}$ in lowest terms.
   a. $\frac{24}{20}$
   b. $\frac{12}{10}$
   c. $\frac{6}{5}$
   d. $\frac{16}{5}$

Adding and Subtracting Fractions

Adding and subtracting fractions that have the same denominators involves adding or subtracting the numerators. The denominator will stay the same. Therefore, the decomposition process can be made simpler, and the fractions do not have to be broken into unit fractions.

For example, for $4\frac{7}{8} - 2\frac{6}{8}$, the answer is found by adding the answers to both:

$$4 - 2 \text{ and } \frac{7}{8} - \frac{6}{8} \text{ becomes } 2 + \frac{1}{8} = 2\frac{1}{8}$$

A common mistake would be to add the denominators so that $\frac{1}{4} + \frac{1}{4} = \frac{1}{8}$ or to add numerators and denominators so that $\frac{1}{4} + \frac{1}{4} = \frac{2}{8}$. However, conceptually, it is known that two quarters make a half, so neither one of these are correct.

If two fractions have different denominators, equivalent fractions must be used to add or subtract them. The fractions must be converted into fractions that have common denominators. A **least common denominator** or the product of the two denominators can be used as the common denominator.

For example, In the problem $\frac{5}{6} + \frac{2}{3}$, either 6, which is the least common denominator, or 18, which is the product of the denominators, can be used. In order to use 6, $\frac{2}{3}$ must be converted to sixths. A number line can be used to show the equivalent fraction is $\frac{4}{6}$. What happens is that $\frac{2}{3}$ is multiplied by a fractional form of 1 to obtain a denominator of 6. Hence:

$$\frac{2}{3} \times \frac{2}{2} = \frac{4}{6}$$

Therefore, the problem is now $\frac{5}{6} + \frac{4}{6} = \frac{9}{6}$, which can be simplified into $\frac{3}{2}$. In order to use 18, both fractions must be converted into having 18 as their denominator. $\frac{5}{6}$ would have to be multiplied by $\frac{3}{3}$, and $\frac{2}{3}$ would need to be multiplied by $\frac{6}{6}$. The addition problem would be $\frac{15}{18} + \frac{12}{18} = \frac{27}{18}$, which reduces into $\frac{3}{2}$.

It is always possible to find a common denominator by multiplying the denominators. However, when the denominators are large numbers, this method is unwieldy, especially if the answer must be provided in its simplest form. Thus, it's beneficial to find the **least common denominator** of the fractions—the least common denominator is incidentally also the **least common multiple**.

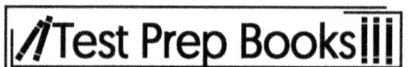

Once equivalent fractions have been found with common denominators, simply add or subtract the numerators to arrive at the answer.

$$\frac{3}{12} + \frac{11}{20} = \frac{15}{60} + \frac{33}{60} = \frac{48}{60} = \frac{4}{5}$$

$$\frac{5}{6} - \frac{7}{18} = \frac{15}{18} - \frac{7}{18} = \frac{8}{18} = \frac{4}{9}$$

Examples

Example 1: $\frac{1}{2} + \frac{3}{4} = ?$

The answer can be found by finding the lowest common denominator, then adding the new fractions together.

$$\frac{1}{2} + \frac{3}{4} = \frac{2}{4} + \frac{3}{4} = \frac{5}{4}$$

Example 2: $\frac{7}{9} - \frac{4}{15} =$

Once again, find the lowest common denominator, then subtract the new fractions.

$$\frac{7}{9} - \frac{4}{15} = \frac{35}{45} - \frac{12}{45} = \frac{23}{45}$$

Practice Questions

1. What two fractions add up to $\frac{7}{6}$?

   a. $\frac{2}{3} + \frac{5}{3}$

   b. $\frac{1}{5} + \frac{6}{5}$

   c. $\frac{1}{6} + \frac{6}{6}$

   d. $\frac{1}{2} + \frac{6}{4}$

2. A closet is filled with red, blue, and green shirts. If $\frac{1}{3}$ of the shirts are green and $\frac{2}{5}$ are red, what fraction of the shirts are blue?

   a. $\frac{4}{15}$

   b. $\frac{1}{5}$

   c. $\frac{7}{15}$

   d. $\frac{1}{2}$

**Numbers and Operations
Fractions**

3. Shawna buys $2\frac{1}{2}$ gallons of paint. If she uses $\frac{1}{3}$ of it on the first day, how much does she have left?

   a. $1\frac{5}{6}$ gallons

   b. $1\frac{1}{2}$ gallons

   c. $1\frac{2}{3}$ gallons

   d. 2 gallons

4. $4\frac{1}{3} + 3\frac{3}{4} =$

   a. $6\frac{5}{12}$

   b. $8\frac{1}{12}$

   c. $8\frac{2}{3}$

   d. $7\frac{7}{12}$

Multiplying and Dividing Fractions

Of the four basic operations that can be performed on fractions, the one that involves the least amount of work is multiplication. To multiply two fractions, simply multiply the numerators together, multiply the denominators together, and place the products of each as a fraction. Whole numbers and mixed numbers can also be expressed as a fraction, as described above, to multiply with a fraction.

Because multiplication is commutative, multiplying a fraction by a whole number is the same as multiplying a whole number by a fraction. The problem involves adding a fraction a specific number of times.

For example, the problem $3 \times \frac{1}{4}$ can be translated into adding the unit fraction three times:

$$\frac{1}{4} + \frac{1}{4} + \frac{1}{4} = \frac{3}{4}$$

Similarly, In the problem $4 \times \frac{2}{5}$, the fraction can be decomposed into $\frac{1}{5} + \frac{1}{5}$ and then added four times to obtain $\frac{8}{5}$. Also, both of these answers can be found by just multiplying the whole number by the numerator of the fraction being multiplied.

The whole numbers can be written in fraction form as:

$$\frac{3}{1} \times \frac{1}{4} = \frac{3}{4}$$

Multiplying a fraction times a fraction involves multiplying the numerators together separately and the denominators together separately.

$$\frac{3}{8} \times \frac{2}{3} = \frac{3 \times 2}{8 \times 3} = \frac{6}{24}$$

Dividing a fraction by a fraction is actually a multiplication problem. It involves flipping the divisor and then multiplying normally.

$$\frac{22}{5} \div \frac{1}{2} = \frac{22}{5} \times \frac{2}{1} = \frac{44}{5}$$

The same procedure can be implemented for division problems involving fractions and whole numbers. The whole number can be rewritten as a fraction over a denominator of 1, and then division can be completed.

A common denominator approach can also be used in dividing fractions. Considering the same problem, $\frac{22}{5} \div \frac{1}{2}$, a common denominator between the two fractions is 10. $\frac{22}{5}$ would be rewritten as $\frac{22}{5} \times \frac{2}{2} = \frac{44}{10}$, and $\frac{1}{2}$ would be rewritten as:

$$\frac{1}{2} \times \frac{5}{5} = \frac{5}{10}$$

Dividing both numbers straight across results in:

$$\frac{44}{10} \div \frac{5}{10} = \frac{44/5}{10/10} = \frac{44/5}{1} = \frac{44}{5}$$

Many real-world problems will involve the use of fractions. Key words include actual fraction values, such as *half, quarter, third, fourth*, etc. The best approach to solving word problems involving fractions is to draw a picture or diagram that represents the scenario being discussed, while deciding which type of operation is necessary in order to solve the problem. A phrase such as "one fourth of 60 pounds of coal" creates a scenario in which multiplication should be used, and the mathematical form of the phrase is $\frac{1}{4} \times 60$.

Examples

Example 1: Multiply $4 \times \frac{2}{5}$.

In this example, we can write the whole number 4 as $\frac{4}{1}$. Entering it into the equation gives us $\frac{4}{1} \times \frac{2}{5} = \frac{8}{5}$, which could be also written as $1\frac{3}{5}$.

Example 2: Multiply and reduce $\frac{5}{15} \times \frac{225}{30}$.

An easy way to multiply two fractions and simplify is to rewrite each value as its prime factorization and then cross out any common factor between the numerator and denominator.

$$\frac{5}{15} \times \frac{225}{30} = \frac{5}{5 \times 3} \times \frac{5 \times 5 \times 3 \times 3}{5 \times 3 \times 2} = \frac{5}{2}.$$

**Numbers and Operations
Fractions**

Practice Questions

1. Simplify the following fraction:

$$\frac{\frac{5}{7}}{\frac{9}{11}}$$

   a. $\frac{55}{63}$

   b. $\frac{7}{1000}$

   c. $\frac{13}{15}$

   d. $\frac{5}{11}$

2. Last year, the New York City area received approximately $27\frac{3}{4}$ inches of snow. The Denver area received approximately 3 times as much snow as New York City. How much snow fell in Denver?

   a. 60 inches

   b. $27\frac{1}{4}$ inches

   c. $9\frac{1}{4}$ inches

   d. $83\frac{1}{4}$ inches

3. Divide and reduce $\frac{4}{13} \div \frac{27}{169}$.

   a. $\frac{52}{27}$

   b. $\frac{51}{27}$

   c. $\frac{52}{29}$

   d. $\frac{51}{29}$

4. Multiply and reduce $\frac{15}{23} \times \frac{54}{127}$.

   a. $\frac{810}{2921}$

   b. $\frac{81}{292}$

   c. $\frac{69}{150}$

   d. $\frac{2921}{810}$

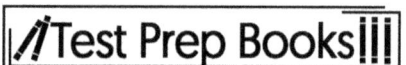

Answer Explanations

Understanding the Unit Fraction as One Part of a Whole

1. D: Even though all of the fractions have the same numerator, this is the one that represents the greatest part of the whole. All other choices are smaller portions of the whole, as seen by this graphic representation.

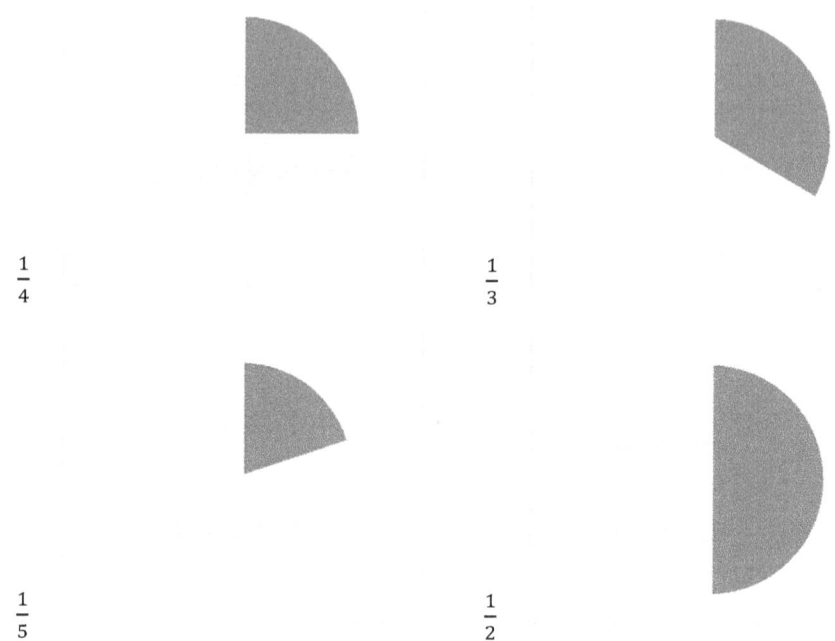

2. B: The pie was split into 8 parts, and 5 were taken by family members. Therefore, $\frac{5}{8}$ of the pie was eaten. There were three pieces left, which represents $\frac{3}{8}$ of the pie.

3. C: The fraction $\frac{1}{2}$ represents exactly half of the whole. The fraction $\frac{4}{6}$ represents more than one half of a whole (4 of 6 equal parts), and the fractions $\frac{3}{9}$ and $\frac{1}{3}$ represent less than a half of a whole (3 out of 9 or 1 out of 3 equal parts). The value $\frac{5}{10}$ is equivalent to the fraction $\frac{1}{2}$. If a pie was sliced into 10 equal parts and 5 were eaten, exactly half of the pie would be eaten.

4. D: 7 of the bags were distributed to kids, so that means 13 were leftover and uneaten. Then, 2 more bags were left uneaten. In total 15 out of the 20 bags were left uneaten, and the equivalent fraction is $\frac{15}{20}$.

5. B: Because 6 out of the 21 students wear glasses, $21 - 6 = 15$ students do not wear glasses. Therefore, 15 out of 21 students don't wear glasses, and the corresponding fraction is $\frac{15}{21}$.

Proper Fractions, Improper Fractions, and Mixed Numbers

1. B: To rewrite a mixed number as an improper fraction, multiply the whole number times the denominator and add the numerator. Then, write this value over the existing denominator. Therefore,

Numbers and Operations Fractions

$$4\frac{11}{12} = \frac{4 \times 12 + 11}{12} = \frac{59}{12}$$

2. A: Divide 54 by 15:

$$15\overline{)54}$$
$$-45$$
$$9$$

The result is $3\frac{9}{15}$. Reduce the remainder for the final answer, $3\frac{3}{5}$.

3. D: The original number was $8\frac{3}{7}$. Multiply the denominator by the whole number portion. Add the numerator and put the total over the original denominator.

$$\frac{(8 \times 7) + 3}{7} = \frac{59}{7}$$

4. C: To compare the fractions, write the mixed numbers as improper fractions. Because all the values have the same denominator, the one with the largest numerator is the largest amount.

$$4\frac{2}{13} = \frac{4 \times 13 + 2}{13} = \frac{54}{13} \text{ and } 6\frac{1}{13} = \frac{6 \times 13 + 1}{13} = \frac{79}{13}$$

The other two options are given as improper fractions: $\frac{55}{13}$ and $\frac{65}{13}$. Therefore, the largest value is $6\frac{1}{13} = \frac{79}{13}$.

5. D: To write an improper fraction as a mixed number, divide the numerator by the denominator. Keep the whole number and then write the remainder over the original denominator. $-117 \div 15 = -7R12$. Therefore, the equivalent mixed number is $-7\frac{12}{15}$.

Representing Fractions using Models

1. D: This solution shows the strip separated into 5 pieces, which is necessary for it to be filled in to show $\frac{3}{5}$. Choice A shows the strip filled to $\frac{1}{2}$, and Choice B shows the strip filled to $\frac{2}{4}$, which is also $\frac{1}{2}$. Neither of these selections is correct. While Choice C shows 3 portions filled, the total number of portions is only 4, making the fraction filled $\frac{3}{4}$. This is also an incorrect choice.

2. A: The light gray portion represents $\frac{4}{5}$ and the dark gray portion represents $\frac{3}{5}$, to total $\frac{7}{5}$. Choice B is not correct because it misrepresents the dark gray portion. Choice C is not correct because it misrepresents the light gray portion. Choice D is not correct because it includes the 1 with the dark gray portion.

3. B: Each fully shaded circle represents a whole, and there are two of them, so the whole number portion is 2. The other circle is divided into three equal parts, and one part is shaded in. The shaded in portion of this circle is $\frac{1}{3}$. Putting these values together shows that $2\frac{1}{3}$ of the circles is shaded in.

Composing and Decomposing Fractions

1. A: $\frac{8}{7}$ is the same as $8 \times \frac{1}{7}$, which is represented by the first option: $\frac{1}{7}+\frac{1}{7}+\frac{1}{7}+\frac{1}{7}+\frac{1}{7}+\frac{1}{7}+\frac{1}{7}+\frac{1}{7}$. This can be thought of as cutting a pie into seven slices and then serving 8 slices. Since you need more slices than you have in your pie, you actually need to cut up two pies and take one piece from the second pie. This is because $\frac{8}{7}$ is an improper fraction, which means the numerator (top number) is greater than the denominator (bottom number).

2. B: Each $\frac{1}{5}$ fraction can be considered as a piece of a pie cut into 5 equal parts. There are 7 of them in the expression, and the first 5 create a whole (five equal parts). Therefore, $\frac{1}{5}+\frac{1}{5}+\frac{1}{5}+\frac{1}{5}+\frac{1}{5}=1$. There are two left over, which can be represented as $\frac{2}{5}$. Putting these together we have $1\frac{2}{5}$. An equivalent expression would be $\frac{7}{5}$.

3. C: Each fraction in the problem has a denominator of 9, so the whole is broken up into 9 equal parts in each case. The correct choice is the one that adds to 8 equal parts in the numerator. Option A adds to 7 equal parts, and Options B and D add to 9 equal parts (which is the entire whole). Option C adds to 8 equal parts, which is equivalent to the fraction $\frac{8}{9}$.

4. D: The righthand side of the equals sign shows the fraction $\frac{5}{5}$, which represents a whole divided into 5 equal parts. Therefore, the values in the numerators on the left-hand side must have a sum of 5. Right now, $2 + 1 = 3$, so there are 3 equal parts accounted for. 2 more need to be added to have a sum of 5. Therefore, the missing value is 2.

5. A: Each fraction has a denominator of 8, which means a whole divided into 8 equal parts. However, the quantity on the right side shows $\frac{11}{8}$, which is equal to one whole plus 3 out of 8 equal parts. Therefore, to obtain $\frac{11}{8}$ on the lefthand side, 8 out of 8 equal parts must be added. The equivalent fraction is $\frac{8}{8}$. This quantity is equal to 1.

Representing Equivalent Fractions

1. B: $\frac{1}{2}$ is the same fraction as $\frac{4}{8}$, and would both fill up the same portion of a number line.

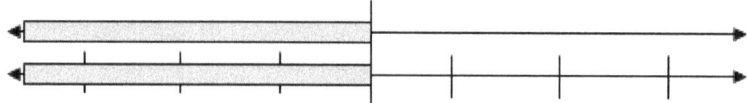

None of the other choices represent equivalent portions to each other, as seen below.

Choice A:

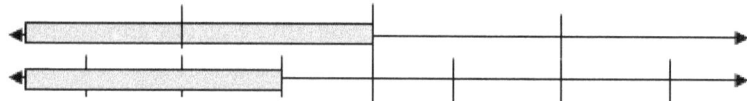

Choice C:

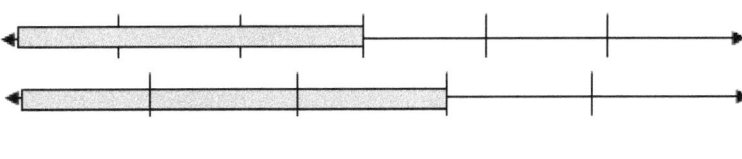

Choice D:

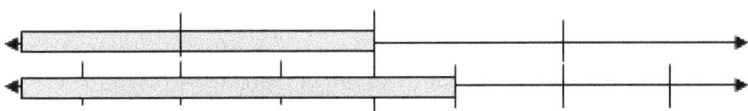

2. **D:** An equivalent fraction is found by multiplying the numerator and the denominator by the same amount. Option A is equivalent to $\frac{2}{5}$ since it is obtained by multiplying the numerator and the denominator both by 8. Option B is equivalent to $\frac{2}{5}$ since it is obtained by multiplying the numerator and the denominator both by 4. Option C is equivalent to $\frac{2}{5}$ since it is obtained by multiplying the numerator and the denominator both by 2. Option D is not equivalent to $\frac{2}{5}$ since the same number cannot be multiplied by both the numerator and the denominator to obtain $\frac{6}{10}$.

3. **A:** To add the fractions, the denominators must both be 8. To turn the denominator into 8 in the second expression, the denominator of 2 must be multiplied by 4. To keep the fraction as an equivalent fraction, the numerator of 1 must be multiplied by the same number. Therefore, the equivalent fraction to add is $\frac{1\times4}{2\times4} = \frac{4}{8}$.

4. **D:** Because all the answer choices are written as improper fractions, rewrite $3\frac{4}{5}$ as an improper fraction.

$$3\frac{4}{5} = \frac{3 \times 5 + 4}{5} = \frac{19}{5}$$

Equivalent fractions are obtained by multiplying both the numerator and the denominator by the same value. If both the numerator and denominator are multiplied by 2, $\frac{38}{10}$ is obtained. Therefore, this is the equivalent fraction.

5. **C:** A fraction in lowest terms is an equivalent fraction that does not have any common factors between the numerator and the denominator. Given the fraction $\frac{96}{80}$, the largest common factor between 96 and 80 is 16. Therefore, divide both the numerator and denominator by 16 to obtain the fraction in lowest terms.

$$\frac{96}{80} = \frac{96 \div 16}{80 \div 16} = \frac{6}{5}$$

Adding and Subtracting Fractions

1. **C:** To add fractions, the denominator must be the same. This is the only choice with both denominators of 6. Adding the numerators totals 7, for a fraction of $\frac{7}{6}$. Choice A equals $\frac{7}{3}$, Choice B equals $\frac{7}{5}$, and Choice D equals $\frac{8}{4}$ or 2.

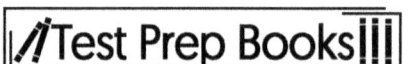

2. A: The total fraction taken up by green and red shirts will be $\frac{1}{3} + \frac{2}{5} = \frac{5}{15} + \frac{6}{15} = \frac{11}{15}$. The remaining fraction is $1 - \frac{11}{15} = \frac{15}{15} - \frac{11}{15} = \frac{4}{15}$.

3. C: If she has used $\frac{1}{3}$ of the paint, she has $\frac{2}{3}$ remaining. $2\frac{1}{2}$ gallons are the same as $\frac{5}{2}$ gallons. The calculation is $\frac{2}{3} \times \frac{5}{2} = \frac{5}{3} = 1\frac{2}{3}$ gallons.

4. B: Writing out this problem can add the whole numbers together.

$$4\frac{1}{3} + 3\frac{3}{4} = 4 + 3 + \frac{1}{3} + \frac{3}{4} = 7 + \frac{1}{3} + \frac{3}{4}$$

Adding the fractions gives:

$$\frac{1}{3} + \frac{3}{4} = \frac{4}{12} + \frac{9}{12} = \frac{13}{12} = 1 + \frac{1}{12}$$

Thus,

$$7 + 1 + \frac{1}{12} = 8\frac{1}{12}$$

Multiplying and Dividing Fractions

1. A: First simplify the larger fraction by separating it into two. When dividing one fraction by another, remember to invert the second fraction and multiply the two as follows:

$$\frac{5}{7} \times \frac{11}{9}$$

The resulting fraction $\frac{55}{63}$ cannot be simplified further, so this is the answer to the problem.

2. D: To find Denver's total snowfall, 3 must be multiplied times $27\frac{3}{4}$. In order to easily do this, the mixed number should be converted into an improper fraction.

$$27\frac{3}{4} = \frac{27 \times 4 + 3}{4} = \frac{111}{4}$$

Therefore, Denver had approximately $\frac{3 \times 111}{4} = \frac{333}{4}$ inches of snow. The improper fraction can be converted back into a mixed number through division.

$$\frac{333}{4} = 83\frac{1}{4} \text{ inches}$$

3. A: First, set up the division problem.

$$\frac{4}{13} \div \frac{27}{169}$$

Numbers and Operations
Decimals

Flip the second fraction and multiply.

$$\frac{4}{13} \times \frac{169}{27}$$

Simplify and reduce with cross multiplication.

$$\frac{4}{1} \times \frac{13}{27}$$

Multiply across the top and across the bottom to solve.

$$\frac{4 \times 13}{1 \times 27} = \frac{52}{27}$$

4. A: First, line up the fractions.

$$\frac{15}{23} \times \frac{54}{127}$$

Multiply across the top and across the bottom:

$$\frac{15 \times 54}{23 \times 127} = \frac{810}{2921}$$

Decimals

Relating Decimals to Fractions

Fractions with denominators of 10 or 100 can easily be converted to decimal notation. This is because the base-10 system we use for place value has a specific place for tenths and hundredths. The tenths place is one place to the right of the decimal point, so one tenth or $\frac{1}{10}$ is written as .1 (you can also include the zero to the left of the decimal point without changing the value: 0.1). As an example, the fraction $\frac{4}{10}$, which is read as "four tenths," can be written .4.

The same concept applies for fractions with a denominator of 100 because these fractions represent parts of one hundred, or hundredths, just like the place value two spaces to the right of the decimal point. $\frac{7}{100}$ is written .07.

Basically, because a fraction can be thought of as a division problem (the numerator (or top number) is divided by the denominator (or bottom number), to convert a fraction to a decimal, the numerator is divided by the denominator.

Decimals are designated by a decimal point which indicates that what follows the point is a value that is less than 1 and is added to the integer number preceding the decimal point. The digit immediately following the decimal point is in the tenths place, the digit following the tenths place is in the hundredths place, and so on.

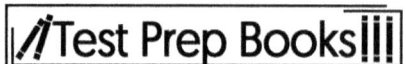

Numbers and Operations
Decimals

As an example, the decimal number 1.735 has a value greater than 1 but less than 2. The 7 represents seven tenths of the unit 1 (0.7 or $\frac{7}{10}$); the 3 represents three hundredths of 1 (0.03 or $\frac{3}{100}$); and the 5 represents five thousandths of 1 (0.005 or $\frac{5}{1000}$).

Examples

Example 1: Convert $\frac{3}{8}$ to a decimal.

$\frac{3}{8}$ can be converted to a decimal by dividing 3 by 8 ($\frac{3}{8} = 0.375$). Therefore, the fraction $\frac{3}{8}$ is equivalent to the decimal 0.375.

Example 2: Change 4.8 to a fraction and simplify.

To convert a decimal to a fraction, remember that any number to the left of the decimal point will be a whole number. Then, since 0.8 goes to the tenths place, it can be placed over 10 to get $4\frac{8}{10}$. However, as both 8 and 10 can be divided by 2, the fraction can be simplified to get $4\frac{4}{5}$.

Practice Questions

1. Convert $\frac{3}{25}$ to a decimal.
    a. 0.15
    b. 0.1
    c. 0.9
    d. 0.12

2. Change 9.3 to a fraction.
    a. $9\frac{3}{10}$
    b. $\frac{903}{1,000}$
    c. $\frac{9.03}{100}$
    d. $3\frac{9}{10}$

3. Rewrite $\frac{82}{10}$ as a decimal.
    a. 0.82
    b. 8.2
    c. 82.0
    d. 8.21

Numbers and Operations
Decimals

4. Rewrite $\frac{15}{9}$ as a decimal.
   a. 1.7
   b. 1.6
   c. $1.\overline{6}$
   d. 1.59

5. Convert 4.679 to a fraction.
   a. $\frac{4,679}{100}$
   b. $4\frac{679}{100}$
   c. $4\frac{679}{10,000}$
   d. $4\frac{679}{1,000}$

Adding and Subtracting Decimals

Addition with Decimals

To add decimal numbers, each number needs to be lined up by the decimal point in vertical columns. For each number being added, the zeros to the right of the last number need to be filled in so that each of the numbers has the same number of places to the right of the decimal. Then, the columns can be added together.

Here is an example of $2.45 + 1.3 + 8.891$ written in column form:

$$\begin{array}{r} 2.450 \\ 1.300 \\ + 8.891 \end{array}$$

Zeros have been added in the columns so that each number has the same number of places to the right of the decimal. Added together, the correct answer is 12.641:

$$\begin{array}{r} 2.450 \\ 1.300 \\ + 8.891 \\ \hline 12.641 \end{array}$$

Subtraction with Decimals

Subtracting decimal numbers is the same process as adding decimals.

Here is $7.89 - 4.235$ written in column form:

$$\begin{array}{r} 7.890 \\ - 4.235 \\ \hline 3.655 \end{array}$$

A zero has been added in the column so that each number has the same number of places to the right of the decimal.

53

Examples

Example 1: Add 5.8791 + 2.835.

To add decimals, line them up vertically with decimal points aligning. Then, add each top digit to its corresponding bottom digit, working from right to left. If a sum is greater than 9, a 1 is carried over to the next digit and added to those values. Notice that a 0 is added to 2.835 so that the values have the same number of decimal places.

$$\begin{array}{r} 111 \\ 5.8791 \\ +2.8350 \\ \hline 8.7141 \end{array}$$

Example 2: Subtract 4.575 − 3.258.

To subtract decimals, line them up vertically with decimal points aligning. Then, subtract each bottom digit from the top digit working from right to left. If the digit on top is smaller than the digit on the bottom, then a 1 must be borrowed from the next digit to the left. This decreases the left value by 1 and adds 10 to the right value.

$$\begin{array}{r} 4.56\cancel{7}15 \\ -3.258 \\ \hline 1.317 \end{array}$$

Practice Questions

1. 3.4 + 2.35 + 4 =
    a. 5.35
    b. 9.2
    c. 9.75
    d. 10.25

2. Add 1.001 + 5.629.
    a. 4.472
    b. 4.628
    c. 5.630
    d. 6.630

3. Subtract 701.1 − 52.33.
    a. 753.43
    b. 648.77
    c. 652.77
    d. 638.43

Numbers and Operations
Decimals

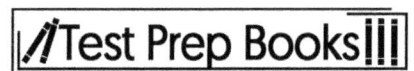

4. Subtract $-3 - 2.452$.
   a. -0.548
   b. -5.452
   c. 0.548
   d. 5.452

5. Subtract $6 - 4.316$.
   a. 1.794
   b. 1.784
   c. 1.684
   d. 2.684

Multiplying and Dividing Decimals

Multiplication with Decimals

The simplest way to multiply decimals is to calculate the product as if the decimals are not there, then count the number of decimal places in the original problem. Use that total to place the decimal the same number of places over in your answer, counting from right to left.

For example, 0.5×1.25 can be rewritten and multiplied as 5×125, which equals 625. Then the decimal is added three places from the right for .625.

The final answer will have the same number of decimal places as the total number of decimal places in the problem. The first number has one decimal place, and the second number has two decimal places. Therefore, the final answer will contain three decimal places:

$$0.5 \times 1.25 = 0.625$$

Division with Decimals

Dividing a decimal by a whole number entails using long division first by ignoring the decimal point. Then, the decimal point is moved the number of places given in the problem.

For example, $6.8 \div 4$ can be rewritten as $68 \div 4$, which is 17. There is one non-zero integer to the right of the decimal point, so the final solution would have one decimal place to the right of the solution. In this case, the solution is 1.7.

Dividing a decimal by another decimal requires changing the divisor to a whole number by moving its decimal point. The decimal place of the dividend should be moved by the same number of places as the divisor. Then, the problem is the same as dividing a decimal by a whole number.

As an example, $5.72 \div 1.1$ has a divisor with one decimal point in the denominator. The expression can be rewritten as $57.2 \div 11$ by moving each number one decimal place to the right to eliminate the decimal. The long division can be completed as $572 \div 11$ with a result of 52. Since there is one non-zero integer to the right of the decimal point in the problem, the final solution is 5.2.

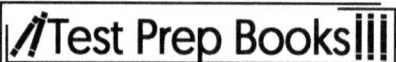

Examples

Example 1: Solve 8 ÷ 0.16.

8 ÷ 0.16 has a divisor with two decimal points in the denominator. The expression can be rewritten as 800 ÷ 16 by moving each number two decimal places to the right to eliminate the decimal in the divisor. The long division can be completed with a result of 50.

Example 2: Solve 5.392 × 0.01.

To multiply decimals, remove the decimals and multiply them as whole numbers. In this example, 5392 × 1 = 5392. Then, count the number of decimal points in the original problem. There are 5 in total. The decimal in 5392 must be moved 5 places to the left, adding any zeros if necessary. Therefore, the answer is 0.05392.

Practice Questions

1. 5.88 × 3.2 =
    a. 18.816
    b. 16.44
    c. 20.352
    d. 17

2. Divide 1,015 ÷ 1.4.
    a. 7,250
    b. 0.725
    c. 7.25
    d. 725

3. Multiply 12.4 × 0.2.
    a. 12.6
    b. 2.48
    c. 12.48
    d. 2.6

4. Divide 852.6 ÷ 0.02.
    a. 42,630
    b. 42.63
    c. 4,263
    d. 0.4263

5. Multiply 5.637 × 23.21.
    a. 13.083477
    b. 130.83477
    c. 130.8347
    d. 1308.3477

**Numbers and Operations
Decimals**

6. Divide 3434.78 ÷ 5.26.
   a. 65.3
   b. 6.52
   c. 653
   d. 6.53

Answer Explanations

Relating Decimals to Fractions

1. D: The fraction is converted so that the denominator is 100 by multiplying the numerator and denominator by 4, to get $\frac{3}{25} = \frac{12}{100}$. Dividing a number by 100 just moves the decimal point two places to the left, with a result of 0.12.

2. A: To convert a decimal to a fraction, remember that any number to the left of the decimal point will be a whole number. Then, since 0.3 goes to the tenths place, the three can be placed over 10, giving a final answer of $9\frac{3}{10}$.

3. B: To convert a fraction to a decimal, divide the numerator by the denominator. Therefore,

$$\frac{82}{10} = 82 \div 10 = 8.2$$

This is read as eight and two tenths.

4. C: To convert a fraction to a decimal, divide the numerator by the denominator. It is true that $\frac{15}{9} = 1.666\ldots$ This is a repeating decimal. A bar is placed over the 6 in the decimal form to show it repeats. Therefore, the correct response is $1.\overline{6}$. The value 1.7 is a rounded approximation of $\frac{15}{9}$.

5. D: To convert 4.679 to a fraction, the 4 can remain as a whole number if the fraction is written as a mixed number. Looking at the decimal portion of the number, the right-most value (the 9) is in the thousandths place. Therefore, 679 needs to be written over a denominator of 1,000. Therefore, the correct response is $4\frac{679}{1,000}$.

Adding and Subtracting Decimals

1. C: The decimal points are lined up, with zeroes put in as needed. Then, the numbers are added just like integers:

$$\begin{array}{r} 3.40 \\ 2.35 \\ +4.00 \\ \hline 9.75 \end{array}$$

2. D: Set up the problem, with the larger number on top and numbers lined up at the decimal. Add, carrying anything over 9 into the next column to the left. Solve from right to left to find the answer of 6.630.

3. B: Set up the problem, with the larger number on top and numbers lined up at the decimal. Insert 0 in any blank spots to the right of the decimal as placeholders. Begin subtracting with the far right column. Borrow 10 from the column to the left, when necessary. Once operations are complete, the answer is 648.77.

4. B: To subtract two negative numbers, add the positive values and then attach a negative sign. -3 can be written as -3.000 so that each decimal has the same number of units. Then, add each place value individually from right to left. $3.000 + 2.452 = 5.452$. Therefore, the answer is -5.452.

5. C: To subtract decimals, line them up vertically with decimal points aligning. Then, subtract each bottom digit from the top digit working from right to left. If the digit on top is smaller than the digit on the bottom, then a 1 must be borrowed from the next digit to the left. If a 1 is borrowed from a 0, then move to the next digit to the left and borrow a 1 from that column.

$$\begin{array}{r} 5\cancel{6}.\cancel{9}0\ \cancel{9}0\ 10 \\ -\ 4\ .\ 3\ 1\ 6 \\ \hline 1\ .\ 6\ 8\ 4 \end{array}$$

Multiplying and Dividing Decimals

1. A: This problem can be multiplied as 588×32, except at the end, the decimal point needs to be moved three places to the left. Performing the multiplication will give 18,816; moving the decimal place over three places results in 18.816.

2. D: Set up the division problem.

$$1.4\overline{\smash{)}1\ 0\ 1\ 5}$$

Move the decimal over one place to the right in both numbers.

$$14\overline{\smash{)}1\ 0\ 1\ 5\ 0}$$

14 does not go into 1 or 10 but does go into 101 so start there.

$$\begin{array}{r} 7\ 2\ 5 \\ 14\overline{\smash{)}1\ 0\ 1\ 5\ 0} \\ -\ 9\ 8 \\ \hline 3\ 5 \\ -\ 2\ 8 \\ \hline 7\ 0 \\ -\ 7\ 0 \\ \hline 0 \end{array}$$

The result is 725.

3. B: Set up the problem, with the larger number on top. Multiply as if there are no decimal places. Add the answer rows together. Count the number of decimal places that were in the original numbers ($1 + 1 = 2$). Place the decimal 2 places to the right for the final solution of 2.48.

Numbers and Operations
Percentages

4. A: To divide a decimal by a decimal, move the decimal point in the divisor (in this case the 0.02) all the way to the right. The result is 2. Then, move the decimal point to the right the same number of units in the dividend (852.6). The result is 85,260. Then, divide these two new values to obtain the result. $85,260 \div 2 = 42,630$.

5. B: To multiply decimals, remove the decimals and multiply them as whole numbers. In this example, $5637 \times 2321 = 13,083,477$. Then, count the total number of values in decimal places in the original problem. There are 5 total. Finally, move the decimal point in 13,083,477 five places to the left. Therefore, the result is 130.83477.

6. C: To divide a decimal by a decimal, move the decimal point in the divisor all the way to the right, counting the number of place values. Therefore, 5.26 turns into 526 by moving the decimal point 2 units to the right. Then, move the decimal point to the right 2 places in the dividend. In this example, the dividend turns into 343,478. Then, divide the two new values. $343,478 \div 526 = 653$.

Percentages

Representing Percents

Think of percentages as fractions with a denominator of 100. In fact, percentage means "per hundred." The basic percent equation is the following:

$$\frac{is}{of} = \frac{\%}{100}$$

The placement of numbers in the equation depends on what the question asks.

Examples

Example 1: Find 40% of 80.

Basically, the problem is asking, "What is 40% of 80?" The 40% is the percent, and 80 is the number to find the percent "of." The equation is:

$$\frac{x}{80} = \frac{40}{100}$$

Solving the equation by cross-multiplication, the problem becomes $100x = 80(40)$. Solving for x gives the answer:

$$x = 32$$

Example 2: What percent of 100 is 20?

The 20 fills in the "is" portion, while 100 fills in the "of." The question asks for the percent, so that will be x, the unknown. The following equation is set up:

$$\frac{20}{100} = \frac{x}{100}$$

Cross-multiplying yields the equation $100x = 20(100)$. Solving for x gives the answer of 20%.

Practice Questions

1. 6 is 30% of what number?
    a. 18
    b. 20
    c. 24
    d. 26

2. What is 39% of 164?
    a. 63.96
    b. 23.78
    c. 6,396
    d. 2.38

3. 30% of what number is 30?
    a. 1
    b. 10
    c. 30
    d. 100

4. Which of the following is NOT a way to write 40 percent of N?
    a. $(0.4)N$
    b. $\frac{2}{5}N$
    c. $40N$
    d. $\frac{4N}{10}$

Using Percents to Relate Numerical Data

In some cases, it is useful to compare numerical data and determine the relationship between values. One of the best ways to mathematically compare two values is to compute the percentage difference between the two values. For example, consider a given music shop that had a net profit of $120,000 in the first year of operation and $185,000 over the second year. Rather than simply finding the net difference between the two years (using subtraction), the business owner may want to know by what percentage his profit increased; in other words, how much his profit in the second year increased relative to his first year. In such cases, the percentage change is desired.

Problems dealing with percentages may involve an original value, a change in that value, and a percentage change. A problem will provide two pieces of information and ask to find the third. To do so, this formula is used: $\frac{change}{original\ value} \times 100 =$ percent change.

Numbers and Operations
Percentages

Examples

Example 1: Attendance at a baseball stadium has dropped 16% from last year. Last year's average attendance was 40,000. What is this year's average attendance?

Using the formula and information, the change is unknown (x), the original value is 40,000, and the percent change is 16%. The formula can be written as:

$$\frac{x}{40,000} \times 100 = 16$$

When solving for x, it is determined the change was 6,400. The problem asked for this year's average attendance, so to calculate, the change (6,400) is subtracted from last year's attendance (40,000) to determine this year's average attendance is 33,600.

Example 2: A store advertises that all its merchandise has been reduced by 25%. The new price of a pair of shoes is $60. What was the original price?

This problem can be solved by writing a proportion. Two ratios should be written comparing the cost and the percent of the original cost. The new cost is 75% of the original cost (100% − 25%); and the original cost is 100% of the original cost. The unknown original cost can be represented by x. The proportion would be set up as: $\frac{60}{75} = \frac{x}{100}$. Solving the proportion, it is determined the original cost was $80.

Practice Questions

1. A couple buys a house for $150,000. They sell it for $165,000. By what percentage did the house's value increase?
    a. 18%
    b. 13%
    c. 10%
    d. 12%

2. After a 20% discount, Frank purchased a new refrigerator for $850. How much did he save from the original price?
    a. $170
    b. $212.50
    c. $105.75
    d. $200

3. Keith's bakery had 252 customers go through its doors last week. This week, that number increased to 378. Express this increase as a percentage.
    a. 26%
    b. 50%
    c. 35%
    d. 12%

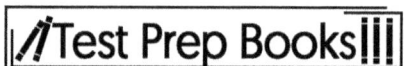

Numbers and Operations
Percentages

4. A traveler takes an hour to drive to a museum, spends 3 hours and 30 minutes there, and takes half an hour to drive home. What percentage of their time was spent driving?
   a. 15%
   b. 30%
   c. 40%
   d. 60%

Converting Between Percentages, Decimals, and Fractions

Decimals and Percentages: Since a percentage is based on "per hundred," decimals and percentages can be converted by multiplying or dividing by 100. Practically speaking, this always amounts to moving the decimal point two places to the right or left, depending on the conversion. To convert a percentage to a decimal, move the decimal point two places to the left and remove the % sign. To convert a decimal to a percentage, move the decimal point two places to the right and add a % sign.

Example

$$65\% = 0.65$$
$$0.33 = 33\%$$
$$0.215 = 21.5\%$$
$$99.99\% = 0.9999$$
$$500\% = 5.00$$
$$7.55 = 755\%$$

Fractions and Percentages: Remember that a percentage is a number per one hundred. So, a percentage can be converted to a fraction by making the number in the percentage the numerator and putting 100 as the denominator:

$$43\% = \frac{43}{100}$$

$$97\% = \frac{97}{100}$$

Note that the percent symbol (%) kind of looks like a 0, a 1, and another 0. So, think of a percentage like 54% as 54 over 100.

To convert a fraction to a percent, follow the same logic. If the fraction happens to have 100 in the denominator, you're in luck. Just take the numerator and add a percent symbol:

$$\frac{28}{100} = 28\%$$

Otherwise, divide the numerator by the denominator to get a decimal, then convert the decimal to a percentage:

$$\frac{9}{12} = 0.75 = 75\%$$

Numbers and Operations
Percentages

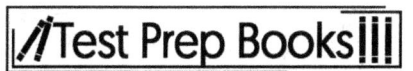

Another option is to make the denominator equal to 100. Be sure to multiply the numerator by the same number as the denominator:

$$\frac{3}{20} \times \frac{5}{5} = \frac{15}{100} = 15\%$$

Fractions and Decimals: To convert a fraction to a decimal divide the numerator by the denominator:

$$\frac{5}{20} = 0.25$$

The other option is to multiply the numerator and denominator by whatever is needed to make the denominator equal to 100. Once the denominator is equal to 100, the numerator can be directly made a decimal:

$$\frac{5}{20} \times \frac{5}{5} = \frac{25}{100} = 0.25$$

To convert a fraction to a decimal follow the same logic, then simplify if possible:

$$0.65 = \frac{65}{100} = \frac{13}{20}$$

Examples

Example 1: Convert $\frac{1}{8}\%$ to a decimal.

First, convert the fraction to a decimal by division. $1 \div 8 = 0.125$. Therefore, $\frac{1}{8}\% = 0.125\%$. Finally, convert the percent to a decimal by moving the decimal point two places to the left. The corresponding decimal is 0.00125.

Example 2: Convert 35% to a reduced fraction.

To convert a percent to a fraction, drop the percent symbol and write the number over a denominator of 100. This results in $\frac{35}{100}$. This fraction is not reduced because both the numerator and the denominator share a common factor of 5. Dividing a 5 out of both results in $\frac{7}{20}$.

Practice Questions

1. How will $\frac{4}{5}$ be written as a percent?
   a. 40 percent
   b. 125 percent
   c. 90 percent
   d. 80 percent

2. Convert $\frac{5}{8}$ to the nearest hundredth.
   a. 0.62
   b. 1.05
   c. 0.63
   d. 1.60

3. Change 0.56 to a fraction.
   a. $\frac{5.6}{100}$
   b. $\frac{14}{25}$
   c. $\frac{56}{1000}$
   d. $\frac{56}{10}$

4. Change $3\frac{3}{5}$ to a decimal.
   a. 3.6
   b. 4.67
   c. 5.3
   d. 0.28

5. Arrange the following numbers from least to greatest value: $0.85, \frac{4}{5}, \frac{2}{3}, \frac{91}{100}$
   a. $0.85, \frac{4}{5}, \frac{2}{3}, \frac{91}{100}$
   b. $\frac{4}{5}, 0.85, \frac{91}{100}, \frac{2}{3}$
   c. $\frac{2}{3}, \frac{4}{5}, 0.85, \frac{91}{100}$
   d. $0.85, \frac{91}{100}, \frac{4}{5}, \frac{2}{3}$

Answer Explanations

Representing Percents

1. B: 30% is $\frac{3}{10}$. The number itself must be $\frac{10}{3}$ of 6, or:

$$\frac{10}{3} \times 6 = 10 \times 2 = 20$$

2. A: This question involves the percent formula. Since we're beginning with a percent, also known as a number over 100, we'll put 39 on the right side of the equation:

$$\frac{x}{164} = \frac{39}{100}$$

Numbers and Operations
Percentages

Now, multiply 164 and 39 to get 6,396, which then needs to be divided by 100.

$$6{,}396 \div 100 = 63.96$$

3. D: The following equation uses the clues and numbers in the problem:

$$\frac{30}{x} = \frac{30}{100}$$

Cross-multiplying results in the equation $30(100) = 30x$. Solving for x gives the answer $x = 100$.

4. C: $40N$ would be 4,000% of N. All of the other coefficients are equivalent to $\frac{40}{100}$ or 40%.

Using Percents to Relate Numerical Data

1. C: The value went up by:

$$\$165{,}000 - \$150{,}000 = \$15{,}000$$

Out of $150,000, this is $\frac{15{,}000}{150{,}000} = \frac{1}{10}$. Convert this to having a denominator of 100, the result is $\frac{10}{100}$ or 10%.

2. B: Since $850 is the price *after* a 20% discount, $850 represents 80% of the original price. To determine the original price, set up a proportion with the ratio of the sale price (850) to original price (unknown) equal to the ratio of sale percentage (where x represents the unknown original price):

$$\frac{850}{x} = \frac{80}{100}$$

To solve a proportion, cross multiply the numerators and denominators and set the products equal to each other: $(850)(100) = (80)(x)$. Multiplying each side results in the equation $85{,}000 = 80x$.

To solve for x, divide both sides by 80: $\frac{85{,}000}{80} = \frac{80x}{80}$, resulting in $x = 1062.5$. Remember that x represents the original price. Subtracting the sale price from the original price ($1062.50 - $850) indicates that Frank saved $212.50.

3. B: First, calculate the difference between the larger value and the smaller value:

$$378 - 252 = 126$$

To calculate this difference as a percentage of the original value, and thus calculate the percentage *increase*, divide 126 by 252, then multiply by 100 to reach the percentage 50%, Choice *B*.

4. B: The total trip time is $1 + 3.5 + 0.5 = 5$ hours. The total time driving is $1 + 0.5 = 1.5$ hours. So, the fraction of time spent driving is $\frac{1.5}{5}$ or $\frac{3}{10}$. To get the percentage, convert this to a fraction out of 100. The numerator and denominator are multiplied by 10, with a result of $\frac{30}{100}$. The percentage is the numerator in a fraction out of 100, so 30%.

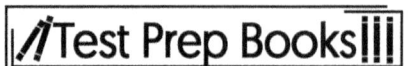

Converting Between Percentages, Decimals, and Fractions

1. D: To convert a fraction to a percent, the fraction is first converted to a decimal. To do so, the numerator is divided by the denominator: $4 \div 5 = 0.8$. To convert a decimal to a percent, the number is multiplied by 100: $0.8 \times 10 = 80\%$.

2. C: Dividing 5 by 8 results in 0.625. Of the options provided, only Choice C correctly rounds 0.625 up to the nearest hundredth of 0.63.

3. B: Since 0.56 goes to the hundredths place, it can be placed over 100:

$$\frac{56}{100}$$

Essentially, the way we got there is by multiplying the numerator and denominator by 100:

$$\frac{0.56}{1} \times \frac{100}{100} = \frac{56}{100}$$

Then, the fraction can be simplified down to $\frac{14}{25}$:

$$\frac{56}{100} \div \frac{4}{4} = \frac{14}{25}$$

4. A: Divide 3 by 5 to get 0.6 and add that to the whole number 3, to get 3.6. An alternative is to incorporate the whole number 3 earlier on by creating an improper fraction: $\frac{18}{5}$. Then, dividing 18 by 5 produces the answer of 3.6.

5. C: The first step is to depict each number using decimals. $\frac{91}{100} = 0.91$. Dividing the numerator by the denominator of $\frac{4}{5}$ to convert it to a decimal yields 0.80, while $\frac{2}{3}$ becomes 0.66 recurring. Rearrange each expression in ascending order to find the order listed in Choice C.

Arithmetic Operations

Understanding the Relationship Between Addition and Subtraction

Addition is the combination of two numbers so their quantities are added together cumulatively. The sign for an addition operation is the + symbol. For example, $9 + 6 = 15$. The 9 and 6 combine to achieve a cumulative value, called a sum. Addition holds the commutative property, which means that numbers in an addition equation can be switched without altering the result. The formula for the **commutative property** is $a + b = b + a$.

Let's look at a few examples to see how the commutative property works:

$$7 = 3 + 4 = 4 + 3 = 7$$

$$20 = 12 + 8 = 8 + 12 = 20$$

Addition also holds the **associative property**, which means that the grouping of numbers doesn't matter in an addition problem. In other words, the presence or absence of parentheses is irrelevant. The formula for the associative property is $(a + b) + c = a + (b + c)$.

Here are some examples of the associative property at work:

$$30 = (6 + 14) + 10 = 6 + (14 + 10) = 30$$

$$35 = 8 + (2 + 25) = (8 + 2) + 25 = 35$$

Addition and subtraction are **inverse operations**. Adding a number and then subtracting the same number will cancel each other out, resulting in the original number, and vice versa.

$$8 + 7 - 7 = 8$$

$$137 - 100 + 100 = 137$$

Subtraction is taking away one number from another, so their quantities are reduced. The sign designating a subtraction operation is the – symbol, and the result is called the difference. For example, $9 - 6 = 3$. The number 6 detracts from the number 9 to reach the difference 3.

Unlike addition, subtraction follows neither the commutative nor associative properties. The order and grouping in subtraction impact the result.

$$15 = 22 - 7 \neq 7 - 22 = -15$$

$$3 = (10 - 5) - 2 \neq 10 - (5 - 2) = 7$$

Practice Questions

1. Which of the following expressions best exemplifies the additive and subtractive identity?
   a. $5 + 2 - 0 = 5 + 2 + 0$
   b. $6 + x = 6 - 6$
   c. $9 - 9 = 0$
   d. $8 + 2 = 10$

2. Which of the following shows the commutative property of addition?
   a. $7 + 2 = 2 + 7$
   b. $7 + 7 = 14$
   c. $(2 + 8) + 2 = 2 + (8 + 2)$
   d. $9 + 0 = 0$

3. Which of the following highlights the associative property of addition?
   a. $11 + 2 = 2 + 11$
   b. $7 + 8 + 2 = 17$
   c. $(6 + 4) + 1 = 6 + (4 + 1)$
   d. $9 + 9 = 18$

4. Which of the following equations does NOT use the associative property properly?
   a. $(4 + 2) + 6 = 4 + (2 + 6)$
   b. $(9 - 2) - 1 = 9 - (2 - 1)$
   c. $(10 + 2 + 4) + 8 = 10 + (2 + 4 + 8)$
   d. $100 + (6 + 5) + (20 + 10) = (100 + 6) + (5 + 20) + 10$

5. Which of the following equations uses the commutative property properly?
   a. $9 - 4 + 5 = 4 - 9 + 5$
   b. $5 + 9 - 2 = 9 + 5 - 2$
   c. $10 - 5 - 2 = 2 - 5 - 10$
   d. $7 - 4 = 4 - 7$

Solving Addition and Subtraction Problems

There are set columns for addition: ones, tens, hundreds, thousands, ten-thousands, hundred-thousands, millions, and so on. To add how many units there are total, each column needs to be combined, starting from the right, or the ones column.

| THOUSANDS | HUNDREDS | TENS | ONES |

Every 10 units in the ones column equals one in the tens column, and every 10 units in the tens column equals one in the hundreds column, and so on.

For example, the number 5432 has 2 ones, 3 tens, 4 hundreds, and 5 thousands. The number 371 has 3 hundreds, 7 tens and 1 one. To combine, or add, these two numbers, simply add up how many units of each column exist. The best way to do this is by lining up the columns:

$$\begin{array}{r} 5\ 4\ 3\ 2 \\ +\ \ \ \ 3\ 7\ 1 \\ \hline \end{array}$$

The ones column adds $2 + 1$ for a total (sum) of 3. The tens column adds $3 + 7$ for a total of 10; since 10 of that unit was collected, add 1 to the hundreds column to denote the total in the next column:

$$\begin{array}{r} 1\ \ \ \ \ \ \ \\ 5\ 4\ 3\ 2 \\ +\ \ \ \ 3\ 7\ 1 \\ \hline 0\ 3 \end{array}$$

When adding the hundreds column this extra 1 needs to be combined, so it would be the sum of 4, 3, and 1.

$$4 + 3 + 1 = 8$$

The last, or thousands, column listed would be the sum of 5. Since there are no other numbers in this column, that is the final total.

Numbers and Operations
Arithmetic Operations

The answer would look as follows:

```
  5 4 3 2
+   3 7 1
---------
  5 8 0 3
```

Examples

Example 1: Find the sum of 9,734 and 895.

Set up the problem:

```
  9 7 3 4
+   8 9 5
---------
```

Total the columns:

```
  9 7 3 4
+   8 9 5
---------
1 0 6 2 9
```

In this example, another column (ten-thousands) is added to the left of the thousands column, to denote a carryover of 10 units in the thousands column. The final sum is 10,629.

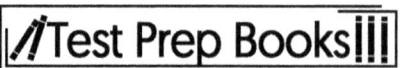

Example 2: Subtract 325 − 77.

When working through subtraction problems involving larger numbers, it's necessary to regroup the numbers. Let's work through a practice problem using regrouping.

$$\begin{array}{r} 3\,2\,5 \\ -\ 7\,7 \\ \hline \end{array}$$

Here, it is clear that the ones and tens columns for 77 are greater than the ones and tens columns for 325. To subtract this number, borrow from the tens and hundreds columns. When borrowing from a column, subtracting 1 from the lender column will add 10 to the borrower column:

$$\begin{array}{r} 3\text{-}1\ \ 10+2\text{-}1\ \ 10+5 \\ -\qquad\ \ 7\qquad\ \ 7 \end{array} = \begin{array}{r} 2\ \ 11\ \ 15 \\ -\qquad 7\ \ 7 \\ \hline 2\ \ 4\ \ 8 \end{array}$$

After ensuring that each digit in the top row is greater than the digit in the corresponding bottom row, subtraction can proceed as normal, and the answer is found to be 248.

Practice Questions

1. Add 103,678 + 487.
    a. 103,191
    b. 103,550
    c. 104,265
    d. 104,165

2. Subtract 112,076 − 1,243.
    a. 109,398
    b. 113,319
    c. 113,833
    d. 110,833

3. Add 5,089 + 10,323.
    a. 15,402
    b. 15,412
    c. 5,234
    d. 15,234

4. Subtract 9,576 − 891.
    a. 10,467
    b. 9,685
    c. 8,325
    d. 8,685

Numbers and Operations
Arithmetic Operations

5. Subtract $148,928 - 3,409$.
   a. 145,519
   b. 145,529
   c. 145,518
   d. 151,977

Representing Multiplication Facts

Multiplication is when we add equal amounts. The answer to a multiplication problem is called a **product**. Products stand for the total number of items within different groups. The symbol for multiplication is × or ·. We say 2×3 or $2 \cdot 3$ means "2 times 3."

As an example, let's say that there are three sets of four apples. The goal is to know how many apples there are in total. Three sets of four apples gives $4 + 4 + 4 = 12$. Also, three times four apples gives $3 \times 4 = 12$.

Therefore, for any whole numbers a and b, where a is not equal to zero, $a \times b = b + b + \cdots b$, where b is added a times. Also, $a \times b$ can be thought of as the number of units in a rectangular block consisting of a rows and b columns.

For example, 3×7 is equal to the number of squares in the following rectangle:

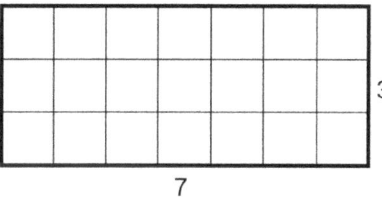

The answer is 21, and there are 21 squares in the rectangle.

When any number is multiplied by one (for example, $8 \times 1 = 8$), the value of original number does not change. Therefore, 1 is the **multiplicative identity**. For any whole number a, $1 \times a = a$. Also, any number multiplied by zero results in zero. Therefore, for any whole number a, $0 \times a = 0$.

Another method of multiplication can be done with the use of an **area model**. An area model is a rectangle that is divided into rows and columns that match up to the number of place values within each number.

For example, let's solve 29×65. These two numbers can be split into simpler numbers: $29 = 25 + 4$ and $65 = 60 + 5$. The products of those 4 numbers are found within the rectangle and then summed up to get the answer. Here is the actual area model:

	25	4
60	60x25 1,500	60x4 240
5	5x25 125	5x4 20

$$\begin{array}{r} 1,500 \\ 240 \\ 125 \\ + 20 \\ \hline 1,885 \end{array}$$

The entire process is:

$$(60 \times 25) + (5 \times 25) + (60 \times 4) + (5 \times 4)$$

$$1,500 + 240 + 125 + 20 = 1,885$$

Like addition, multiplication holds the commutative and associative properties:

$$115 = 23 \times 5 = 5 \times 23 = 115$$

$$84 = 3 \times (7 \times 4) = (3 \times 7) \times 4 = 84$$

Multiplication also follows the **distributive property**, which allows the multiplication to be distributed through parentheses. The formula for distribution is $a \times (b + c) = ab + ac$.

Example

$$45 = 5 \times 9 = 5(3 + 6) = (5 \times 3) + (5 \times 6) = 15 + 30 = 45$$

$$20 = 4 \times 5 = 4(10 - 5) = (4 \times 10) - (4 \times 5) = 40 - 20 = 20$$

Examples

Example 1: A fruit seller packed 64 baskets of blueberries. Each basket contained 112 blueberries. How many blueberries in total did they pack?

Because each basket contained 112 blueberries, and there were 64 baskets packed, the total number of blueberries is found by multiplying 112 by 64. Therefore, there were $112 \times 64 = 7,168$ blueberries in total.

Numbers and Operations
Arithmetic Operations

Example 2: Sam had a garage sale. He was selling his baseball cards. He had 64 pages of cards, and each page held 9 cards. If he sold each card for $2, how much money would he make if he sold all 64 pages of cards?

Each page held 9 cards, so Sam was selling $64 \times 9 = 576$ cards. If he sold each card for $2, he could make $576 \times \$2 = \$1,176$ at the garage sale.

Practice Questions

1. Ming would like to share his collection of 16 baseball cards with his three friends. He has decided that he will divide the collection equally among himself and his friends. Which of the following shows the correct grouping of Ming's cards?

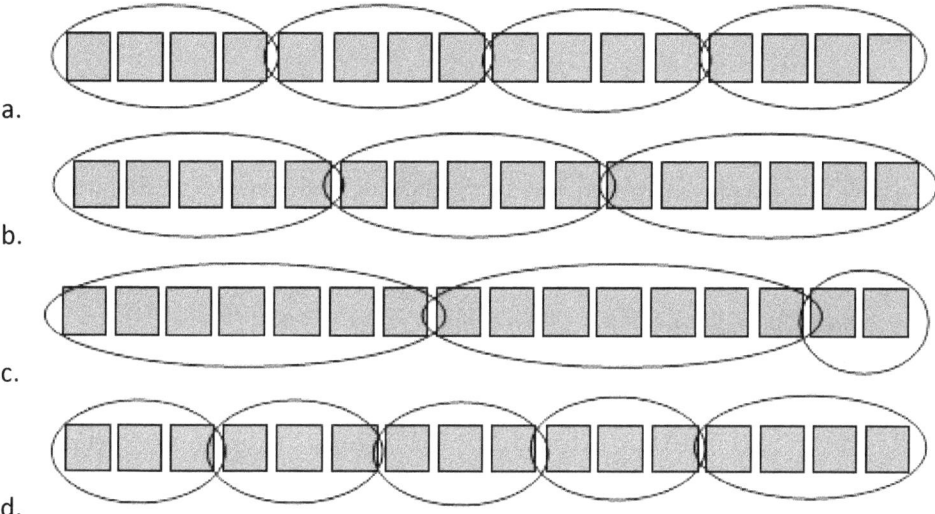

a.

b.

c.

d.

2. At the store, Jan spends $90 on apples and oranges. Apples cost $1 each and oranges cost $2 each. If Jan buys the same number of apples as oranges, how many oranges did she buy?
   a. 20
   b. 25
   c. 30
   d. 35

3. A grocery store had a sale on eggs. There were 88 dozen eggs on sale. How many individual eggs were they selling at a sale price?
   a. 880
   b. 8,812
   c. 1,056
   d. 100

4. The monthly salary of a bank employee is $6,745. What is her annual income by salary?
   a. $80,940
   b. $67,450
   c. $40,470
   d. $202,350

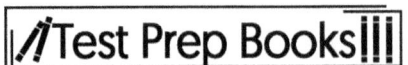

5. Krystal has 4 bags with 5 marbles in each bag. Mark has 7 bags with 3 marbles in each bag. How many more marbles does Mark have?
   a. 21
   b. 1
   c. 3
   d. 2

Understanding the Relationship Between Multiplication and Division

Division and multiplication are inverses of each other in the same way that addition and subtraction are opposites. Therefore, multiplying by a number and then dividing by the same number results in the original number, and vice versa.

For example, $8 \times 2 \div 2 = 8$ and $12 \div 4 \times 4 = 12$.

Inverse operations are used to work backwards to solve problems.

The signs designating the division operation are the $\div$ and / symbols. In division, the second number divides into the first.

The number before the division sign is called the **dividend** or, if expressed as a fraction, the **numerator.** For example, in $a \div b$, a is the dividend, while in $\frac{a}{b}$, a is the numerator.

The number after the division sign is called the **divisor** or, if expressed as a fraction, the **denominator**. For example, in $a \div b$, b is the divisor, while in $\frac{a}{b}$, b is the denominator.

Division is based on dividing a given number into parts. The simplest problem involves dividing a number into equal parts.

For example, if a pack of 20 pencils is to be divided among 10 children, you would have to divide 20 by 10. In this example, each child would receive 2 pencils. The equation for this problem is written as $20 \div 10 = 2$, or $20/10 = 2$. This means "20 divided by 10 is equal to 2." Division can be explained as the following: for any whole numbers a and b, where b is not equal to zero, $a \div b = c$ if—and only if—$a = b \times c$. This means, division can be thought of as a multiplication problem with a missing part. For instance, calculating $20 \div 10$ is the same as asking the following: "If there are 20 items in total with 10 in each group, how many are in each group?" Therefore, 20 is equal to ten times what value? This question is the same as asking, "If there are 20 items in total with 2 in each group, how many groups are there?" The answer to each question is 2.

Numbers and Operations
Arithmetic Operations

Like subtraction, division doesn't follow the commutative property, as it matters which number comes before the division sign, and division doesn't follow the associative or distributive properties for the same reason.

Example

$$\frac{3}{2} = 9 \div 6 \neq 6 \div 9 = \frac{2}{3}$$

$$2 = 10 \div 5 = (30 \div 3) \div 5 \neq 30 \div (3 \div 5) = 30 \div \frac{3}{5} = 50$$

$$25 = 20 + 5 = (40 \div 2) + (40 \div 8) \neq 40 \div (2 + 8) = 40 \div 10 = 4$$

Practice Questions

1. What other operation could be utilized to teach the process of dividing 9453 by 24 besides division?
    a. Multiplication
    b. Addition
    c. Exponents
    d. Subtraction

2. Which of the following highlights the associative property of multiplication?
    a. $(2 \times 4) \times 3 = (4 \times 2) \times 3$
    b. $(5 \times 6) \times 2 = 5 \times (6 \times 2)$
    c. $5 \times (3 \times 8) \times 2 = 2 \times (3 \times 8) \times 5$
    d. $4 \times 3 = 3 \times 4$

3. Which of the following highlights the commutative property of multiplication?
    a. $(5 \times 8) \times 2 = 5 \times (8 \times 2)$
    b. $3 \times 2 \times 9 = 3 \times (2 \times 9)$
    c. $6 \times 3 \times 2 = 2 \times 3 \times 6$
    d. $2 \times (9 \times 10) \times 4 = (2 \times 9) \times 10 \times 4$

4. Which of the following uses the commutative property correctly?
    a. $12 \div 4 \times 3 = 12 \div 3 \times 4$
    b. $18 \div 4 = 4 \div 18$
    c. $12 \times 4 \div 3 = 4 \times 12 \div 3$
    d. $24 \div 2 \times 3 = 3 \times 2 \div 24$

Solving Multiplication and Division Problems

Multiplication Problems

One of the quickest methods to multiply larger numbers involves an algorithm to line up the products. For larger-number multiplication, how the numbers are lined up can ease the process. It is simplest to put the number with the most digits on top and the number with fewer digits on the bottom. If they have the same number of digits, select one for the top and one for the bottom. Line up the problem and begin by multiplying the far-right column on the top and the far-right column on the bottom. If the answer to a column is more than 9, the one digit will be written below that column and the tens place

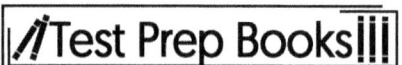

digit will carry to the top of the next column to be added after those digits are multiplied. Write the answer below that column. Move to the next column to the left on the top, and multiply it by the same far right column on the bottom. Keep moving to the left one column at a time on the top number until the end.

If there is more than one column to the bottom number, move to the row below the first strand of answers, mark a zero in the far-right column, and then begin the multiplication process again with the far-right column on top and the second column from the right on the bottom. For each digit in the bottom number, there will be a row of answers, each padded with the respective number of zeros on the right. Finally, add up all of the answer rows for one total number.

Examples

Example 1: Multiply 37×8.

To solve this problem, line up the numbers, placing the one with the most digits on top.

$$\begin{array}{r} 3\ 7 \\ \times\ \ \ 8 \\ \hline \end{array}$$

Multiply the far-right column on the top with the far-right column on the bottom (7×8). Write the answer, 56, as below: The ones value, 6, gets recorded, the tens value, 5, is carried.

$$\begin{array}{r} ^{+5} \\ 3\ 7 \\ \times\ \ \ 8 \\ \hline 6 \end{array}$$

Move to the next column left on the top number and multiply with the far-right bottom (3×8). Remember to add any carry over after multiplying: $3 \times 8 = 24, 24 + 5 = 29$. Since there are no more digits on top, write the entire number below.

$$\begin{array}{r} ^{+5} \\ 3\ 7 \\ \times\ \ \ 8 \\ \hline 2\ 9\ 6 \end{array}$$

The solution is 296.

Example 2: Multiply 512×36.

Line up the numbers (the one with the most digits on top) to multiply. Begin with the right column on top and the right column on bottom (2×6).

Numbers and Operations
Arithmetic Operations

```
  5 1 2
X   3 6
```

Move one column left on top and multiply by the far-right column on the bottom (1 × 6). Add the carry over after multiplying: $1 \times 6 = 6, 6 + 1 = 7$.

```
      +1
    5 1 2
x     3 6
      7 2
```

Move one column left on top and multiply by the far-right column on the bottom (5 × 6). Since this is the last digit on top, write the whole answer below.

```
    5 1 2
X     3 6
    3 0 7 2
```

Now to the second column on the bottom number. Starting on the far-right column on the top, repeat this pattern for the next number left on the bottom (2 × 3). Write the answers below the first line of answers; remember to begin with a zero placeholder on the far right.

```
    5 1 2
X     3 6
    3 0 7 2
        6 0
```

Continue the pattern (1 × 3).

```
    5 1 2
X     3 6
    3 0 7 2
      3 6 0
```

Since this is the last digit on top, write the whole answer below.

```
      5 1 2
x       3 6
      3 0 7 2
    1 5 3 6 0
```

Now add the answer rows together. Pay attention to ensure they are aligned correctly.

```
      5 1 2
x       3 6
      3 0 7 2
    1 5 3 6 0
```

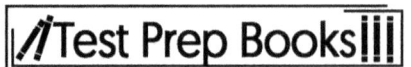

18432

The solution is 18,432.

Division Problems

Dividing a number by a single digit or two digits can be turned into repeated subtraction problems. An area model can be used throughout the problem that represents multiples of the divisor.

Examples

Example 1: Divide $\frac{8,580}{55}$ or $8,580 \div 55$.

The answer to $8580 \div 55$ can be found by subtracting 55 from 8580 one at a time and counting the total number of subtractions necessary. However, a simpler process involves using larger multiples of 55. First, $100 \times 55 = 5,500$ is subtracted from 8,580, and 3,080 is left over. Next, $50 \times 55 = 2,750$ is subtracted from 3,080 to obtain 380. $5 \times 55 = 275$ is subtracted from 330 to obtain 55, and finally, $1 \times 55 = 55$ is subtracted from 55 to obtain zero. Therefore, there is no remainder, and the answer is:

$$100 + 50 + 5 + 1 = 156$$

Here is a picture of the area model and the repeated subtraction process:

```
         8580 ÷ 55

              55
       100 | 5500 |         55 | 8580
        50 | 2750 |             -5500  (100 x 55)
         5 |  275 |              3080
         1 |   55 |             -2750  (50 x 55)
                                  330
                                 -275  (5 x 55)
                                   55
                                  -55  (1 x 55)
                                    0
```

Numbers and Operations
Arithmetic Operations

Example 2: Divide $\frac{1,050}{42}$ or $1,050 \div 42$.

Set up the problem with the denominator being divided into the numerator.

$$42\overline{)1050}$$

Check for divisibility into the first unit of the numerator, 1. 42 cannot go into 1, so add on the next unit in the denominator, 0. 42 cannot go into 10, so add on the next unit in the denominator, 5. 42 can be divided into 105, two times. Write the 2 over the 5 in 105 and multiply 42×2. Write the 84 under 105 for subtraction and note the remainder, 21 is less than 42.

$$\begin{array}{r} 2 \\ 42\overline{)1050} \\ -84 \\ \hline 21 \end{array}$$

Drop the next digit in the numerator down to the remainder (making 21 into 210) to create a number 42 can divide into. 42 divides into 210 five times. Write the 5 over the 0 and multiply 42×5.

$$\begin{array}{r} 25 \\ 42\overline{)1050} \\ -84 \\ \hline 210 \end{array}$$

Write the 210 under 210 for subtraction. The remainder is 0.

$$\begin{array}{r} 25 \\ 42\overline{)1050} \\ -84 \\ \hline 210 \\ -210 \\ \hline 0 \end{array}$$

The solution is 25.

Practice Questions

1. Multiply $13,114 \times 191$.
    a. 2,504,774
    b. 250,477
    c. 150,474
    d. 2,514,774

2. What is the product of 26×12?
   a. 78
   b. 202
   c. 302
   d. 312

3. Which of the following equations is correct?
   a. $123 \div 4 = 33$
   b. $123 \div 4 = 30 + 3$
   c. $123 \div 4 = 30 \text{ R } 3$
   d. $123 \div 4 = 3 \text{ R } 30$

4. $864 \div 36 =$
   a. 24
   b. 25
   c. 34
   d. 18

5. Divide $1350 \div 15$.
   a. 90
   b. 9
   c. 15
   d. 135

Interpreting Remainders

If a divisor doesn't divide into a dividend an integer number of times, whatever is left over is termed the remainder. The remainder can be further divided out into decimal form by using long division; however, this doesn't always give a quotient with a finite number of decimal places, so the remainder can also be expressed as a fraction over the original divisor.

Numbers and Operations
Arithmetic Operations

Example

Example 1: Divide $\frac{375}{4}$ or $375 \div 4$.

Set up the problem.

$$4\overline{)375}$$

4 cannot divide into 3, so add the next unit from the numerator, 7. 4 divides into 37 nine times, so write the 9 above the 7. Multiply $4 \times 9 = 36$. Write the 36 under the 37 for subtraction. The remainder is 1 (1 is less than 4).

$$\begin{array}{r} 9 \\ 4\overline{)375} \\ -36 \\ \hline 1 \end{array}$$

Drop the next digit in the numerator, 5, making the remainder 15. 4 divides into 15, three times, so write the 3 above the 5. Multiply 4×3. Write the 12 under the 15 for subtraction, remainder is 3 (3 is less than 4).

$$\begin{array}{r} 93 \\ 4\overline{)375} \\ -36 \\ \hline 15 \\ -12 \\ \hline 3 \end{array}$$

The solution is 93 remainder 3 or $93\frac{3}{4}$ (the remainder can be written over the original denominator).

Practice Questions

1. Divide $1{,}202 \div 44$, expressing the result with a remainder written as a fraction.

    a. $27\frac{2}{7}$

    b. $2\frac{7}{22}$

    c. $7\frac{2}{7}$

    d. $27\frac{7}{22}$

2. Divide $188 \div 16$, expressing the result with a remainder written as a fraction.
    a. $1\frac{3}{4}$
    b. $111\frac{3}{4}$
    c. $11\frac{3}{4}$
    d. $10\frac{3}{4}$

3. Divide $25,654 \div 12$, expressing the result with a remainder written as a fraction.
    a. $2138\frac{5}{6}$
    b. $2137\frac{5}{6}$
    c. $2137\frac{10}{11}$
    d. $213\frac{5}{6}$

Operations with Negative Numbers

For addition, if all numbers are either positive or negative, simply add them together. For example, $4 + 4 = 8$ and $-4 + -4 = -8$. However, things get tricky when some of the numbers are negative, and some are positive.

Take $6 + (-4)$ as an example. First, take the absolute values of the numbers, which are 6 and 4. Second, subtract the smaller value from the larger. The equation becomes $6 - 4 = 2$. Third, place the sign of the original larger number on the sum. Here, 6 is the larger number, and it's positive, so the sum is 2.

Here's an example where the negative number has a larger absolute value: $(-6) + 4$. The first two steps are the same as the example above. However, on the third step, the negative sign must be placed on the sum, as the absolute value of (-6) is greater than 4. Thus, $-6 + 4 = -2$.

The absolute value of numbers implies that subtraction can be thought of as flipping the sign of the number following the subtraction sign and simply adding the two numbers. This means that subtracting a negative number will in fact be adding the positive absolute value of the negative number.

Example

$$-6 - 4 = -6 + -4 = -10$$

$$3 - -6 = 3 + 6 = 9$$

$$-3 - 2 = -3 + -2 = -5$$

Numbers and Operations
Arithmetic Operations

For multiplication and division, if both numbers are positive, then the product or quotient is always positive. If both numbers are negative, then the product or quotient is also positive. However, if the numbers have opposite signs, the product or quotient is always negative.

Simply put, the product in multiplication and quotient in division is always positive, unless the numbers have opposing signs, in which case it's negative.

Example

$$(-6) \times (-5) = 30$$

$$(-50) \div 10 = -5$$

$$8 \times |-7| = 56$$

$$(-48) \div (-6) = 8$$

If there are more than two numbers in a multiplication problem, then whether the product is positive or negative depends on the number of negative numbers in the problem. If there is an odd number of negatives, then the product is negative. If there is an even number of negative numbers, then the result is positive.

Example

$$(-6) \times 5 \times (-2) \times (-4) = -240$$

$$(-6) \times 5 \times 2 \times (-4) = 240$$

Practice Questions

1. Add $-15 + (-21)$.
    a. -36
    b. -6
    c. 6
    d. 36

2. Add $-16 + 21$.
    a. -5
    b. 5
    c. -37
    d. 37

3. Add $19 + (-29)$.
    a. 10
    b. -48
    c. -10
    d. 48

4. Subtract $-16 - (-15)$.
   a. 1
   b. 31
   c. −31
   d. −1

5. Perform the indicated operations: $-5 \times 18 \div (-3)$.
   a. −30
   b. 30
   c. 270
   d. −80

Answer Explanations

Understanding the Relationship Between Addition and Subtraction

1. A: The additive and subtractive identity is 0. When added or subtracted to any number, 0 does not change the original number.

2. A: The commutative property of addition states that addition can be computed in any order. The equation $7 + 2 = 2 + 7$ shows this property because no matter what order the digits are added, the result is 9.

3. C: The associative property of addition states that addition can be computed by grouping the numbers in any combination. In this case, the grouping is done with parentheses. Following order of operations, $(6 + 4) + 1 = 6 + (4 + 1)$ can be simplified to $10 + 1 = 6 + 5$, which are both equal to 11.

4. B: The associative property only holds for addition and not subtraction. Changing the order of the numbers that you subtract first does change the result. Therefore, Options A, C, and D are correct uses of the associative property. When computing Option B, we obtain $8 - 1 = 9 - 3$. These two sides are not equal because 7 does not equal 6.

5. B: The commutative property only holds for addition, and it does not hold for subtraction. This is because order does matter when computing subtraction, but not addition. Option B is the only option that uses the commutative property for addition and not subtraction. It does not change the order of subtraction. Also, this is the only equation that has equality on either side. If the expressions are simplified, the result is $14 = 14$.

Solving Addition and Subtraction Problems

1. D: Set up the problem and add each column, starting on the far right (ones). Add, carrying anything over 9 into the next column to the left. Solve from right to left to find 104,165.

2. D: Set up the problem, with the larger number on top. Begin subtracting with the far-right column (ones). Borrow 10 from the column to the left, when necessary to reach the answer of 110,833.

3. B: Set up the problem and add each column, starting on the far right (ones). Add, carrying anything over 9 into the next column to the left. Solve from right to left to find 15,412.

**Numbers and Operations
Arithmetic Operations**

4. D: Set up the problem, with the larger number on top. Begin subtracting with the far-right column (ones). Borrow 10 from the column to the left, when necessary. This process finds the answer, 8,685.

5. A: To subtract, line each number up vertically, making sure place values are aligned. Then, subtract each individual place value from right to left. If a value on top is less than a value on the bottom, a one must be borrowed from the value to the left. This will add ten to the current digit.

$$\begin{array}{r} 1 \\ 1\ 4\ 8\ 9\ \cancel{2}\ 18 \\ -\ \ \ \ 3\ 4\ 0\ 9 \\ \hline 1\ 4\ 5\ 5\ 1\ 9 \end{array}$$

Representing Multiplication Facts

1. A: This choice shows that Ming plus his three friends $(1 + 3 = 4)$ is the number of divisions necessary to split the lot of cards evenly $(16 \div 4 = 4)$. There would need to be four groups of 4 cards each, or $\frac{4}{16}$, which is $\frac{1}{4}$ of the total cards. The other choices do not correctly divide the cards into even groupings.

2. C: One apple/orange pair costs $3 total. Therefore, Jan bought $90 \div 3 = 30$ total pairs, and hence, she bought 30 oranges.

3. C: Each dozen holds 12 eggs. Therefore, there were $88 \times 12 = 1,056$ total eggs on sale.

4. A: A year has 12 months, so the monthly salary needs to be multiplied by 12 to obtain her annual salary. $\$6,745 \times 12 = \$80,940$.

5. B: Krystal has $4 \times 5 = 20$ marbles. Mark has $7 \times 3 = 21$ marbles. Therefore, Mark has $21 - 20 = 1$ more marble than Krystal.

Understanding the Relationship Between Multiplication and Division

1. D: Division can be computed as a repetition of subtraction problems by subtracting multiples of 24.

2. B: The associative property of multiplication states that the way in which factors are grouped within a multiplication expression does not matter. Option *B* groups 5 and 6 on the righthand side, and it groups 6 and 2 on the lefthand side. Notice that each side is equal to 60, so the grouping does not matter since the same result is found. The other options utilize the commutative property of multiplication.

3. C: The commutative property of multiplication states that changing the order in which the factors of a multiplication expression is given does not change the result. Option *C* changes the order of the factors on both sides of the equals sign, but each side equals 36, showing that order does not matter. The other options involve grouping with parentheses, which demonstrates the associative property.

4. C. The commutative property only holds for multiplication, and it does not hold for division. Therefore, order does matter when dividing, but it does not when multiplying. Options *A, B,* and *D* all swap the order of division and the expressions on the lefthand side do not equal those on the righthand side. Option *C* switches the order of multiplication, which correctly demonstrates the commutative property. Both sides equal the same quantity.

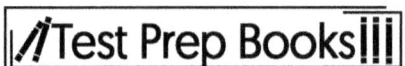

Solving Multiplication and Division Problems

1. A: Line up the numbers (the number with the most digits on top) to multiply. Begin with the right column on top and the right column on bottom.

Move one column left on top and multiply by the far-right column on the bottom. Remember to add the carry over after you multiply. Continue that pattern for each of the numbers on the top row.

Starting on the far-right column on top repeat this pattern for the next number left on the bottom. Write the answers below the first line of answers; remember to begin with a zero placeholder. Continue for each number in the top row.

Starting on the far-right column on top, repeat this pattern for the next number left on the bottom. Write the answers below the first line of answers. Remember to begin with zero placeholders.

Once completed, ensure the answer rows are lined up correctly, then add.

2. D: This answer is the only one that carries out proper multiplication to get the correct result (as seen below).

$$\begin{array}{r} 2^16 \\ \times 1\ 2 \\ \hline 5\ 2 \\ +2^16\ 0 \\ \hline 3\ 1\ 2 \end{array}$$

The calculation for Choice A is incorrect, as it does not place the zero marker for the second row of numbers being multiplied. The calculation for Choice B is incorrect, as it does not carry any of the ones necessary to multiply the numbers. The calculation for Choice C is incorrect, as it does not carry the one in the multiplication portion of the problem.

3. C: If an array were to be used, 123 items could be divided up into 4 groups of 30, with 3 left over. Choices A, C, and D are misrepresentations of the correct grouping and not equal to 30 with a remainder of 3.

4. A: The long division would be completed as follows:

$$\begin{array}{r} 24 \\ 36\overline{)864} \\ -72\downarrow \\ \hline 144 \end{array}$$

5. A: This problem can be done via long division. $135 \div 15 = 9$ and since there is only a 0 left in the dividend, the final answer is 90. Also, the fact that division is the inverse operation of multiplication can be used to determine the correct answer. Multiply each option by 15 to see if 1350 is obtained. The only correct option is A because $90 \times 15 = 1350$.

Numbers and Operations
Arithmetic Operations

Interpreting Remainders

1. D: Set up the division problem.

$$44 \overline{)1202}$$

44 does not go into 1 or 12 but will go into 120 so start there.

$$\begin{array}{r} 27 \\ 44 \overline{)1202} \\ -88 \\ \hline 322 \\ -308 \\ \hline 14 \end{array}$$

The answer is $27\frac{14}{44}$. Reduce the fraction for the final answer: $27\frac{7}{22}$.

2. C: Set up the division problem.

$$16 \overline{)188}$$

16 does not go into 1 but does go into 18 so start there.

$$\begin{array}{r} 11 \\ 16 \overline{)188} \\ -16 \\ \hline 28 \\ -16 \\ \hline 12 \end{array}$$

The result is $11\frac{12}{16}$. Reduce the fraction for the final answer: $11\frac{3}{4}$.

3. B: 12 goes into 25 two times, so the 2 is written over the 5. Then, 12 is multiplied times 2 and this amount is written below the 25. 24 is subtracted from 25 and the 6 from the next place value is brought down. The division process is repeated until the last digit of 4 is used. There is a remainder of 10. This value is written over the divisor of 12 and then reduced into a simplified fraction: $\frac{10}{12} = \frac{5}{6}$. Therefore, the answer is $2137\frac{5}{6}$.

```
             2  1  3  7
         ┌─────────────
    1 2  │  2  5  6  5  4
         -2  4
         ─────
             1  6
           -  1  2
             ─────
                 4  5
               -  3  6
                 ─────
                    9  4
                  -  8  4
                    ─────
                       1  0
```

Operations with Negative Numbers

1. A: To add two negative values, add them together as you would positive values and reattach the negative symbol. $15 + 21 = 36$. Therefore, the answer is –36.

2. B: The absolute value of –16 is 16, and the absolute value of 21 is 21. Between 21 and –16, the value with the larger absolute value is 21, which is the positive addend. Therefore, the answer to this addition problem is positive. Subtract $21 - 16 = 5$. The answer is positive 5.

3. C: The absolute value of –29 is 29, and the absolute value of 19 is 19. Between –29 and 19, the value with the larger absolute value is –29, which is the negative addend. Therefore, the answer to this addition problem is negative. Subtract $29 - 19 = 10$. The answer is –10.

4. D: Subtracting a negative number turns the operation into adding a positive number. Therefore, the problem can be turned into $-16 + 15$. In this addition problem, the addend with the larger absolute value is negative. $16 - 15 = 1$. Therefore, the result is –1.

5. B: Multiplication and division need to be performed from left to right. First, the multiplication is computed. A negative number times a positive number results in a negative number. Therefore, $-5 \times 18 = -90$. A negative number divided by a negative number results in a positive number. The solution is $-90 \div (-3) = 30$.

Estimation and Rounding

Rounding Whole Numbers to a Given Place Value

Estimation is finding a value that is close to a solution but is not the exact answer. For example, if there are values in the thousands to be multiplied, then each value can be estimated to the nearest thousand and the calculation performed. This value provides an approximate solution that can be determined very quickly.

Numbers and Operations
Estimation and Rounding

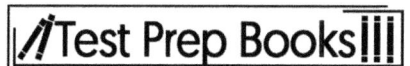

When estimating, it's often convenient to **round** a number, which means to give an approximate figure to make it easier to compare amounts or perform mental math. Round up when the digit is 5 or more. The digit used to determine the rounding, and all subsequent digits, become 0, and the selected place value is increased by 1.

Round down when rounding on any digit that is below 5. The rounded digit, and all subsequent digits, becomes 0, and the preceding digit stays the same.

As examples, 92 rounded to the nearest ten is 90, while 75 rounded to the nearest ten is 80. 839 rounded to the nearest hundred is 800, while 380 rounded to the nearest hundred is 400. 22.643 rounded to the nearest hundredth is 22.64, while 22.697 rounded to the nearest hundredth is 22.70.

The same estimation strategies and techniques used when working with standard math problems can be employed when working with real-life situations. Estimation is frequently used in calculations involving money, such as for determining if one has enough money for a purchase, how much one needs to save weekly to buy a desired product, or how much a restaurant bill will sum to.

Example

Example 1: Round 399,981 to the nearest hundred.

The rightmost 9 is in the hundreds place. The value to the right is 8 which is greater than or equal to 5, so the 9 gets rounded up. Because the 9 becomes 1, a 1 is added to the next place value to the left. The 9 in the thousands place becomes 10, so a 1 is added to the next place value to the left. That is also a 9, so a 1 gets added to the leftmost place value. All of the digits turn into 0 besides the 4 in the hundred-thousands place. The result is 400,000.

Practice Questions

1. How will the number 84,789 be written if rounded to the nearest hundred?
    a. 84,800
    b. 84,700
    c. 84,780
    d. 85,000

2. Round 458,912 to the nearest ten thousand.
    a. 459,000
    b. 450,000
    c. 460,000
    d. 458,900

3. Round 42,498,212 to the nearest million.
    a. 43,000,000
    b. 42,000,000
    c. 40,000,000
    d. 42,500,000

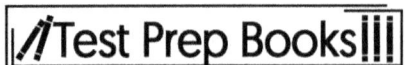

Rounding Decimals

As mentioned, sometimes when performing operations such as multiplying numbers, the result can be estimated by rounding.

For example, to estimate the value of 11.2×2.01, each number can be rounded to the nearest integer. This will yield a result of 22.

Rounding numbers helps with estimation because it changes the given number to a simpler, although less accurate, number than the exact given number. Rounding allows for easier calculations, which estimate the results of using the exact given number. The accuracy of the estimate and ease of use depends on the place value to which the number is rounded. First, the place value is specified. Then, the digit to its right is looked at. For example, if rounding to the nearest hundreds place, the digit in the tens place is used. If it is a zero, one, 2, 3, or 4, the digit being rounded to is left alone. If it is a 5, 6, 7, 8 or 9, the digit being rounded to is increased by one. All other digits before the decimal point are then changed to zeros, and the digits in decimal places are dropped. If a decimal place is being rounded to, all digits that come after are just dropped.

For example, if 845,231.45 was to be rounded to the nearest thousands place, the answer would be 845,000. The 5 would remain the same due to the 2 in the hundreds place.

Examples

Example 1: Round to the nearest tenth: 4.567

If 4.567 were to be rounded to the nearest tenths place, the answer would be 4.6. The 5 increased to 6 due to the 6 in the hundredths place, and the rest of the decimal is dropped.

Practice Questions

1. When rounding 245.2678 to the nearest thousandth, which place value would be used to decide whether to round up or round down?
    a. Ten-thousandth
    b. Thousandth
    c. Hundredth
    d. Thousand

2. Round to the nearest tenth: 8.067
    a. 8.07
    b. 8.1
    c. 8.00
    d. 8.11

3. Round 45.7891 to the nearest hundred-thousandth.
    a. 45.8
    b. 45.79
    c. 45.7
    d. 45.789

Numbers and Operations
Estimation and Rounding

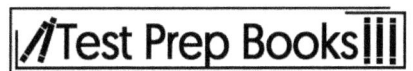

Using Estimation to Solve Problems

Prior to performing operations and calculating the answer to a problem involving addition, subtraction, multiplication, or division, it is helpful to estimate the result. Doing so will enable the test taker to determine whether his or her computed answer is logical within the context of a given problem and prevent careless errors. For example, it is unfortunately common under the pressure of a testing situation for test takers to inadvertently perform the incorrect operation or make a simple calculation error on an otherwise easy math problem. By quickly estimating the answer by eyeballing the numbers, rounding if needed, and performing some simple mental math, test takers can establish an approximate expected outcome before calculating the specific answer. The derived result after computation can then be evaluated by its nearness to the expected answer. This is performed by approximating given values to perform mental math. Numbers should be rounded to the nearest value possible to check the initial results.

Once a result is determined to be logical within the context of a given problem, the result should be evaluated by its nearness to the expected answer. This is performed by approximating given values to perform mental math. Numbers should be rounded to the nearest value possible to check the initial results.

When rounding, the place-value that is used in rounding can make a difference. Suppose the student had rounded to the nearest hundred for the estimation. The result ($400 + 100 + 100 + 0 = 600$; $600 \div 4 = 150$) will show that the answer is reasonable but not as close to the actual value as rounding to the nearest ten.

Examples

Example 1: A problem states that a customer is buying a new sound system for their home. The customer purchases a stereo for $435, 2 speakers for $67 each, and the necessary cables for $12. The customer chooses an option that allows him to spread the costs over equal payments for 4 months. How much will the monthly payments be?

After making calculations for the problem, a student determines that the monthly payment will be $145.25. To check the accuracy of the results, the student rounds each cost to the nearest ten ($440 + 70 + 70 + 10$) and determines that the total is approximately $590. Dividing by 4 months gives an approximate monthly payment of $147.50. Therefore, the student can conclude that the solution of $145.25 is very close to what should be expected.

Practice Questions

1. What is $\frac{420}{100}$ rounded to the nearest whole number?
    a. 4
    b. 3
    c. 5
    d. 6

2. Which is closest to 17.8×9.9?
    a. 140
    b. 180
    c. 200
    d. 350

3. Alex needs to purchase carpet for his bedroom, which is 16.5 feet long by 19.5 feet wide. Which of the following is the best approximation for how much carpet he should buy?
    a. 340 ft^2
    b. 304 ft^2
    c. 400 ft^2
    d. 37 ft^2

Answer Explanations

Rounding Whole Numbers to a Given Place Value

1. A: The hundred place value is located three digits to the left of the decimal point (the digit 7). The digit to the right of the place value is examined to decide whether to round up or keep the digit. In this case, the digit 8 is 5 or greater so the hundred place is rounded up. When rounding up, any digits to the left of the place value being rounded remain the same and any to its right are replaced with zeros. Therefore, the number is rounded to 84,800.

2. C: The 5 is in the ten-thousands place. The value to the right of the 5 is 8, which is greater than or equal to 5. Therefore, the 5 gets rounded up to 6. The rest of the digits to the right of the ten-thousands place turn into zeros. The correct choice is 460,000.

3. B: The leftmost 2 is in the millions place. The value to its right is 4, which is less than 5. Therefore, the digit in the millions place is kept, and the values to the right become zeros. The result is 42,000,000.

Rounding Decimals

1. A: The place value to the right of the thousandth place, which would be the ten-thousandth place, is what gets used. The value in the thousandth place is 7. The number in the place value to its right is greater than 4, so the 7 gets bumped up to 8. Everything to its right turns to a zero, to get 245.2680. The zero is dropped because it is part of the decimal, to get 245.268.

2. B: To round 8.067 to the nearest tenths, use the digit in the hundredths. The 6 in the hundredths is greater than 5, so round up in the tenths. In 8.067, the 0 becomes a 1. This results in 8.1.

3. D: The 9 is in the hundred-thousandth place. The digit to its right is a 1, so the digit in the hundred-thousandth place stays the same, and all other digits to its right are dropped. The result is 45.789.

Using Estimation to Solve Problems

1. A: Dividing by 100 involves mean shifting the decimal point of the numerator to the left by 2. The result is 4.2 and rounds to 4.

2. B: Instead of multiplying these out, the product can be estimated by using $18 \times 10 = 180$. The error here should be lower than 15, since it is rounded to the nearest integer, and the numbers add to something less than 30.

Numbers and Operations
Translating Phrases and Sentences

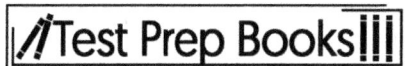

3. A: 16.5 rounds to 17 feet and 19.5 rounds to 20 feet, since both digits in the tens place are greater than or equal to 5. The amount of carpet needed is a measure of area, which is length times width. Therefore, the best approximation is $17 \times 20 = 340$ ft^2.

Translating Phrases and Sentences

Translating Phrases and Sentences into Expressions, Equations, and Inequalities

To translate a word problem into an expression, look for a series of key words indicating addition, subtraction, multiplication, or division:

> Addition: add, altogether, together, plus, increased by, more than, in all, sum, and total
> Subtraction: minus, less than, difference, decreased by, fewer than, remain, and take away
> Multiplication: *times*, *twice*, *of*, *double*, and *triple*
> Division: divided by, cut up, half, quotient of, split, and shared equally

If a question asks to give words to a mathematical expression and says "equals," then an = sign must be included in the answer. Similarly, "less than or equal to" is expressed by the inequality symbol ≤, and "greater than or equal" to is expressed as ≥. Furthermore, "less than" is represented by <, and "greater than" is expressed by >.

Equations use the equals sign because the numeric expressions on either side of the symbol (=) are equivalent. In contrast, inequalities compare values or expressions that are unequal. Although not always true, linear equations that include a variable often have just one value for the variable that makes the statement true. Linear inequalities generally have an infinite number of values that make the statement true.

Practice Questions

1. Write the expression for six less than three times the sum of twice a number and one.
   a. $2x + 1 - 6$
   b. $3x + 1 - 6$
   c. $3(x + 1) - 6$
   d. $3(2x + 1) - 6$

2. What would the equation be for the following problem?
   3 times the sum of a number and 7 is greater than or equal to 32
   a. $3(7n) > 32$
   b. $3 \times n + 7 \geq 32$
   c. $3n + 21 > 32$
   d. $3(n + 7) \geq 32$

Applying Operations to Real-World Contexts

There are a variety of real-world situations in which one or more of the operators is used to solve a problem. The tables below display the most common scenarios, along with examples.

Addition & Subtraction

	Unknown Result	Unknown Change	Unknown Start
Adding to	5 students were in class. 4 more students arrived. How many students are in class? $5 + 4 = ?$	8 students were in class. More students arrived late. There are now 18 students in class. How many students arrived late? $8 + ? = 18$ Solved by inverse operations $18 - 8 = ?$	Some students were in class early. 11 more students arrived. There are now 17 students in class. How many students were in class early? $? + 11 = 17$ Solved by inverse operations $17 - 11 = ?$
Taking from	15 students were in class. 5 students left class. How many students are in class now? $15 - 5 = ?$	12 students were in class. Some students left class. There are now 8 students in class. How many students left class? $12 - ? = 8$ Solved by inverse operations $8 + ? = 12 \rightarrow 12 - 8 = ?$	Some students were in class. 3 students left class. Then there were 13 students in class. How many students were in class before? $? - 3 = 13$ Solved by inverse operations $13 + 3 = ?$

	Unknown Total	Unknown Addends (Both)	Unknown Addends (One)
Putting together/ taking apart	The homework assignment is 10 addition problems and 8 subtraction problems. How many problems are in the homework assignment? $10 + 8 = ?$	Bobby has $9. How much can Bobby spend on candy and how much can Bobby spend on toys? $9 = ? + ?$	Bobby has 12 pairs of pants. 5 pairs of pants are shorts, and the rest are long. How many pairs of long pants does he have? $12 = 5 + ?$ Solved by inverse operations $12 - 5 = ?$

94

Numbers and Operations
Translating Phrases and Sentences

	Unknown Difference	Unknown Larger Value	Unknown Smaller Value
Comparing	Bobby has 5 toys. Tommy has 8 toys. How many more toys does Tommy have than Bobby? $5+?=8$ Solved by inverse operations $8-5=?$ Bobby has $6. Tommy has $10. How many fewer dollars does Bobby have than Tommy? $10-6=?$	Tommy has 2 more toys than Bobby. Bobby has 4 toys. How many toys does Tommy have? $2+4=?$ Bobby has 3 fewer dollars than Tommy. Bobby has $8. How many dollars does Tommy have? $?-3=8$ Solved by inverse operations $8+3=?$	Tommy has 6 more toys than Bobby. Tommy has 10 toys. How many toys does Bobby have? $?+6=10$ Solved by inverse operations $10-6=?$ Bobby has $5 less than Tommy. Tommy has $9. How many dollars does Bobby have? $9-5=?$

Multiplication and Division

	Unknown Product	Unknown Group Size	Unknown Number of Groups
Equal groups	There are 5 students, and each student has 4 pieces of candy. How many pieces of candy are there in all? $5 \times 4=?$	14 pieces of candy are shared equally by 7 students. How many pieces of candy does each student have? $7 \times ?=14$ Solved by inverse operations $14 \div 7=?$	If 18 pieces of candy are to be given out 3 to each student, how many students will get candy? $? \times 3=18$ Solved by inverse operations $18 \div 3=?$

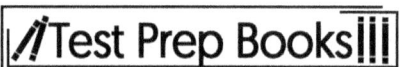

**Numbers and Operations
Translating Phrases and Sentences**

	Unknown Product	Unknown Factor	Unknown Factor
Arrays	There are 5 rows of students with 3 students in each row. How many students are there? $5 \times 3 = ?$	If 16 students are arranged into 4 equal rows, how many students will be in each row? $4 \times ? = 16$ Solved by inverse operations $16 \div 4 = ?$	If 24 students are arranged into an array with 6 columns, how many rows are there? $? \times 6 = 24$ Solved by inverse operations $24 \div 6 = ?$

	Larger Unknown	Smaller Unknown	Multiplier Unknown
Comparing	A small popcorn costs $1.50. A large popcorn costs 3 times as much as a small popcorn. How much does a large popcorn cost? $1.50 \times 3 = ?$	A large soda costs $6 and that is 2 times as much as a small soda costs. How much does a small soda cost? $2 \times ? = 6$ Solved by inverse operations $6 \div 2 = ?$	A large pretzel costs $3 and a small pretzel costs $2. How many times as much does the large pretzel cost as the small pretzel? $? \times 2 = 3$ Solved by inverse operations $3 \div 2 = ?$

Practice Questions

1. Katie works at a clothing company and sold 192 shirts over the weekend. $\frac{1}{3}$ of the shirts that were sold were patterned, and the rest were solid. Which mathematical expression would calculate the number of solid shirts Katie sold over the weekend?

   a. $192 \times \frac{1}{3}$
   b. $192 \div \frac{1}{3}$
   c. $192 \times (1 - \frac{1}{3})$
   d. $192 \div 3$

2. Carey bought 184 pounds of fertilizer to use on her lawn. Each segment of her lawn required $11\frac{1}{2}$ pounds of fertilizer to do a sufficient job. If a student were asked to determine how many segments could be fertilized with the amount purchased, what operation would be necessary to solve this problem?

   a. Multiplication
   b. Division
   c. Addition
   d. Subtraction

Numbers and Operations
Translating Phrases and Sentences

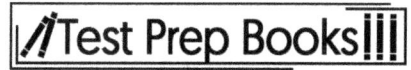

3. Consider a four-year private institution that you would like to attend for college. The tuition per year is $22,000 and it is estimated that room and board will be $5,000 per year and books will cost you $500 per year. If a scholarship pays for 25% of your total expenses, how much will you have to have in a savings account if you would like to have the total amount available before you even attend?
   a. $82,500
   b. $110,000
   c. $88,000
   d. $27,500

4. Katie has $\frac{1}{3}$ of a pizza left over, but Michelle comes home and eats half of what is left. Which of the following expressions represent how much pizza is left?
   a. $\frac{1}{3} - \frac{1}{2}$
   b. $\frac{1}{3} + \frac{1}{2}$
   c. $\left(\frac{1}{2}\right)\left(\frac{1}{3}\right)$
   d. $\frac{1}{2} \div \frac{1}{3}$

5. Kyle traveled 225 miles in 6 hours. Which of the following is the correct expression for the average speed that he was traveling?
   a. 225×6 mph
   b. $225 + 6$ mph
   c. $225 \div 6$ mph
   d. 225 mph

Answer Explanations

Translating Phrases and Sentences into Expressions, Equations, and Inequalities

1. D: The expression is three times the sum of twice a number and 1, which is $3(2x + 1)$. Then, 6 is subtracted from this expression, which gives $3(2x + 1) - 6$.

2. D: 3 times the sum of a number and 7 is greater than or equal to 32 can be translated into equation form utilizing these mathematical operators and numbers.

Applying Operations to Real-World Contexts

1. C: $\frac{1}{3}$ of the shirts sold were patterned. Therefore, $1 - \frac{1}{3} = \frac{2}{3}$ of the shirts sold were solid. Anytime "of" a quantity appears in a word problem, multiplication needs to be used. Therefore:

$$192 \times \frac{2}{3} = 192 \times \frac{2}{3} = \frac{384}{3} = 128 \text{ solid shirts were sold}$$

The entire expression is $192 \times \left(1 - \frac{1}{3}\right)$.

2. B: This is a division problem because the original amount needs to be split up into equal amounts. The mixed number $11\frac{1}{2}$ should be converted to an improper fraction first:

$$11\frac{1}{2} = \frac{(11 \times 2) + 1}{2} = \frac{23}{2}$$

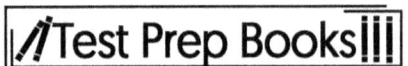

Numbers and Operations
Translating Phrases and Sentences

Carey needs to determine how many times $\frac{23}{2}$ goes into 184. This is a division problem:

$$184 \div \frac{23}{2} = ?$$

The fraction can be flipped, and the problem turns into the multiplication:

$$184 \times \frac{2}{23} = \frac{368}{23}$$

This improper fraction can be simplified into 16 because $368 \div 23 = 16$. The answer is 16 lawn segments.

3. A: Total tuition for four years is:

$$\$22{,}000 \times 4 = \$88{,}000$$

Total room and board for four years is:

$$\$5{,}000 \times 4 = \$20{,}000$$

Total cost of books for 4 years is $\$500 \times 4 = \$2{,}000$. Therefore, it is estimated that you will spend $\$110{,}000$ on college. Your scholarship is going to pay 25% of this cost, which is:

$$0.25 \times \$110{,}000 = \$27{,}500$$

Therefore, you will be responsible for:

$$\$110{,}000 - \$27{,}500 = \$82{,}500$$

Therefore, to obtain your goal, you will need to have $\$82{,}500$ in your account before college starts.

4. C: The amount of pizza left over is half of $\frac{1}{3}$. In math, the word "of" is represented by multiplication and "half" is the fraction $\frac{1}{2}$. The correct expression is $\left(\frac{1}{2}\right)\left(\frac{1}{3}\right)$, which is equal to $\frac{1}{6}$.

5. C: The units are miles per hour. In order to find the average speed, the total distance must be divided by the total number of hours. Therefore, the correct answer is $225 \div 6$ mph. This stems from the distance formula, distance = rate × time.

Patterns, Relationships, and Algebraic Reasoning

Creating Patterns

Generating a Numerical Pattern

Patterns are an important part of mathematics. When mathematical calculations are completed repeatedly, patterns can be recognized. Recognizing patterns is an integral part of mathematics because it helps you understand relationships between different ideas.

Example
Given the sequence of numbers 7, 14, 21, 28, 35, …, the next number in the sequence would be 42. This is because the sequence lists all multiples of 7, starting at 7.

Sequences can also be built from addition, subtraction, and division. Being able to recognize the relationship between the values that are given is the key to finding out the next number in the sequence.

Patterns within a sequence can come in 2 distinct forms. The items either repeat in a constant order, or the items change from one step to another in some consistent way. The core is the smallest unit, or number of items, that repeats in a repeating pattern.

Example
The pattern ○○▲○○▲○… has a core that is ○○▲.

Knowing only the core, the pattern can be extended. Knowing the number of steps in the core allows the identification of an item in each step without drawing/writing the entire pattern out.

Example
Suppose you must find the tenth item in the previous pattern. Because the core consists of three items (○○▲), the core repeats in multiples of 3. In other words, steps 3, 6, 9, 12, etc. will be ▲ completing the core with the core starting over on the next step. For the above example, the 9th step will be ▲ and the 10th will be ○.

Practice Questions

1. What is the 42nd item in the pattern: ▲○○□▲○○□▲…?
    a. ○
    b. ▲
    c. □
    d. None of the above

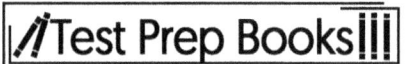

Patterns, Relationships, and Algebraic Reasoning
Creating Patterns

2. What is the 25th symbol in the following pattern: ΩΨΦΦΥΩΨΦΦΥ...?
   a. Ω
   b. Ψ
   c. Φ
   d. Υ

3. Determine the next term in the pattern: ∩U ⊢◁ ∩∩UU ◁◁⊢⊢ ∩∩ ...
   a. ∩
   b. U
   c. ⊢
   d. ◁

Making Conjectures, Predictions, or Generalizations Based on Patterns

The most common patterns where each item changes from one step to the next are arithmetic and geometric sequences. In an arithmetic sequence, the items increase or decrease by a constant difference. In other words, the same thing is added or subtracted to each item or step to produce the next. To determine if a sequence is arithmetic, see what must be added or subtracted to step one to produce step two. Then, check if the same thing is added/subtracted to step two to produce step three. The same thing must be added/subtracted to step three to produce step four, and so on.

Example

Consider the pattern 13, 10, 7, 4, ... To get from step one (13) to step two (10) by adding or subtracting requires subtracting by 3. The next step is checking if subtracting 3 from step two (10) will produce step three (7), and subtracting 3 from step three (7) will produce step four (4). In this case, the pattern holds true. Therefore, this is an arithmetic sequence in which each step is produced by subtracting 3 from the previous step. To extend the sequence, 3 is subtracted from the last step to produce the next. The next three numbers in the sequence are 1, -2, -5.

A geometric sequence is one in which each step is produced by multiplying or dividing the previous step by the same number. To see if a sequence is geometric, decide what step one must be multiplied or divided by to produce step two. Then check if multiplying or dividing step two by the same number produces step three, and so on.

Example

Consider the pattern 2, 8, 32, 128, ... To get from step one (2) to step two (8) requires multiplication by 4. The next step determines if multiplying step two (8) by 4 produces step three (32), and multiplying step three (32) by 4 produces step four (128). In this case, the pattern holds true. Therefore, this is a geometric sequence in which each step is found by multiplying the previous step by 4. To extend the sequence, the last step is multiplied by 4 and repeated. The next three numbers in the sequence are 512; 2,048; 8,192.

Arithmetic and geometric sequences can also be represented by shapes.

Patterns, Relationships, and Algebraic Reasoning
Creating Patterns

> **Example**
>
> An arithmetic sequence could consist of shapes with three sides, four sides, and five sides. A geometric sequence could consist of eight blocks, four blocks, and two blocks (each step is produced by dividing the number of blocks in the previous step by 2).

Practice Questions

1. What is the next number in the following series: 1, 3, 6, 10, 15, 21, ... ?
    a. 26
    b. 27
    c. 28
    d. 29

2. What is the next value in the numerical sequence 0, 1, 1, 2, 3, 5, ...?
    a. 5
    b. 6
    c. 7
    d. 8

3. What is the next value in the numerical sequence 4, 9, 18, 23, 46, 51, ...?
    a. 56
    b. 102
    c. 55
    d. 94

Recognizing the Difference Between Additive and Multiplicative Patterns

When given two number patterns, the corresponding terms should be examined to determine if a relationship exists between them. Corresponding terms between patterns are the pairs of numbers which appear in the same step of the two sequences.

> **Example**
>
> Consider the following patterns 1, 2, 3, 4,... and 3, 6, 9, 12, ... The corresponding terms are: 1 and 3; 2 and 6; 3 and 9; and 4 and 12. To identify the relationship, each pair of corresponding terms is examined. You can also examine the possibilities of performing an operation (+, −, ×, ÷) to each sequence. In this case:
>
> $1 + 2 = 3$ or $1 \times 3 = 3$
>
> $2 + 4 = 6$ or $2 \times 3 = 6$
>
> $3 + 6 = 9$ or $3 \times 3 = 9$
>
> $4 + 8 = 12$ or $4 \times 3 = 12$
>
> The pattern is that the number from the first sequence multiplied by 3 equals the number in the second sequence.

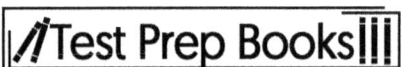

Patterns, Relationships, and Algebraic Reasoning
Creating Patterns

By assigning each sequence a label (input and output) or variable (x and y), the relationship can be written as an equation. The first sequence represents the inputs, or x, and the second sequence represents the outputs, or y. So, the relationship can be expressed as: $y = 3x$.

Examples

Example 1: Write an equation to describe the relationship between the values for a and the values for b, considering the following sets of numbers:

a	2	4	6	8
b	6	8	10	12

To write a rule for the relationship between the values for a and the values for b, the corresponding terms (2 and 6; 4 and 8; 6 and 10; 8 and 12) are examined. The possibilities for producing b from a are:

$2 + 4 = 6$ or $2 \times 3 = 6$

$4 + 4 = 8$ or $4 \times 2 = 8$

$6 + 4 = 10$

$8 + 4 = 12$ or $8 \times 1.5 = 12$

The pattern is that adding 4 to the value of a produces the value of b. The relationship can be written as the equation $a + 4 = b$.

Practice Questions

1. Given $a = 4b$, if $b = 5$, what is the value of a?
   a. 4
   b. 9
   c. 20
   d. 5

2. Given $a = 12 + b$, if $b = 9$, what is the value of a?
   a. 21
   b. 20
   c. 108
   d. 3

Patterns, Relationships, and Algebraic Reasoning
Creating Patterns

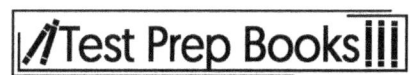

3. Which of the following is the correct equation for the variables a and b given the following table of values?

a	4	6	8	10
b	12	18	24	30

a. $a = 3b$
b. $b = 3a$
c. $a = 3 + b$
d. $b = 4a$

Answer Explanations

Generating a Numerical Pattern

1. A: The core of the pattern consists of 4 items: ▲○○□. Therefore, the core repeats in multiples of 4, with the pattern starting over on the next step. The closest multiple of 4 to 42 is 40. Step 40 is the end of the core (□), so step 41 will start the core over (▲) and step 42 is ○.

2. D: The pattern repeats itself after every five symbols. Therefore, every fifth symbol is a Y. The tenth, fifteenth, and twentieth symbols are Ys; any term that is a multiple of 5 will also be a Y. Therefore, Y is the 25th symbol.

3. A: The four symbols are placed in the following order: ∩∪⊢⊲. However, they are first repeated once, then twice, and so on. The next symbol will be a ∩ because it needs to be repeated three times to follow the pattern.

Making Conjectures, Predictions, or Generalizations Based on Patterns

1. C: Each number in the sequence is adding one more than the difference between the previous two.

For example, $10 - 6 = 4, 4 + 1 = 5$.

Therefore, the next number after 10 is $10 + 5 = 15$.

Going forward, $21 - 15 = 6, 6 + 1 = 7$. The next number is $21 + 7 = 28$.

Therefore, the difference between numbers is the set of whole numbers starting at 2: 2, 3, 4, 5, 6, 7….

2. D: Each value after the first and second numbers can be found by adding the two previous numbers together. For example, $1 + 2 = 3, 2 + 3 = 5$. Therefore, the next value is $3 + 5 = 8$. This is the start of a famous sequence of numbers known as the Fibonacci sequence.

3. B: The second number of the sequence is found by adding 5 to 4 to obtain 9, and then the third number is found by doubling 9 to obtain 18. This pattern is repeated. 18 plus 5 is 23, and then 23 is doubled to obtain 46. 5 is added to 46 to obtain 51, so the next number in the sequence is $51 \times 2 = 102$.

Recognizing the Difference Between Additive and Multiplicative Patterns

1. C: There is a multiplicative relationship between the variables a and b. Given b, a can be found by multiplying 5 times b. Therefore, $a = 4 \times 5 = 20$.

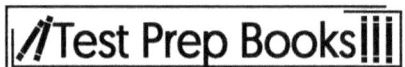

2. A: There is an additive relationship between the variables a and b. Given b, a can be found by adding 12 to b. Therefore, $a = 12 + 9 = 21$.

3. B: Each value in the row for b can be found by multiplying the corresponding value in the row for a times 3. This can be represented by the equation $b = 3a$.

Comparing and Ordering Rational Numbers

Comparing and Ordering Whole Numbers

In order to compare whole numbers with many digits, place value can be used. In each number to be compared, it is necessary to find the highest place value in which the numbers differ and to compare the value within that place value.

For example, $4,523,345 < 4,532,456$ because of the values in the ten thousands place.

A similar process can be used for decimals. However, number lines can also be used. Tick marks can be placed within two whole numbers on the number line that represent tenths, hundredths, etc. Each number being compared can then be plotted. The value farthest to the right on the number line is the largest.

Practice Questions

1. Which of the following numbers is greater than (>) 220,058?
    a. 220,158
    b. 202,058
    c. 220,008
    d. 217,058

2. Which of the following numbers has the greatest value?
    a. 34,560
    b. 8,634
    c. 43,650
    d. 50,643

3. Which of the following numbers has the least value?
    a. 26,200
    b. 8,325
    c. 91,650
    d. 10,211

Comparing and Ordering Fractions, Decimals, and Percentages

To compare decimals and order them by their value, utilize a method similar to that of ordering large numbers.

Patterns, Relationships, and Algebraic Reasoning
Comparing and Ordering Rational Numbers

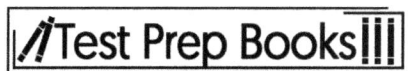

The main difference is where the comparison will start. Assuming that any numbers to left of the decimal point are equal, the next numbers to be compared are those immediately to the right of the decimal point. If those are equal, then move on to compare the values in the next decimal place to the right.

Comparing decimals is regularly exemplified with money because the "cents" portion of money ends in the hundredths place. When paying for gasoline or meals in restaurants, and even in bank accounts, if enough errors are made when calculating numbers to the hundredths place, they can add up to dollars and larger amounts of money over time.

Now that decimal ordering has been explained, let's expand and consider all real numbers. Whether the question asks to order the numbers from greatest to least or least to greatest, the crux of the question is the same—convert the numbers into a common format. Generally, it's easiest to write the numbers as whole numbers and decimals so they can be placed on a number line.

Examples

Example 1: Which number is greater, 12.35 or 12.38?

Check that the values to the left of the decimal point are equal: 12 = 12. Those are equal in value.

Next, compare the values of the decimal place to the right of the decimal: 12.3 = 12.3. Those are also equal in value.

Finally, compare the value of the numbers in the next decimal place to the right on both numbers: 12.3**5** and 12.3**8**. Here the 5 is less than the 8, so the final way to express this inequality is:

12.35 < 12.38

Example 2: Order the following rational numbers from greatest to least:

$\sqrt{36}$, 0.65, 78%, $\frac{3}{4}$, 7, 90%, $\frac{5}{2}$

Of the seven numbers, the whole number (7) and decimal (0.65) are already in an accessible form, so concentrate on the other five.

First, the square root of 36 equals 6. (If the test asks for the root of a non-perfect root, determine which two whole numbers the root lies between.) Next, convert the percentages to decimals. A percentage means "per hundred," so this conversion requires moving the decimal point two places to the left, leaving 0.78 and 0.9.

Lastly, evaluate the fractions:

$$\frac{3}{4} = \frac{75}{100} = 0.75 \;; \frac{5}{2} = 2\frac{1}{2} = 2.5$$

Now, the only step left is to list the numbers in the request order:

$$7, \sqrt{36}, \frac{5}{2}, 90\%, 78\%, \frac{3}{4}, 0.65$$

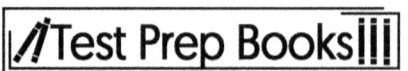
Patterns, Relationships, and Algebraic Reasoning
Comparing and Ordering Rational Numbers

Example 3: Order the following rational numbers from least to greatest:

$$2.5, \sqrt{9}, -10.5, 0.853, 175\%, \sqrt{4}, \frac{4}{5}$$

Changing each of these into a more accessible form will help to solve the problem. $\sqrt{9} = 3$, $175\% = 1.75$, $\sqrt{4} = 2$, and $\frac{4}{5} = 0.8$. Thus, from least to greatest, the answer is:

$$-10.5, \frac{4}{5}, 0.853, 175\%, \sqrt{4}, 2.5, \sqrt{9}$$

Practice Questions

1. Chris walks $\frac{4}{7}$ of a mile to school and Tina walks $\frac{5}{9}$ of a mile. Which student covers more distance on the walk to school?
   a. Chris, because $\frac{4}{7} > \frac{5}{9}$
   b. Chris, because $\frac{4}{7} < \frac{5}{9}$
   c. Tina, because $\frac{5}{9} > \frac{4}{7}$
   d. Tina, because $\frac{5}{9} < \frac{4}{7}$

2. Arrange the following numbers from least to greatest value: $0.85, \frac{4}{5}, \frac{2}{3}, \frac{91}{100}$
   a. $0.85, \frac{4}{5}, \frac{2}{3}, \frac{91}{100}$
   b. $\frac{4}{5}, 0.85, \frac{91}{100}, \frac{2}{3}$
   c. $\frac{2}{3}, \frac{4}{5}, 0.85, \frac{91}{100}$
   d. $0.85, \frac{91}{100}, \frac{4}{5}, \frac{2}{3}$

3. Which of the following is largest?
   a. 0.45
   b. 0.096
   c. 0.3
   d. 0.313

4. Which of the following numbers has the greatest value?
   a. 1.43785
   b. 1.07548
   c. 1.43592
   d. 0.89409

Answer Explanations

Comparing and Ordering Whole Numbers
1. A: This choice can be determined by comparing the place values, beginning with that which is the farthest left; hundred-thousands, then ten-thousands, then thousands, then hundreds. It is in the

Patterns, Relationships, and Algebraic Reasoning
Solving Equations in One Variable

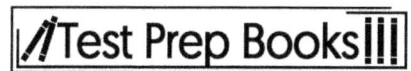

hundreds place that Choice *A* is larger. Choice *B* is smaller in the ten-thousands place, Choice *C* is smaller in the tens place, and Choice *D* is smaller in the ten-thousands place.

2. D: Compare each number figure out which overall number is greatest. While Choice *B* begins with the largest number, the 8 is only in the thousands place. The other choices all have numbers in the ten-thousands place. Of these options, Choice *D* is the largest, as 50,643 is greater than 43,650 or 34,560.

3. B: Compare each number to figure out which overall number has the least value. Choice *D* begins with a 1, but it is in the ten-thousands place. The only number choice that does not have a number in the ten-thousands place is Choice *B*, which only goes up to the thousands place. Of the options presented, Choice *B* is the smallest.

Comparing and Ordering Fractions, Decimals, and Percentages

1. A: In order to compare the fractions $\frac{4}{7}$ and $\frac{5}{9}$, a common denominator must be used. The least common denominator is 63, which is found by multiplying the two denominators together (7×9). The conversions are as follows:

$$\frac{4}{7} \times \frac{9}{9} = \frac{36}{63}$$

$$\frac{5}{9} \times \frac{7}{7} = \frac{35}{63}$$

Although they walk nearly the same distance, $\frac{4}{7}$ is slightly more than $\frac{5}{9}$ because $\frac{36}{63} > \frac{35}{63}$. Remember, the sign > means "is greater than." Therefore, Chris walks further than Tina, and Choice *A* correctly shows this expression in mathematical terms.

2. C: The first step is to depict each number using decimals. $\frac{91}{100} = 0.91$. Dividing the numerator by denominator of $\frac{4}{5}$ to convert it to a decimal yields 0.80, while $\frac{2}{3}$ becomes 0.66 recurring. Rearrange each expression in ascending order, as found in Choice *C*.

3. A: Figure out which is largest by looking at the first non-zero digits. Choice *B*'s first non-zero digit is in the hundredths place. The other four all have non-zero digits in the tenths place, so it must be *A*, *C*, or *D*. Of these, *A* has the largest first non-zero digit.

4. A: Compare each number after the decimal point to figure out which overall number is greatest. In Choices *A* (1.43785) and *C* (1.43592), both have the same tenths place (4) and hundredths place (3). However, the thousandths place is greater in Choice *A* (7), so *A* has the greatest value overall.

Solving Equations in One Variable

Solving Problems involving Four Operations

Order of Operations
When solving equations with multiple operations, special rules apply. These rules are known as the Order of Operations. The order is as follows: Parentheses, Exponents, Multiplication and Division from

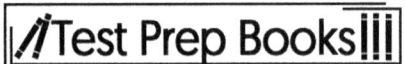

left to right, and Addition and Subtraction from left to right. A popular pneumonic device to help remember the order is Please Excuse My Dear Aunt Sally (PEMDAS).

Examples

Example 1: Solve $4 + (3 \times 2)^2 \div 4$.

First, solve the operation within the parentheses: $4 + 6^2 \div 4$.

Second, solve the exponent: $4 + 36 \div 4$.

Third, solve the division operation: $4 + 9$.

Fourth, finish the operation with addition for the answer, 13.

Example 2: Solve $2 \times (6 + 3) \div (2 + 1)^2$.

First, solve the operations within the parentheses: $2 \times 9 \div (3)^2$

Second, solve the exponent: $2 \times 9 \div 9$

Third, solve the multiplication operation: $18 \div 9$

Fourth, finish the operation with division for the answer, 2.

Parentheses

Parentheses separate different parts of an equation, and operations within them should be thought of as taking place before the outside operations take place. Practically, this means that the distinction between what is inside and outside of the parentheses decides the order of operations that the equation follows. Failing to solve operations inside the parentheses before addressing the part of the equation outside of the parentheses will lead to incorrect results.

Example

Let's analyze $5 - (3 + 25)$. The addition operation within the parentheses must be solved first. So $3 + 25 = 28$, leaving $5 - (28) = -23$. If this was solved in the incorrect order of operations, the solution might be found to be $5 - 3 + 25 = 2 + 25 = 27$, which would be wrong.

Equations often feature multiple layers of parentheses. To differentiate them, square brackets [ ] and braces { } are used in addition to parentheses. The innermost parentheses must be solved before working outward to larger brackets.

Example

In $\{2 \div [5 - (3 + 1)]\}$, solving the innermost parentheses $(3 + 1)$ leaves $\{2 \div [5 - (4)]\}$. $[5 - (4)]$ is now the next smallest, which leaves $\{2 \div [1]\}$ in the final step, and 2 as the answer.

Patterns, Relationships, and Algebraic Reasoning
Solving Equations in One Variable

Practice Questions

1. In the following expression, which operation should be completed first? $5 \times 6 + 4 \div 2 - 1$.
    a. Multiplication
    b. Addition
    c. Division
    d. Subtraction

2. What is the solution to $9 \times 9 \div 9 + 9 - 9 \div 9$?
    a. 1
    b. 17
    c. 81
    d. 9

3. Solve the following:

$$4 \times 7 + (25 - 21)^2 \div 2$$

    a. 512
    b. 36
    c. 60.5
    d. 22

4. What is the value of the expression: $7^2 - 3 \times (4 + 2) + 15 \div 5$?
    a. 12.2
    b. 40.2
    c. 34
    d. 58.2

5. Which of the following is the correct order of operations?
    a. Parentheses, Exponents, Multiplication, Division, Addition, Subtraction
    b. Exponents, Parentheses, Multiplication, Division, Addition, Subtraction
    c. Parentheses, Exponents, Addition, Multiplication, Division, Subtraction
    d. Parentheses, Exponents, Division, Addition, Subtraction, Multiplication

Solving Problems with an Unknown

Solving equations with one variable is the process of isolating a variable on one side of the equation. The letters in an equation are variables as they stand for unknown quantities that you are trying to solve for. The numbers attached to the variables by multiplication are called coefficients. X is commonly used as a variable, though any letter can be used. For example, in $3x - 7 = 20$, the variable is $3x$, and it needs to be isolated. The numbers (also called constants) are -7 and 20. That means $3x$ needs to be on one side of the equals sign (either side is fine), and all the numbers need to be on the other side of the equals sign.

To accomplish this, the equation must be manipulated by performing opposite operations of what already exists. Remember that addition and subtraction are opposites and that multiplication and division are opposites. Any action taken to one side of the equation must be taken on the other side to maintain equality.

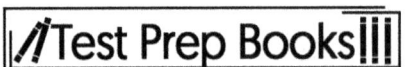

Example

In $3x - 7 = 20$, Since the 7 is being subtracted, it can be moved to the right side of the equation by adding seven to both sides:

$$3x - 7 = 20$$

$$3x - 7 + 7 = 20 + 7$$

$$3x = 27$$

Now that the variable $3x$ is on one side and the constants (now combined into one constant) are on the other side, the 3 needs to be moved to the right side. 3 and x are being multiplied together, so 3 then needs to be divided from each side.

$$\frac{3x}{3} = \frac{27}{3}$$

$$x = 9$$

Now that x has been completely isolated, we know its value.

The solution is found to be $x = 9$. This solution can be checked for accuracy by plugging $x = 9$ in the original equation. After simplifying the equation, $20 = 20$ is found, which is a true statement:

$$3 \times 9 - 7 = 20$$

$$27 - 7 = 20$$

$$20 = 20$$

Evaluating Expressions for Given Values

An algebraic expression is a statement written in mathematical symbols, typically including one or more unknown values represented by variables. For example, the expression $2x + 3$ states that an unknown number (x) is multiplied by 2 and added to 3. If given a value for the unknown number, or variable, the value of the expression is determined. For example, if the value of the variable x is 4, the value of the expression 4 is multiplied by 2, and 3 is added. This results in a value of 11 for the expression.

When given an algebraic expression and values for the variable(s), the expression is evaluated to determine its numerical value. To evaluate the expression, the given values for the variables are substituted (or replaced), and the expression is simplified using the order of operations. Parenthesis should be used when substituting.

Example

Example 1: Evaluate $a - 2b + ab$ for $a = 3$ and $b = -1$.

To evaluate, any variable a is replaced with 3 and any variable b with -1, producing:

$$(3) - 2(-1) + (3)(-1)$$

Next, the order of operations is used to calculate the value of the expression, which is 2.

Patterns, Relationships, and Algebraic Reasoning
Solving Equations in One Variable

Practice Questions

1. If $2x + 6 = 20$, what is x?
   a. 3
   b. 4
   c. 7
   d. 9

2. Suppose $\frac{x+2}{x} = 2$. What is x?
   a. -1
   b. 2
   c. 0
   d. 4

3. What is the value of b in this equation?

$$5b - 4 = 2b + 17$$

   a. 13
   b. 24
   c. 7
   d. 21

4. Given the equation $5x + 6 = 81$, determine the value of x.
   a. 15
   b. 87
   c. $\frac{87}{5}$
   d. 5

Answer Explanations

Solving Problems Involving Four Operations

1. A: Using the order of operations, multiplication and division are computed first from left to right. Multiplication is on the left; therefore, the multiplication should be performed first.

2. B: According to order of operations, multiplication and division must be completed first from left to right. Then, addition and subtraction are completed from left to right. Therefore:

$$9 \times 9 \div 9 + 9 - 9 \div 9$$

$$81 \div 9 + 9 - 9 \div 9$$

$$9 + 9 - 1$$

$$18 - 1$$

$$17$$

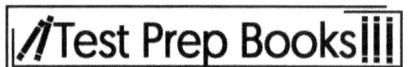

Patterns, Relationships, and Algebraic Reasoning
Solving Equations in One Variable

3. B: To solve this correctly, keep in mind the order of operations with the mnemonic PEMDAS (Please Excuse My Dear Aunt Sally). This stands for Parentheses, Exponents, Multiplication, Division, Addition, Subtraction. Taking it step by step, solve inside the parentheses first:

$$4 \times 7 + (4)^2 \div 2$$

Then, apply the exponent:

$$4 \times 7 + 16 \div 2$$

Multiplication and division are both performed next:

$$28 + 8$$

Addition and subtraction are done last.

$$28 + 8 = 36$$

The solution is 36.

4. C: When performing calculations consisting of more than one operation, the order of operations should be followed: *Parenthesis, Exponents, Multiplication/Division, Addition/Subtraction*. Parenthesis:

$$7^2 - 3 \times (4 + 2) + 15 \div 5$$
$$7^2 - 3 \times (6) + 15 \div 5$$

Exponents:

$$7^2 - 3 \times 6 + 15 \div 5 = 49 - 3 \times 6 + 15 \div 5$$

Multiplication/Division (from left to right):

$$49 - 3 \times 6 + 15 \div 5 = 49 - 18 + 3$$

Addition/Subtraction (from left to right):

$$49 - 18 + 3 = 34$$

5. A: Order of operations follows PEMDAS—Parentheses, Exponents, Multiplication and Division from left to right, and Addition and Subtraction from left to right.

Solving Problems with an Unknown

1. C: Begin by subtracting 6 from both sides to get $2x = 14$. Dividing both sides by 2 results in $x = 7$.

2. B: Multiply both sides by x to get $x + 2 = 2x$. Then, subtract x from both sides to get $-x = -2$, or $x = 2$.

3. C: To solve for the value of b, both sides of the equation need to be equalized.

Start by cancelling out the lower value of -4 by adding 4 to both sides:

$$5b - 4 = 2b + 17$$

Patterns, Relationships, and Algebraic Reasoning
Solving Real-World Problems with Rational Numbers

$$5b - 4 + 4 = 2b + 17 + 4$$
$$5b = 2b + 21$$

The variable b is the same on each side, so subtract the lower $2b$ from each side:

$$5b = 2b + 21$$
$$5b - 2b = 2b + 21 - 2b$$
$$3b = 21$$

Then divide both sides by 3 to get the value of b:

$$3b = 21$$
$$\frac{3b}{3} = \frac{21}{3}$$
$$b = 7$$

4. A: First, subtract 6 from both sides of the equation to obtain $5x = 75$. Then, divide both sides by 5 to obtain $x = \frac{75}{5} = 15$.

Solving Real-World Problems with Rational Numbers

Using Rational Numbers

When rational and irrational numbers interact, there are different types of number outcomes. For example, when adding or multiplying two rational numbers, the result is a rational number. No matter what two fractions are added or multiplied together, the result can always be written as a fraction.

Example

The following expression shows two rational numbers multiplied together:

$$\frac{3}{8} \times \frac{4}{7} = \frac{12}{56}$$

The product of these two fractions is another fraction that can be simplified to $\frac{3}{14}$.

As another interaction, rational numbers added to irrational numbers will always result in irrational numbers. No part of any fraction can be added to a never-ending, non-repeating decimal to make a rational number. The same result is true when multiplying a rational and irrational number. Taking a fractional part of a never-ending, non-repeating decimal will always result in another never-ending, non-repeating decimal. For example, the product of rational and irrational numbers is shown in the following expression: $2 \times \sqrt{7}$.

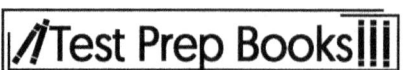 Patterns, Relationships, and Algebraic Reasoning
Solving Real-World Problems with Rational Numbers

The last type of interaction concerns two irrational numbers, where the sum or product may be rational or irrational depending on the numbers being used. For example, the following expression shows a rational sum from two irrational numbers:

$$\sqrt{3} + (6 - \sqrt{3}) = 6$$

The product of two irrational numbers can be rational or irrational.

Example

A rational result can be seen in the following expression:

$$\sqrt{2} \times \sqrt{8} = \sqrt{2 \times 8} = \sqrt{16} = 4$$

An irrational result can be seen in the following:

$$\sqrt{3} \times \sqrt{2} = \sqrt{6}$$

Practice Questions

1. What is the product of two irrational numbers?
    a. An irrational number
    b. A rational number
    c. A contradictory number
    d. A rational or an irrational number

2. Which of the following is an irrational number?
    a. π
    b. 0.5
    c. $0.\overline{3}$
    d. 5

3. What is the sum of two irrational numbers?
    a. A rational number
    b. An irrational number
    c. A whole number
    d. A rational or an irrational number

Understanding Exponents

An **exponent** is an operation used as shorthand for a number multiplied or divided by itself for a defined number of times.

Example

$$3^7 = 3 \times 3 \times 3 \times 3 \times 3 \times 3 \times 3$$

In this example, the 3 is called the **base**, and the 7 is called the **exponent**. The exponent is typically expressed as a superscript number near the upper right side of the base but can also be identified as the

Patterns, Relationships, and Algebraic Reasoning
Solving Real-World Problems with Rational Numbers

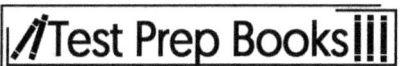

number following a caret symbol (^). This operation is verbally expressed as "3 to the 7th power" or "3 raised to the power of 7." Common exponents are 2 and 3. A base raised to the power of 2 is referred to as having been "squared," while a base raised to the power of 3 is referred to as having been "cubed."

Several special rules apply to exponents. First, the **Zero Power Rule** finds that any number raised to the zero power equals 1. As examples, 100^0, 2^0, $(-3)^0$ and 0^0 all equal 1 because the bases are raised to the zero power.

Second, exponents can be negative. With negative exponents, the equation is expressed as a fraction, as in the following example:

$$3^{-7} = \frac{1}{3^7} = \frac{1}{3 \times 3 \times 3 \times 3 \times 3 \times 3 \times 3}$$

Third, the **Power Rule** concerns exponents being raised by another exponent. When this occurs, the exponents are multiplied by each other:

$$(x^2)^3 = x^6 = (x^3)^2$$

Fourth, when multiplying two exponents with the same base, the **Product Rule** requires that the base remains the same, and the exponents are added. For example, $a^x \times a^y = a^{x+y}$. Since addition and multiplication are commutative, the two terms being multiplied can be in any order. For example:

$$x^3 x^5 = x^{3+5} = x^8 = x^{5+3} = x^5 x^3$$

Fifth, when dividing two exponents with the same base, the **Quotient Rule** requires that the base remains the same, but the exponents are subtracted. So, $a^x \div a^y = a^{x-y}$. Since subtraction and division are not commutative, the two terms must remain in order. For example:

$$x^5 x^{-3} = x^{5-3} = x^2 = x^5 \div x^3 = \frac{x^5}{x^3}$$

Additionally, 1 raised to any power is still equal to 1, and any number raised to the power of 1 is equal to itself:

$$a^1 = a \text{ and } 14^1 = 14$$

There are additional rules for exponents. For any numbers a, b, m, n, the following hold true:

$$(a \times b)^m = a^m \times b^m$$

$$(a \div b)^m = a^m \div b^m$$

Any number, including a fraction, can be an exponent. The same rules apply.

Practice Questions

1. Which of the following is the result of simplifying the expression: $\frac{4a^{-1}b^3}{a^4b^{-2}} \times \frac{3a}{b}$?
   a. $12a^3b^5$
   b. $12\frac{b^4}{a^4}$
   c. $\frac{12}{a^4}$
   d. $7\frac{b^4}{a}$

2. What is the simplified quotient of $\frac{5x^3}{3x^2y} \div \frac{25}{3y^9}$?
   a. $\frac{125x}{9y^{10}}$
   b. $\frac{x}{5y^8}$
   c. $\frac{5}{xy^8}$
   d. $\frac{xy^8}{5}$

3. Simplify $\frac{4x^{-2}y^3z^8}{5x^2y^3z^{-1}} \div \frac{x^2}{y^{-3}}$
   a. $\frac{4x^6z^9}{5y^3}$
   b. $\frac{4z^9}{5x^6y^3}$
   c. $\frac{4y^9z^9}{5x^3}$
   d. $\frac{4y^3z^9}{5x^2}$

Understanding Roots

The **square root** symbol is expressed as $\sqrt{}$ and is commonly known as the radical. Taking the root of a number is the inverse operation of multiplying that number by itself some number of times. For example, squaring the number 7 is equal to 7×7, or 49. Finding the square root is the opposite of finding an exponent, as the operation seeks a number that when multiplied by itself, equals the number in the square root symbol.

Example

$\sqrt{36} = 6$ because 6 multiplied by 6 equals 36. Note, the square root of 36 is also -6 since $-6 \times -6 = 36$. This can be indicated using a **plus/minus** symbol like this: ± 6.

**Patterns, Relationships, and Algebraic Reasoning
Solving Real-World Problems with Rational Numbers**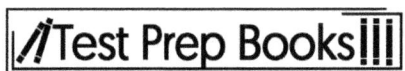

However, square roots are often just expressed as a positive number for simplicity, with it being understood that the true value can be either positive or negative.

Perfect squares are numbers with whole number square roots. The list of perfect squares begins with 0, 1, 4, 9, 16, 25, 36, 49, 64, 81, and 100.

Determining the square root of imperfect squares requires a calculator to reach an exact figure. It's possible, however, to approximate the answer by finding the two perfect squares that the number fits between. For example, the square root of 40 is between 6 and 7 since the squares of those numbers are 36 and 49, respectively.

Square roots are the most common root operation. If the radical doesn't have a number to the upper left of the symbol $\sqrt{}$, then it's a **square root**. Sometimes a radical includes a number in the upper left, like $\sqrt[3]{27}$, as in the other common root type—the **cube root**. Complicated roots, like the cube root, often require a calculator.

Examples

Example 1. Simplify the following: $\left(\sqrt{27} \times \sqrt{3}\right)^3$

First, multiply the radical expressions together under one root: $\sqrt{27} \times \sqrt{3} = \sqrt{27 \times 3} = \sqrt{81}$. The square root of 81 is 9, so the final answer is $9^3 = 729$.

Practice Questions

1. Solve the following: $\left(\sqrt{36} \times \sqrt{16}\right) - 3^2$
    a. 30
    b. 21
    c. 15
    d. 13

2. What is the value of the following expression?
$$\sqrt{8^2 + 6^2}$$
    a. 14
    b. 10
    c. 9
    d. 100

3. What is the solution to the radical equation $\sqrt[3]{2x + 11} + 9 = 12$?
    a. −8
    b. 8
    c. 0
    d. 12

4. Simplify the following: $10^2 + \left(4\sqrt{100} - 2\sqrt{49}\right)$
    a. 126
    b. 103

c. 154
d. 74

Writing Equations and Inequalities

A linear expression is a statement about an unknown quantity expressed in mathematical symbols. The statement "five times a number added to forty" can be expressed as $5x + 40$. A linear equation is a statement in which two expressions (at least one containing a variable) are equal to each other. The statement "five times a number added to forty is equal to ten" can be expressed as $5x + 40 = 10$. Real-world scenarios can also be expressed mathematically.

Forms of Linear Equations

Every linear equation can be rewritten algebraically so that it looks like:

$$Ax + By = C$$

First, the ratio of the change in the y coordinate to the change in the x coordinate is constant for any two distinct points on the line. In any pair of points on a line, two points, (x_1, y_1) and (x_2, y_2)—where $x_1 \neq x_2$—the ratio $\frac{y_2-y_1}{x_2-x_1}$ will always be the same, even if another pair of points is used.

This ratio, $\frac{y_2-y_1}{x_2-x_1}$, is called the *slope* of the line and is often denoted with the letter m. If the slope is **positive**, then the line goes upward when moving to the right. If the slope is **negative**, then it moves downward when moving to the right. If the slope is 0, then the line is **horizontal**, and the y-coordinate is constant along the entire line. For lines where the x-coordinate is constant along the entire line, the slope is not defined, and these lines are called **vertical** lines.

The y-coordinate of the point where the line touches the y-axis is called the y-**intercept** of the line. It is often denoted by the letter b, used in the form of the linear equation $y = mx + b$. The x-coordinate of the point where the line touches the x-axis is called the x-**intercept**. It is also called the *zero* of the line.

There are several convenient ways to write down linear equations. The common forms are listed here:

- **Standard Form**: $Ax + By = C$, where the slope is given by $\frac{-A}{B}$, and the y-intercept is given by $\frac{C}{B}$.

- **Slope-Intercept Form**: $y = mx + b$, where the slope is m, and the y-intercept is b.

- **Point-Slope Form**: $y - y_1 = m(x - x_1)$, where m is the slope, and (x_1, y_1) is any point on the line.

- **Two-Point Form**: $\frac{y-y_1}{x-x_1} = \frac{y_2-y_1}{x_2-x_1}$, where (x_1, y_1), and (x_2, y_2) are any two distinct points on the line.

- **Intercept Form**: $\frac{x}{x_1} + \frac{y}{y_1} = 1$, where x_1 is the x-intercept, and y_1 is the y-intercept.

Depending upon the given information, different forms of the linear equation can be easier to write down than others. When given two points, the two-point form is easy to write down. If the slope and a

Patterns, Relationships, and Algebraic Reasoning
Solving Real-World Problems with Rational Numbers

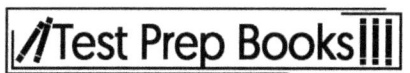

single point is known, the point-slope form is easiest to start with. In general, which form to start with depends upon the given information.

Linear inequalities are a concise mathematical way to express the relationship between unequal values. More specifically, they describe in what way the values are unequal. A value could be greater than ($>$); less than ($<$); greater than or equal to ($\geq$); or less than or equal to ($\leq$) another value.

Common words and phrases that express inequalities are:

Symbol	Phrase
$<$	is under, is below, smaller than, beneath
$>$	is above, is over, bigger than, exceeds
$\leq$	no more than, at most, maximum
$\geq$	no less than, at least, minimum

Example

Example 1: Write a mathematical expression for this scenario: Bob had $20 and Tom had $4. After selling 4 ice cream cones to Bob, Tom has as much money as Bob.

The cost of an ice cream cone is an unknown quantity and can be represented by a variable. The amount of money Bob has after his purchase is four times the cost of an ice cream cone subtracted from his original $20. The amount of money Tom has after his sale is four times the cost of an ice cream cone added to his original $4. This can be expressed as: $20 - 4x = 4x + 4$, where x represents the cost of an ice cream cone.

Example 2: Write a mathematical expression for the statement "five times a number added to forty is more than sixty-five."

The statement "five times a number added to forty is more than sixty-five" can be expressed as $5x + 40 > 65$.

Practice Questions

1. Karen gets paid a weekly salary and a commission for every sale that she makes. The table below shows the number of sales and her pay for different weeks.

Sales	2	7	4	8
Pay	$380	$580	$460	$620

Which of the following equations represents Karen's weekly pay?
    a. $y = 90x + 200$
    b. $y = 90x - 200$
    c. $y = 40x + 300$
    d. $y = 40x - 300$

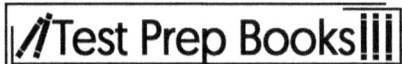

2. The phone bill is calculated each month using the equation $c = 50g + 75$. The cost of the phone bill per month is represented by c, and g represents the gigabytes of data used that month. Identify and interpret the slope of this equation.
    a. 75 dollars per day
    b. 75 gigabytes per day
    c. 50 dollars per day
    d. 50 dollars per gigabyte

3. A company invests $50,000 in a building where they can produce saws. Then, if the cost of producing one saw is $40, which function expresses the amount of money the company pays overall? The variable y is the money paid and x is the number of saws produced.
    a. $y = 50,000x + 40$
    b. $y + 40 = x - 50,000$
    c. $y = 40x - 50,000$
    d. $y = 40x + 50,000$

Solving Linear Equations

When asked to solve a linear equation, one must determine a numerical value for the unknown variable. Given a linear equation involving addition, subtraction, multiplication, and division, isolation of the variable is done by working backward. Addition and subtraction are inverse operations, as are multiplication and division; therefore, they can be used to cancel each other out.

The first steps to solving linear equations are to distribute if necessary and combine any like terms that are on the same side of the equation. Sides of an equation are separated by an = sign. Next, the equation should be manipulated to get the variable on one side. Whatever is done to one side of an equation, must be done to the other side to remain equal. Then, the variable should be isolated by using inverse operations to undo the order of operations backward. Undo addition and subtraction, then undo multiplication and division.

The answer can be checked by substituting the value for the variable into the original equation and ensuring both sides calculate to be equal.

Examples

Example 1: Solve $4(t - 2) + 2t - 4 = 2(9 - 2t)$

Distribute: $4t - 8 + 2t - 4 = 18 - 4t$

Combine like terms: $6t - 12 = 18 - 4t$

Add $4t$ to each side to move the variable: $10t - 12 = 18$

Add 12 to each side to isolate the variable: $10t = 30$

Divide each side by 10 to isolate the variable: $t = 3$

Patterns, Relationships, and Algebraic Reasoning
Solving Real-World Problems with Rational Numbers

Practice Questions

1. If $6t + 4 = 16$, what is t?
    a. 1
    b. 2
    c. 3
    d. 4

2. Solve for x: $\frac{2x}{5} - 1 = 59$.
    a. 60
    b. 145
    c. 150
    d. 115

Solving Linear Inequalities

Linear inequalities and linear equations are both comparisons of two algebraic expressions. However, unlike equations in which the expressions are equal to each other, linear inequalities compare expressions that are unequal. Linear equations typically have one value for the variable that makes the statement true. Linear inequalities generally have an infinite number of values that make the statement true.

When solving a linear inequality, the solution is the set of all numbers that makes the statement true. For example, the inequality $x + 2 \geq 6$ has a solution set of 4 and every number greater than 4 (4.0001, 5, 12, 107, etc.). Adding 2 to 4 or any number greater than 4 would result in a value that is greater than or equal to 6. Therefore, $x \geq 4$ would be the solution set.

Solution sets for linear inequalities often will be displayed using a number line. If a value is included in the set ($\geq$ or $\leq$), there is a shaded dot placed on that value and an arrow extending in the direction of the solutions. For a variable $>$ or $\geq$ a number, the arrow would point right on the number line (the direction where the numbers increase); and if a variable is $<$ or $\leq$ a number, the arrow would point left (where the numbers decrease). If the value is not included in the set ($>$ or $<$), an open circle on that value would be used with an arrow in the appropriate direction.

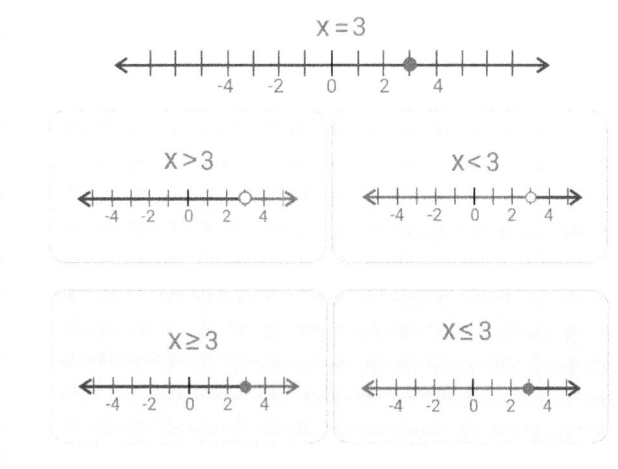

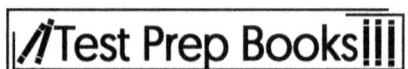

Patterns, Relationships, and Algebraic Reasoning
Solving Real-World Problems with Rational Numbers

Students may be asked to write a linear inequality given a graph of its solution set. To do so, they should identify whether the value is included (shaded dot or open circle) and the direction in which the arrow is pointing.

In order to algebraically solve a linear inequality, the same steps should be followed as in solving a linear equation (see section on *Solving Linear Equations*). The inequality symbol stays the same for all operations EXCEPT when multiplying or dividing by a negative number. If multiplying or dividing by a negative number while solving an inequality, the relationship reverses (the sign flips). Multiplying or dividing by a positive does not change the relationship, so the sign stays the same. In other words, > switches to < and vice versa.

Example

Example 1: Solve $-2(x + 4) \leq 22$ for the value of x.

First, distribute -2 to the binomial by multiplying:

$$-2x - 8 \leq 22$$

Next, add 8 to both sides to isolate the variable:

$$-2x \leq 30$$

Divide both sides by -2 to solve for x:

$$x \geq -15$$

Practice Questions

1. Which inequality represents the number line below?

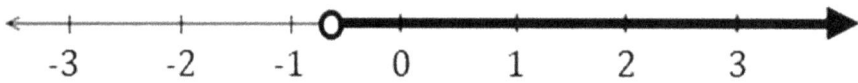

   a. $4x + 5 < 8$
   b. $-4x + 5 < 8$
   c. $-4x + 5 > 8$
   d. $4x - 5 > 8$

2. Which of the following inequalities is equivalent to $3 - \frac{1}{2}x \geq 2$?

   a. $x \geq 2$
   b. $x \leq 2$
   c. $x \geq 1$
   d. $x \leq 1$

3. If $-3(x + 4) \geq x + 8$, what is the value of x?

   a. $x = 4$
   b. $x \geq 2$
   c. $x \geq -5$
   d. $x \leq -5$

Patterns, Relationships, and Algebraic Reasoning
Solving Real-World Problems with Rational Numbers

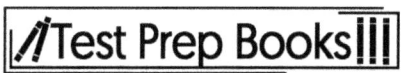

4. Solve $10 - 5x \leq 125$.
   a. $x \leq -23$
   b. $x \leq 23$
   c. $x \geq -23$
   d. $x \geq 23$

Using and Evaluating Algebraic Expressions

Algebraic expressions look similar to equations, but they do not include the equal sign. Algebraic expressions are comprised of numbers, variables, and mathematical operations. Some examples of algebraic expressions are $8x + 7y - 12z$, $3a^2$, and $5x^3 - 4y^4$.

Algebraic expressions consist of variables, numbers, and operations. A **term** of an expression is any combination of numbers and/or variables, and terms are separated by addition and subtraction. For example, the expression $5x^2 - 3xy + 4 - 2$ consists of 4 terms: $5x^2$, $-3xy$, $4y$, and -2. Note that each term includes its given sign (+ or −). The **variable** part of a term is a letter that represents an unknown quantity. The coefficient of a term is the number by which the variable is multiplied. For the term $4y$, the variable is y, and the coefficient is 4. Terms are identified by the power (or exponent) of its variable.

A number without a variable is referred to as a **constant**. If the variable is to the first power (x^1 or simply x), it is referred to as a **linear** term. A term with a variable to the second power (x^2) is **quadratic** and a term to the third power (x^3) is **cubic**.

For example, consider the expression $x^3 + 3x - 1$. The constant is -1. The linear term is $3x$. There is no quadratic term. The cubic term is x^3.

An algebraic expression is simplified by combining like terms. A term is a number, variable, or product of a number, and variables separated by addition and subtraction.

> **Example**
>
> For the algebraic expression $3x^2 - 4x + 5 - 5x^2 + x - 3$, the terms are $3x^2$, $-4x$, 5, $-5x^2$, x, and -3. **Like terms** have the same variables raised to the same powers (exponents). The like terms for the previous example are $3x^2$ and $-5x^2$, $-4x$ and x, 5 and -3. To combine like terms, the coefficients (numerical factor of the term including sign) are added, and the variables and their powers are kept the same. Note that if a coefficient is not written, it is an implied coefficient of 1 ($x = 1x$). The previous example will simplify to $-2x^2 - 3x + 2$.

When adding or subtracting algebraic expressions, each expression is written in parenthesis. The negative sign is distributed when necessary, and like terms are combined.

To evaluate an algebraic expression, the given values for the variables are substituted (or replaced) and the expression is simplified using the order of operations. Parenthesis should be used when substituting.

Examples

Example 1: Add $2a + 5b - 2$ to $a - 2b + 8c - 4$.

The sum is set as follows:

$$(a - 2b + 8c - 4) + (2a + 5b - 2)$$

In front of each set of parentheses is an implied positive one, which, when distributed, does not change any of the terms. Therefore, the parentheses are dropped and like terms are combined:

$$a - 2b + 8c - 4 + 2a + 5b - 2$$

$$3a + 3b + 8c - 6$$

Example 2: Subtract $2a + 5b - 2$ from $a - 2b + 8c - 4$.

The difference is set as follows:

$$(a - 2b + 8c - 4) - (2a + 5b - 2)$$

The implied one in front of the first set of parentheses will not change those four terms. However, distributing the implied -1 in front of the second set of parentheses will change the sign of each of those three terms:

$$a - 2b + 8c - 4 - 2a - 5b + 2$$

Combining like terms yields the simplified expression:

$$-a - 7b + 8c - 2$$

Example 3: Evaluate $a - 2b + ab$ for $a = 3$ and $b = -1$.

To evaluate, any variable a is replaced with 3 and any variable b with -1, producing:

$$(3) - 2(-1) + (3)(-1)$$

Next, the order of operations is used to calculate the value of the expression, which is 2.

Example 4: Evaluate $4|5 - x| + 2y$, $x = 4, y = -3$.

The first step is to substitute 4 in for x and -3 in for y in the expression:

$$4|5 - 4| + 2(-3)$$

Then, the absolute value expression is simplified, which is:

$$|5 - 4| = |1| = 1$$

The expression is $4(1) + 2(-3)$ which can be simplified using the order of operations.

First is the multiplication, $4 + (-6)$; then addition yields an answer of -2.

Patterns, Relationships, and Algebraic Reasoning
Solving Real-World Problems with Rational Numbers

Practice Questions

1. Which of the following is the result after simplifying the expression: $(7n + 3n^3 + 3) + (8n + 5n^3 + 2n^4)$?
   a. $9n^4 + 15n - 2$
   b. $2n^4 + 5n^3 + 15n - 2$
   c. $9n^4 + 8n^3 + 15n$
   d. $2n^4 + 8n^3 + 15n + 3$

2. What is the value of $x^2 - 2xy + 2y^2$ when $x = 2, y = 3$?
   a. 8
   b. 10
   c. 12
   d. 14

3. If $x = 2.6$ and $y = 5.3$, what is the value of $3.2xy - 4.1y$?
   a. -7.95
   b. 33.436
   c. 44.096
   d. 22.366

Identifying Functions

A **function** is defined as a relationship between inputs and outputs where there is only one output value for a given input. The following function is in function notation:

$$f(x) = 3x - 4$$

The $f(x)$ represents the output value for an input of x. If $x = 2$, the equation becomes:

$$f(2) = 3(2) - 4$$

$$6 - 4 = 2$$

The input of 2 yields an output of 2, forming the ordered pair $(2, 2)$. The following set of ordered pairs corresponds to the given function: $(2, 2), (0, -4), (-2, -10)$. The set of all possible inputs of a function is its **domain**, and all possible outputs is called the **range**. By definition, each member of the domain is paired with only one member of the range.

Functions can also be defined recursively. In this form, they are not defined explicitly in terms of variables. Instead, they are defined using previously-evaluated function outputs, starting with either $f(0)$ or $f(1)$. An example of a recursively-defined function is:

$$f(1) = 2$$

$$f(n) = 2f(n - 1) + 2n$$

$$n > 1$$

The domain of this function is the set of all integers.

A function $f(x)$ is a mathematical object which takes one number, x, as an input and gives a number in return. The input is called the **independent variable**. If the variable is set equal to the output, as in $y = f(x)$, then this is called the **dependent variable**. To indicate the dependent value a function, y, gives for a specific independent variable, x, the notation $y = f(x)$ is used.

The **domain** of a function is the set of values that the independent variable is allowed to take. Unless otherwise specified, the domain is any value for which the function is well defined. The **range** of the function is the set of possible outputs for the function.

In many cases, a function can be defined by giving an equation. For instance, $f(x) = x^2$ indicates that given a value for x, the output of f is found by squaring x.

Not all equations in x and y can be written in the form $y = f(x)$. An equation can be written in such a form if it satisfies the **vertical line test**: no vertical line meets the graph of the equation at more than a single point. In this case, y is said to be a *function of x*. If a vertical line meets the graph in two places, then this equation cannot be written in the form $y = f(x)$.

The graph of a function $f(x)$ is the graph of the equation $y = f(x)$. Thus, it is the set of all pairs (x, y) where $y = f(x)$. In other words, it is all pairs $(x, f(x))$. The x-intercepts are called the **zeros** of the function. The y-intercept is given by $f(0)$.

If, for a given function f, the only way to get $f(a) = f(b)$ is for $a = b$, then f is *one-to-one*. Often, even if a function is not one-to-one on its entire domain, it is one-to-one by considering a restricted portion of the domain.

A function $f(x) = k$ for some number k is called a **constant function**. The graph of a constant function is a horizontal line.

The function $f(x) = x$ is called the **identity function**. The graph of the identity function is the diagonal line pointing to the upper right at 45 degrees, $y = x$.

A function is called **monotone** if it is either always increasing or always decreasing. For example, the functions $f(x) = 3x$ and $f(x) = -x^5$ are monotone.

Patterns, Relationships, and Algebraic Reasoning
Solving Real-World Problems with Rational Numbers

An **even function** looks the same when flipped over the y-axis: $f(x) = f(-x)$. The following image shows a graphic representation of an even function.

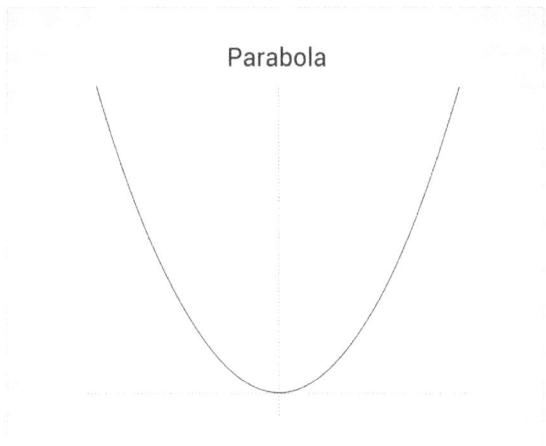

An **odd function** looks the same when flipped over the y-axis and then flipped over the x-axis: $f(x) = -f(-x)$. The following image shows an example of an odd function.

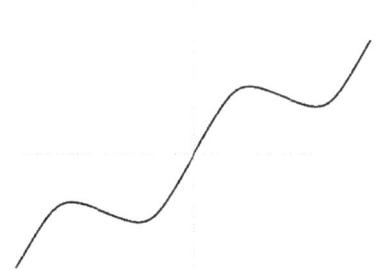

Practice Questions

1. Which equation is NOT a function?
    a. $y = |x|$
    b. $y = \frac{1}{x}$
    c. $x = 3$
    d. $y = 4$

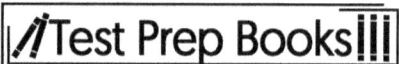

Patterns, Relationships, and Algebraic Reasoning
Solving Real-World Problems with Rational Numbers

2. Is the following function even, odd, neither, or both?
$$y = \frac{1}{2}x^4 + 2x^2 - 6$$
   a. Even
   b. Odd
   c. Neither
   d. Both

3. Is the function $f(x) = -x^5 + 3x^3 - x$ even, odd, neither, or both?
   a. Even
   b. Odd
   c. Neither
   d. Both

4. Is the function $f(x) = x^7 + 11x - 5$ even, odd, neither, or both?
   a. Even
   b. Odd
   c. Neither
   d. Both

Building and Evaluating Functions

Functions can be built out of the context of a situation. For example, the relationship between the money paid for a gym membership and the months that someone has been a member can be described through a function. If the one-time membership fee is $40 and the monthly fee is $30, then the function can be written $f(x) = 30x + 40$. The x-value represents the number of months the person has been part of the gym, while the output is the total money paid for the membership. The table below shows this relationship. It is a representation of the function because the initial cost is $40 and the cost increases each month by $30.

x (months)	y (money paid to gym)
0	40
1	70
2	100
3	130

Functions can also be built from existing functions. For example, a given function $f(x)$ can be transformed by adding a constant, multiplying by a constant, or changing the input value by a constant. The new function $g(x) = f(x) + k$ represents a vertical shift of the original function.

For example, in $f(x) = 3x - 2$, a vertical shift 4 units up would be:
$$g(x) = 3x - 2 + 4 = 3x + 2$$

Multiplying the function times a constant k represents a vertical stretch, based on whether the constant is greater than or less than 1.

Patterns, Relationships, and Algebraic Reasoning
Solving Real-World Problems with Rational Numbers

Example

The function $g(x) = kf(x) = 4(3x - 2) = 12x - 8$ represents a stretch.

Changing the input x by a constant forms the function:

$$g(x) = f(x + k) = 3(x + 4) - 2$$

$$3x + 12 - 2 = 3x + 10$$

This represents a horizontal shift to the left 4 units. If $(x - 4)$ was plugged into the function, it would represent a vertical shift.

A composition function can also be formed by plugging one function into another. In function notation, this is written:

$$(f \circ g)(x) = f(g(x))$$

Example

For two functions $f(x) = x^2$ and $g(x) = x - 3$, the composition function becomes:

$$f(g(x)) = (x - 3)^2$$

$$x^2 - 6x + 9$$

Functions can also be formed from combinations of existing functions.

Given $f(x)$ and $g(x)$, the following can be built:

$$f + g$$

$$f - g$$

$$fg$$

$$\frac{f}{g}$$

The domains of $f + g$, $f - g$, and fg are the intersection of the domains of f and g. The domain of $\frac{f}{g}$ is the same set, excluding those values that make $g(x) = 0$.

Example

$$f(x) = 2x + 3$$

$$g(x) = x + 1$$

then

$$\frac{f}{g} = \frac{2x + 3}{x + 1}$$

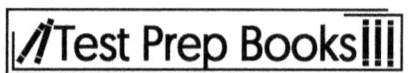

Patterns, Relationships, and Algebraic Reasoning
Solving Real-World Problems with Rational Numbers

Its domain is all real numbers except -1.

To evaluate functions, plug in the given value everywhere the variable appears in the expression for the function.

Example

Find $g(-2)$ where $g(x) = 2x^2 - \frac{4}{x}$. To complete the problem, plug in -2 in the following way:

$$g(-2) = 2(-2)^2 - \frac{4}{-2}$$

$$2 \times 4 + 2$$

$$8 + 2 = 10$$

Practice Questions

1. If $g(x) = x^3 - 3x^2 - 2x + 6$ and $f(x) = 2$, then what is $g(f(x))$?
    a. -26
    b. 6
    c. $2x^3 - 6x^2 - 4x + 12$
    d. -2

2. It costs Shea $12 to produce 3 necklaces. If he can sell each necklace for $20, how much profit would he make if he sold 60 necklaces?
    a. $240
    b. $360
    c. $960
    d. $1200

Answer Explanations

Using Rational Numbers

1. D: The product of two irrational numbers can be rational or irrational. Sometimes, the irrational parts of the two numbers cancel each other out, leaving a rational number. For example, $\sqrt{2} \times \sqrt{2} = 2$ because the roots cancel each other out. Technically, the product of two irrational numbers can be complex because complex numbers can have either the real or imaginary part (in this case, the imaginary part) equal zero and still be considered a complex number.

2. A: An irrational number cannot be written as a ratio of two whole numbers. Choice B can be written as $\frac{1}{2}$, choice C can be written as $\frac{1}{3}$, and choice D can be written as $\frac{5}{1}$. π, pi, cannot be written as a ratio of two whole numbers, so it is the irrational number.

3. B: The addition or subtraction of two irrational numbers will always result in an irrational number, so Choice B is correct. The sum of two irrational numbers will never result in a rational number or a whole number because each initial value cannot be written as a ratio of two whole numbers.

Patterns, Relationships, and Algebraic Reasoning
Solving Real-World Problems with Rational Numbers

Understanding Exponents

1. B: To simplify the given equation, the first step is to make all exponents positive by moving them to the opposite place in the fraction. This expression becomes $\frac{4b^3b^2}{a^1a^4} \times \frac{3a}{b}$. Then the rules for exponents can be used to simplify. Multiplying the same bases means the exponents can be added. Dividing the same bases means the exponents are subtracted. The resulting expression becomes $12\frac{b^4}{a^4}$.

2. D: Dividing rational expressions follows the same rule as dividing fractions. The division is changed to multiplication, and the reciprocal is found in the second fraction. This turns the expression into $\frac{5x^3}{3x^2y} \times \frac{3y^9}{25}$. Multiplying across and simplifying, the final expression is $\frac{xy^8}{5}$.

3. B: First, divide by the fraction by multiplying times its reciprocal:

$$\frac{4x^{-2}y^3z^8}{5x^2y^3z^{-1}} \div \frac{x^2}{y^{-3}} = \frac{4x^{-2}y^3z^8}{5x^2y^3z^{-1}} \cdot \frac{y^{-3}}{x^2} = \frac{4x^{-2}y^3y^{-3}z^8}{5x^2x^2y^3z^{-1}}$$

Then, use the properties of exponents that $a^b a^c = a^{b+c}$ and $\frac{a^b}{a^c} = a^{b-c}$ to simplify.

$$\frac{4x^{-2}y^3y^{-3}z^8}{5x^2x^2y^3z^{-1}} = \frac{4x^{-2}z^8}{5x^4y^3z^{-1}} = \frac{4x^{-6}z^9}{5y^3}$$

Finally, use the fact that $a^{-b} = \frac{1}{a^b}$ to rewrite with positive exponents:

$$\frac{4x^{-6}z^9}{5y^3} = \frac{4z^9}{5x^6y^3}$$

Understanding Roots

1. C: Follow the *order of operations* in order to solve this problem. Solve the parentheses first, and then follow the remainder as usual:

$$(6 \times 4) - 9$$

This equals 24 – 9 or 15, Choice *C*.

2. B: 8 squared is 64, and 6 squared is 36. These should be added together to get $64 + 36 = 100$. Then, the last step is to find the square root of 100 which is 10.

3. B: First, subtract 9 from both sides to isolate the radical. Then, cube each side of the equation to obtain:

$$\sqrt[3]{2x + 11} + 9 = 12$$

$$\sqrt[3]{2x + 11} = 3$$

$$2x + 11 = 27$$

Subtract 11 from both sides, and then divide by 2.

$$2x = 16$$

The result is $x = 8$.

Plug 8 back into the original equation to obtain the true statement to check the answer:

$$\sqrt[3]{16 + 11} + 9$$

$$\sqrt[3]{27} + 9$$

$$3 + 9 = 12$$

4. A: By order of operations, the expression inside the parentheses is simplified. $\sqrt{100} = 10$ and $\sqrt{49} = 7$, so $4\sqrt{100} - 2\sqrt{49} = 4(10) - 2(7) = 40 - 14 = 26$. Therefore, the answer is $10^2 + 26 = 100 + 26 = 126$.

Writing Equations and Inequalities

1. C: In this scenario, the variables are the number of sales and Karen's weekly pay. The weekly pay depends on the number of sales. Therefore, weekly pay is the dependent variable (y), and the number of sales is the independent variable (x). Each pair of values from the table can be written as an ordered pair (x, y): $(2, 380), (7, 580), (4, 460), (8, 620)$. The ordered pairs can be substituted into the equations to see which creates true statements (both sides equal) for each pair. Even if one ordered pair produces equal values for a given equation, the other three ordered pairs must be checked.

The only equation which is true for all four ordered pairs is $y = 40x + 300$:

$$380 = 40(2) + 300 \rightarrow 380 = 380$$

$$580 = 40(7) + 300 \rightarrow 580 = 580$$

$$460 = 40(4) + 300 \rightarrow 460 = 460$$

$$620 = 40(8) + 300 \rightarrow 620 = 620$$

2. D: The slope from this equation is 50, and it is interpreted as the cost per gigabyte used. Since the g-value represents number of gigabytes and the equation is set equal to the cost in dollars, the slope relates these two values. For every gigabyte used on the phone, the bill goes up 50 dollars.

3. D: For manufacturing costs, there is a linear relationship between the cost to the company and the number produced, with a y-intercept given by the base cost of acquiring the means of production, and a slope given by the cost to produce one unit. In this case, that base cost is $50,000, while the cost per unit is $40. So, $y = 40x + 50,000$.

Solving Linear Equations

1. B: First, subtract 4 from each side. This yields $6t = 12$. Now, divide both sides by 6 to obtain $t = 2$.

2. C: Set up the initial equation.

$$\frac{2x}{5} - 1 = 59$$

Patterns, Relationships, and Algebraic Reasoning
Solving Real-World Problems with Rational Numbers

Add 1 to both sides.

$$\frac{2x}{5} - 1 + 1 = 59 + 1$$

Multiply both sides by $\frac{5}{2}$.

$$\frac{2x}{5} \times \frac{5}{2} = 60 \times \frac{5}{2} = 150$$

$$x = 150$$

Solving Linear Inequalities

1. B: The number line shows:

$$x > -\frac{3}{4}$$

Each inequality must be solved for x to determine if it matches the number line. Choice A of $4x + 5 < 8$ results in $x < -\frac{3}{4}$, which is incorrect. Choice C of $-4x + 5 > 8$ yields $x < -\frac{3}{4}$, which is also incorrect. Choice D of $4x - 5 > 8$ results in $x > \frac{13}{4}$, which is not correct. Choice B, $-4x + 5 < 8$, is the only choice that results in the correct answer of $x > -\frac{3}{4}$.

2. B: To simplify this inequality, subtract 3 from both sides to get $-\frac{1}{2}x \geq -1$. Then, multiply both sides by -2 (remembering this flips the direction of the inequality) to get $x \leq 2$.

3. D: When solving a linear equation or inequality:

Distribution is performed if necessary:

$$-3(x + 4) \rightarrow -3x - 12 \geq x + 8$$

This means that any like terms on the same side of the equation/inequality are combined.

The equation/inequality is manipulated to get the variable on one side. In this case, subtracting x from both sides produces:

$$-4x - 12 \geq 8$$

The variable is isolated using inverse operations to undo addition/subtraction. Adding 12 to both sides produces $-4x \geq 20$.

The variable is isolated using inverse operations to undo multiplication/division. Remember if dividing by a negative number, the relationship of the inequality reverses, so the sign is flipped. In this case, dividing by -4 on both sides produces $x \leq -5$.

4. C: First, subtract 10 from both sides. The resulting inequality is $-5x \leq 115$. Then, divide both sides by -5. When an inequality is divided by a negative number on both sides, the sign must be flipped. Therefore, the solution is $x \geq -23$.

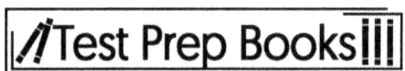

Patterns, Relationships, and Algebraic Reasoning
Solving Real-World Problems with Rational Numbers

Using and Evaluating Algebraic Expressions

1. D: The expression is simplified by collecting like terms. Terms with the same variable and exponent are like terms, and their coefficients can be added.

2. B: Start with the original equation: $x^2 - 2xy + 2y^2$, then replace each instance of x with a 2, and each instance of y with a 3 to get:

$$2^2 - 2 \times 2 \cdot 3 + 2 \times 3^2 = 4 - 12 + 18 = 10$$

3. D: The values for x and y should be plugged into the equation to find the correct answer.

$$3.2(2.6)(5.3) - 4.1(5.3) = 22.366$$

Identifying Functions

1. C: The equation $x = 3$ is not a function because it does not pass the vertical line test. This test is made from the definition of a function, where each x-value must be mapped to one and only one y-value. This equation is a vertical line, so the x-value of 3 is mapped with an infinite number of y-values.

2. A: The equation is *even* because $f(-x) = f(x)$. Plugging in a negative value will result in the same answer as when plugging in the positive of that same value.

$$f(-2) = \frac{1}{2}(-2)^4 + 2(-2)^2 - 6 = 8 + 8 - 6 = 10$$

This function yields the same value as:

$$f(2) = \frac{1}{2}(2)^4 + 2(2)^2 - 6 = 8 + 8 - 6 = 10$$

3. B: A function is odd if $f(-x) = -x$. Plugging in $-x$ into the function results in $f(-x) = -(-x)^7 + 3(-x)^3 - (-x) = x^7 - 3x^3 + x = f(x)$. Therefore, the function is odd.

4. C: A function is odd if $f(-x) = -x$ and is even if $f(-x) = x$. Plugging in $-x$ into the function results in $f(-x) = (-x)^7 + 11(-x) - 5 = x^7 - 11x + 5$. This expression is not equal to $f(x)$ nor $f(-x)$, so the answer is neither.

Building and Evaluating Functions

1. D: This problem involves a composition function, where one function is plugged into the other function. In this case, the $f(x)$ function is plugged into the $g(x)$ function for each x-value. The composition equation becomes:

$$g(f(x)) = 2^3 - 3(2^2) - 2(2) + 6$$

Simplifying the equation gives the answer:

$$g(f(x)) = 8 - 3(4) - 2(2) + 6$$

$$g(f(x)) = 8 - 12 - 4 + 6$$

$$g(f(x)) = -2$$

Patterns, Relationships, and Algebraic Reasoning
Solving Real-World Problems with Proportions

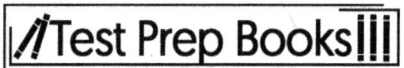

2. C: In order to calculate the profit, we need to create an equation that models the total income minus the cost of the materials. $60 \times 20 = \$1,200$ total income. $60 \div 3 = 20$ sets of materials. $20 \times \$12 = \$240$ cost of materials. $\$1,200 - \$240 = \$960$ profit. Choice A is not correct, as it is only the cost of materials. Choice B is not correct, as it is a miscalculation. Choice D is not correct, as it is the total income from the sale of the necklaces.

Solving Real-World Problems with Proportions

Proportional Relationships

Much like a scale factor can be written using an equation like $2A = B$, a **relationship** is represented by the equation $Y = kX$. X and Y are proportional because as values of X increase, the values of Y also increase. A relationship that is inversely proportional can be represented by the equation $Y = \frac{k}{X}$, where the value of Y decreases as the value of x increases and vice versa.

Proportional reasoning can be used to solve problems involving ratios, percentages, and averages. Ratios can be used in setting up proportions and solving them to find unknowns.

Examples

Example 1: If a student completes an average of 10 pages of math homework in 3 nights, how long would it take the student to complete 22 pages?

Both ratios can be written as fractions. The second ratio would contain the unknown. The following proportion represents this problem, where x is the unknown number of nights:

$$\frac{10 \text{ pages}}{3 \text{ nights}} = \frac{22 \text{ pages}}{x \text{ nights}}$$

Solving this proportion entails cross-multiplying and results in the following equation: $10x = 22 \times 3$. Simplifying and solving for x results in the exact solution: $x = 6.6$ nights. The result would be rounded up to 7 because the homework would actually be completed on the 7th night.

Example 2: If 20% of the class is girls and 30 students are in the class, how many girls are in the class?

This problem uses ratios involving percentages. To set up this problem, it is helpful to use the common proportion: $\frac{\%}{100} = \frac{is}{of}$. Within the proportion, % is the percentage of girls, 100 is the total percentage of the class, *is* is the number of girls, and *of* is the total number of students in the class. Most percentage problems can be written using this language. To solve this problem, the proportion should be set up as $\frac{20}{100} = \frac{x}{30}$, and then solved for x. Cross-multiplying results in the equation $20 \times 30 = 100x$, which results in the solution $x = 6$. There are 6 girls in the class.

Practice Questions

1. If Sarah reads at an average rate of 21 pages in four nights, how long will it take her to read 140 pages?
   a. 6 nights
   b. 26 nights
   c. 8 nights
   d. 27 nights

2. The variable y is directly proportional to x. If $y = 3$ when $x = 5$, then what is y when $x = 20$?
   a. 10
   b. 12
   c. 14
   d. 16

3. If Danny takes 48 minutes to walk 3 miles, how long should it take him to walk 5 miles maintaining the same speed?
   a. 32 min
   b. 64 min
   c. 80 min
   d. 96 min

Representing Relationships using Number Pairs in a Table

Typical representations of real-world situations involve organizing data and systematically applying a calculation to a set of numbers, so as to calculate a systematic output.

For example, a question may tell you the following: A bicycle store is taking inventory of the number of tires on their bikes. Create a table in which to display the possible outputs there could be for two-wheeled bikes and a column to display how these outputs are calculated. How was this table was designed, and how were the calculations that represent the data determined?

Create a table with three categories for the input, the calculation, and the output. The following represent possible products:

Number of Bikes (input)	Calculation of Wheels	Total Number of Wheels (output)
1	1 × 2	2
2	2 × 2	4
3	3 × 2	6
5	5 × 2	10
10	10 × 2	20

Patterns, Relationships, and Algebraic Reasoning
Solving Real-World Problems with Proportions

Or the table could be organized as follows:

Number of Bikes (input)	1	2	3	5	10
Calculation of Wheels	1 × 2	2 × 2	3 × 2	5 × 2	10 × 2
Total Number of Wheels (output)	2	4	6	10	20

Be able to describe the process used to design the table: the categories for input, calculation, and output. Note that the calculations encompass the idea that for every bike there are two wheels. Thus, the multiplication of the number of bikes by the number of wheels (a constant of 2) results in the output for each permutation.

Practice Questions

1. If Amanda can eat two times as many mini cupcakes as Marty, what would the missing values be for the following input-output table?

Input (number of cupcakes eaten by Marty)	Output (number of cupcakes eaten by Amanda)
1	2
3	
5	10
7	
9	18

a. 6, 10
b. 3, 11
c. 6, 14
d. 4, 12

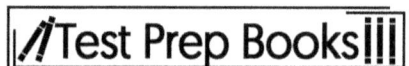

Patterns, Relationships, and Algebraic Reasoning
Solving Real-World Problems with Proportions

2. Which of the following are correct labels for the chart below?

Input	Calculation (Input × 3)	Output
1	1 × 3	3
2	2 × 3	6
3	3 × 3	9
4	4 × 3	12

a. Input: number of chairs; Calculation: number of chairs × number of legs on a chair; Output: number of rubber feet for chairs to order
b. Input: Number of wheels on a tricycle; Calculation: number of tricycles; Output: number of wheels in inventory
c. Input: number of tricycles; Calculation: number of wheels on a tricycle; Output: number of wheels in inventory
d. Input: number of booties for dogs; Calculation: number of dogs; Output: number of booties in inventory

3. Carl's company can mow three times as many yards as Gary's company can in a single day. What are the missing values in the following input-output table?

Input (number of yards mowed by Gary's company)	Output (number of yards mowed by Carl's company)
4	12
6	18
7	
9	27
11	

a. 14, 22
b. 21, 33
c. 10, 14
d. 24, 33

Describing the Coordinate Plane

Algebraic equations can be used to describe geometric figures in the plane. The method for doing so is to use the **Cartesian coordinate plane**. The idea behind these Cartesian coordinates (named for mathematician and philosopher Descartes) is that from a specific point on the plane, known as the **origin**, one can specify any other point by saying *how far to the right or left* and *how far up or down*.

The plane is covered with a grid. The two directions, right to left and bottom to top, are called **axes** (singular **axis**). When working with x and y variables, the x variable corresponds to the right and left axis, and the y variable corresponds to the up and down axis.

Any point on the grid is found by specifying how far to travel from the center along the x-axis and how far to travel along the y-axis. The ordered pair can be written as (x, y). A positive x value means go to the right on the x-axis, while a negative x value means to go to the left. A positive y value means to go up, while a negative value means to go down.

To illustrate, several points are shown in the following figure:

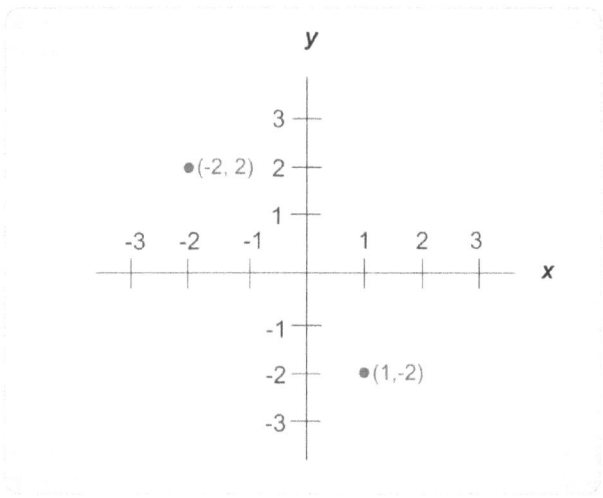

Cartesian Coordinate Plane

The coordinate plane can be divided into four **quadrants**. The upper-right part of the plane is called the first quadrant, where both x and y are positive. The second quadrant is the upper-left, where x is negative, but y is positive. The third quadrant is the lower left, where both x and y are negative. Finally, the fourth quadrant is in the lower right, where x is positive, but y is negative. These quadrants are often written with Roman numerals:

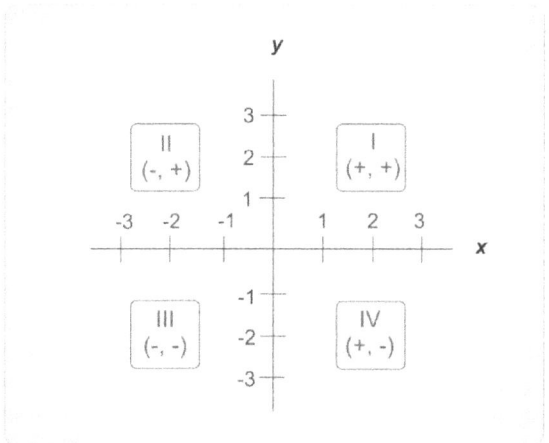

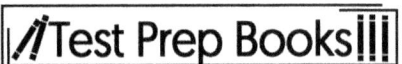

In addition to graphing individual points as shown above, the graph lines and curves in the plane can be graphed corresponding to equations. In general, if there is some equation involving x and y, then the graph of that equation consists of all the points (x, y) in the Cartesian coordinate plane, which satisfy this equation.

For example, given the equation $y = x + 2$, the point $(0, 2)$ is in the graph, since $2 = 0 + 2$ is a true equation. However, the point $(1, 4)$ will *not* be in the graph, because $4 = 1 + 2$ is false.

Practice Questions

1. In which quadrant is the ordered pair $(-3, 3)$?
    a. I
    b. II
    c. III
    d. IV

2. On which axis is the ordered pair $(0, 4)$?
    a. Positive x-axis
    b. Positive y-axis
    c. Negative x-axis
    d. Negative y-axis

3. In which quadrant is the ordered pair $(-10, -24)$?
    a. I
    b. II
    c. III
    d. IV

4. On which axis is the ordered pair $(-5, 0)$?
    a. Positive y-axis
    b. Positive x-axis
    c. Negative y-axis
    d. Negative x-axis

Graphing Ordered Pairs

The coordinate plane represents a representation of real-world space, and any point within the plane can be defined by a set of **coordinates** (x, y). The coordinates consist of two numbers, x and y, which represent a position on each number line. The coordinates can also be referred to as an **ordered pair,** and $(0, 0)$ is the ordered pair known as the **vertex**, or the origin, the point in which the axes intersect. Positive x-coordinates go to the right of the vertex, and positive y-coordinates go up. Negative x-coordinates go left, and negative y-coordinates go down.

Patterns, Relationships, and Algebraic Reasoning
Solving Real-World Problems with Proportions

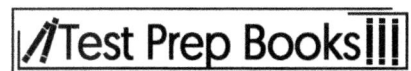

Here is an example of the coordinate plane with a point plotted:

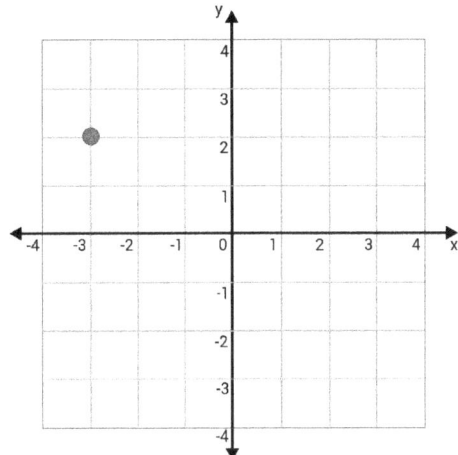

In order to plot a point on the coordinate plane, each coordinate must be considered individually. The value of x represents how many units away from the vertex the point lies on the x-axis. The value of y represents the number of units away from the vertex that the point lies on the y-axis.

For example, when given the ordered pair $(5, 4)$, the x-coordinate, 5, is the distance from the origin along the x-axis, and the y-coordinate, 4, is the distance from the origin along the y-axis. This is determined by counting 5 units to the right from $(0, 0)$ along the x-axis and then counting 4 units up from that point, to reach the point where $x = 5$ and $y = 4$. In order to graph the single point, the point should be marked there with a dot and labeled as $(5, 4)$. Every point on the plane has its own ordered pair.

Examples

Example 1: If the ordered pair $(2, 2)$ is reflected over the y-axis, which quadrant would the new point be in?

The ordered pair $(2, 2)$ is in Quadrant I. If it is reflected over the y-axis, it would mean that the x-coordinate becomes -2, so the new point is $(-2, 2)$. This point is in Quadrant II.

Practice Questions

1. What are the coordinates of the two points marked with dots on this coordinate plane?

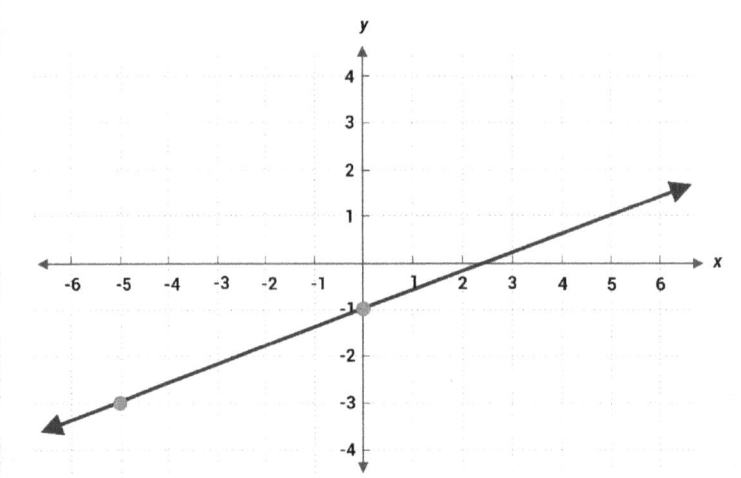

    a. (-3, -5) and (-1, 0)
    b. (5, 3) and (0, 1)
    c. (-5, -3) and (0, -1)
    d. (-3, -5) and (0, -1)

2. If the ordered pair $(-3, -4)$ is reflected over the x-axis, what's the new ordered pair?
    a. $(-3, -4)$
    b. $(3, -4)$
    c. $(3, 4)$
    d. $(-3, 4)$

3. If the ordered pair $(4, -3)$ is reflected over the x-axis, which quadrant would the new point be in?
    a. I
    b. II
    c. III
    d. IV

Answer Explanations

Proportional Relationships

1. D: This problem can be solved by setting up a proportion involving the given information and the unknown value. The proportion is:

$$\frac{21 \text{ pages}}{4 \text{ nights}} = \frac{140 \text{ pages}}{x \text{ nights}}$$

Patterns, Relationships, and Algebraic Reasoning
Solving Real-World Problems with Proportions

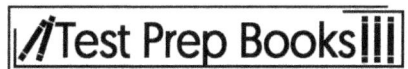

Solving the proportion by cross-multiplying, the equation becomes $21x = 4 \times 140$, where $x = 26.67$. Since it is not an exact number of nights, the answer is rounded up to 27 nights. Twenty-six nights would not give Sarah enough time.

2. B: To be directly proportional means that $y = mx$. If x is changed from 5 to 20, the value of x is multiplied by 4. Applying the same rule to the y-value, also multiply the value of y by 4. Therefore, $y = 12$.

3. C: To solve the problem, a proportion is written consisting of ratios comparing distance and time. One way to set up the proportion is: $\frac{3}{48} = \frac{5}{x} \left(\frac{distance}{time} = \frac{distance}{time} \right)$ where x represents the unknown value of time. To solve a proportion, the ratios are cross-multiplied:

$$(3)(x) = (5)(48) \rightarrow 3x = 240$$

The equation is solved by isolating the variable, or dividing by 3 on both sides, to produce $x = 80$ minutes.

Representing Relationships using Number Pairs in a Table

1. C: The situation can be described by the equation $? \times 2$. Filling in for the missing numbers would result in $3 \times 2 = 6$ and $7 \times 2 = 14$. Therefore, the missing numbers are 6 and 14. The other choices are miscalculations or misidentification of the pattern formed by the table.

2. C: These labels correctly describe a real-world application of the input-output table shown. The number of tricycles would need to be multiplied by 3 (the number of wheels on a tricycle) in order to find the number of total wheels in a store's inventory. Choice A is not a correct modeling of a real-world situation. A stable chair would have 4 legs, not 3. Choice B is incorrect as it mixes up the number of wheels on a tricycle with the number of tricycles. The number of wheels cannot be the variable (changing) item for this calculation. Choice D does something similar to Choice B, by mixing up the variable and the multiplier; dogs would have a set number of paws, not one that would change.

3. B: The number of yards mowed by Carl's company in each row is three times the number of yards mowed by Gary's company. 7 times 3 is 21, and 11 times 3 is 33. Therefore, the two missing values are 21 and 33, making Choice B the correct answer.

Describing the Coordinate Plane

1. B: The quadrant in which the first coordinate is positive, and the second coordinate is negative is the second quadrant. Therefore, the ordered pair is in Quadrant II, so Choice B is correct.

2. B: Because the x-coordinate is 0, the point does not move along the x-axis. It moves up 4 units above the origin along the y-axis. Therefore, this point is on the positive y-axis and Choice B is correct.

3. C: The quadrant in which the first and second coordinates are both negative is the third quadrant. Therefore, the ordered pair is in Quadrant III, which makes Choice C the correct answer.

4. D: Because the y-coordinate is 0, the point does not move along the y-axis. It moves to the left 5 units on the x-axis away from the origin. Therefore, this point is on the negative x-axis and Choice D is correct.

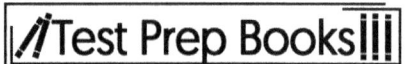

Graphing Ordered Pairs

1: C. The two points are at −5 and 0 for the x-axis and at −3 and at −1 for y-axis respectively. Therefore, the two points have the coordinates of (−5, −3) and (0, −1).

2. D: When an ordered pair is reflected over an axis, the sign of one of the coordinates must change. When it's reflected over the x-axis, the sign of the y-coordinate must change. The x-value remains the same. Therefore, the new ordered pair is (−3, 4).

3. A: The ordered pair (4, −3) is in Quadrant IV. If it is reflected over the x-axis, it would mean that the y-coordinate becomes 3, so the new point is (4, 3). This point is in Quadrant I, so Choice A is correct.

Solving Real-World Problems with Ratios

Ratios and Unit Rates

Ratios are used to show the relationship between two quantities. The ratio of oranges to apples in the grocery store may be 3 to 2. That means that for every 3 oranges, there are 2 apples. This comparison can be expanded to represent the actual number of oranges and apples. Another example may be the number of boys to girls in a math class. If the ratio of boys to girls is given as 2 to 5, that means there are 2 boys to every 5 girls in the class. Ratios can also be compared if the units in each ratio are the same. The ratio of boys to girls in the math class can be compared to the ratio of boys to girls in a science class by stating which ratio is higher and which is lower.

Rates are used to compare two quantities with different units. **Unit rates** are the simplest form of rate. With unit rates, the denominator in the comparison of two units is one.

> **Example**
>
> If someone can type at a rate of 1,000 words in 5 minutes, then his or her unit rate for typing is $\frac{1{,}000 \text{ words}}{5 \text{ minutes}} = 200$ words in one minute or 200 words per minute.

Any rate can be converted into a unit rate by dividing to make the denominator one. 1000 words in 5 minutes has been converted into the unit rate of 200 words per minute.

Ratios and rates can be used together to convert rates into different units. For example, if someone is driving 50 kilometers per hour, that rate can be converted into miles per hour by using a ratio known as the **conversion factor**. Since the given value contains kilometers and the final answer needs to be in miles, the ratio relating miles to kilometers needs to be used.

> **Example**
>
> There are 0.62 miles in 1 kilometer. This, written as a ratio and in fraction form, is $\frac{0.62 \text{ miles}}{1 \text{ km}}$. To convert 50km/hour into miles per hour, the following conversion needs to be set up:
>
> $$\frac{50 \text{ km}}{\text{hour}} \times \frac{0.62 \text{ miles}}{1 \text{ km}} = 31 \text{ miles per hour}$$

The ratio between two similar geometric figures is called the **scale factor**.

Patterns, Relationships, and Algebraic Reasoning
Solving Real-World Problems with Ratios

For example, a problem may depict two similar triangles, A and B. The scale factor from the smaller triangle A to the larger triangle B is given as 2 because the length of the corresponding side of the larger triangle, 16, is twice the corresponding side on the smaller triangle, 8. This scale factor can also be used to find the value of a missing side, x, in triangle A. Since the scale factor from the smaller triangle (A) to larger one (B) is 2, the larger corresponding side in triangle B (given as 25), can be divided by 2 to find the missing side in A ($x = 12.5$). The scale factor can also be represented in the equation $2A = B$ because two times the lengths of A gives the corresponding lengths of B. This is the idea behind similar triangles.

Practice Questions

1. A school has 15 teachers and 20 teaching assistants. They have 200 students. What is the ratio of faculty to students?
    a. 3:20
    b. 4:17
    c. 3:2
    d. 7:40

2. In Jim's school, there are 3 girls for every 2 boys. There are 650 students in total. Using this information, how many students are girls?
    a. 260
    b. 130
    c. 65
    d. 390

3. The hospital has a nurse-to-patient ratio of $1 : 25$. If there is a maximum of 325 patients admitted at a time, how many nurses are there?
    a. 13 nurses
    b. 25 nurses
    c. 325 nurses
    d. 12 nurses

Determining the Constant Rate of Proportionality

Linear relationships may be represented by a table of 2 corresponding values. Certain tables may determine the relationship between the values and predict other corresponding sets. From the table, the constant of proportionality—or the unit rate—can be determined. Proportional relationships will present as a pattern. A simple input-output table can model a pattern that pertains to a specific situation or equation. These can then be utilized in other areas in math, such as graphing.

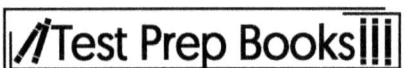

Patterns, Relationships, and Algebraic Reasoning
Solving Real-World Problems with Ratios

Examples

Example 1: For every 1 parakeet the pet store sells, it sells 5 goldfish. Using the following equation to model this situation, fill in numbers missing in the input-output table, to show the total number of pets sold by the store.

$$Total\ number\ of\ pets\ sold\ (t) = number\ of\ parakeets\ (p) + number\ of\ parakeets\ (p) \times 5\ goldfish$$

$$t = p + (p \times 5)$$

$$t = 6p$$

p	t
1	6
2	12
3	
4	24
5	

The missing numbers are 18 and 30.

This can also be shown by using an equation. If 3 is put in for *p*, it would look as follows:

$$t = 6 \times 3$$

$$t = 18$$

If 5 is put in for *p*, it would look as follows:

$$t = 6 \times 5$$

$$t = 30$$

The completed table would appear as follows:

p	t
1	6
2	12
3	18
4	24
5	30

By looking at the completed table, the numeric patterns between consecutive *p* and *t* values (from one row to the next) can be seen. The *p*-values increase by 1, and the *t*-values increase by 6.

146

Patterns, Relationships, and Algebraic Reasoning
Solving Real-World Problems with Ratios

Practice Questions

1. Which table has a constant of proportionality equal to 4? The constant of proportionality is k in the equation $y = kx$.

a.

x	y
1	4
2	7
3	11
4	12

b.

x	y
1	4
2	8
3	12
4	16

c.

x	y
4	1
8	2
12	3
16	4

d.

x	y
1	1
2	2
3	3
4	4

2. What is the constant of proportionality in the equation $12y = 6x$?
   a. 2
   b. 6
   c. $\frac{1}{2}$
   d. 12

3. Find the constant of proportionality in the table below:

x	y
4	10
6	15
8	20
10	25

a. 2.5
b. 5
c. 10
d. 15

Representing the Constant Rate of Change

Rate of change for any line calculates the steepness of the line over a given interval. Rate of change is also known as the slope or rise/run. The slope is given by the change in y divided by the change in x. The formula looks like this:

$$slope = \frac{y_2 - y_1}{x_2 - x_1}$$

Slope can be thought of as determining the rise over run:

$$slope = \frac{rise}{run}$$

The rise being the change vertically on the y-axis and the run being the change horizontally on the x-axis.

The rate of change for a linear function is constant and can be determined based on a few representations. One method is to place the equation in slope-intercept form: $y = mx + b$. Thus, m is the slope, and b is the y-intercept.

The **y-intercept of a linear function** is the value of y when $x = 0$ (the point where the line intercepts the y-axis on the graph of the equation). It is sometimes helpful to think of this as a "starting point" for a linear function.

Patterns, Relationships, and Algebraic Reasoning
Solving Real-World Problems with Ratios

For example, In the graph below, the equation is $y = x + 1$, where the slope is 1 and the y-intercept is 1. For every vertical change of 1 unit, there is a horizontal change of 1 unit. The x-intercept is -1, which is the point where the line crosses the x-axis:

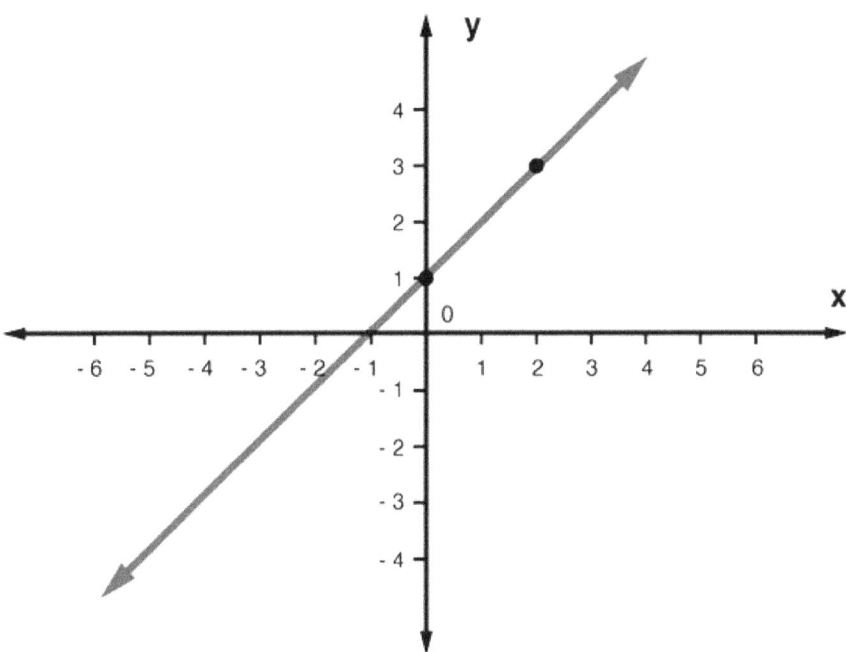

Let's look at an example of a proportional, or linear relationship, seen in the real world.

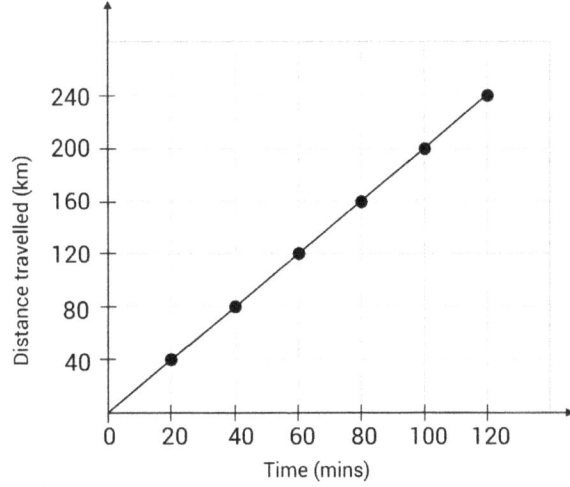

The graph above represents the relationship between distance traveled and time. To find the distance traveled in 80 minutes, the mark for 80 minutes is located at the bottom of the graph. By following this mark directly up on the graph, the corresponding point for 80 minutes is directly across from the 160 kilometer mark. This information indicates that the distance travelled in 80 minutes is 160 kilometers. To predict information not displayed on the graph, the way in which the variables change with respect to one another is determined. In this case, distance increases by 40 kilometers as time increases by 20 minutes. This information can be used to continue the data in the graph or convert the values to a table.

Examples

Example 1: Find the slope of the line in the graph below.

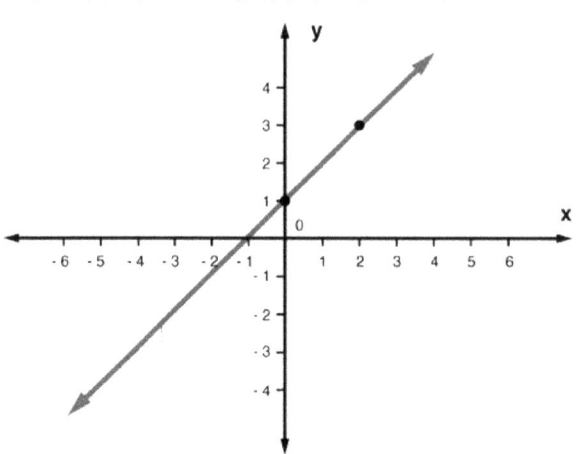

In the graph above, two points are plotted. The first has the coordinates of (0, 1), and the second point is (2, 3). Remember that the x coordinate is always placed first in coordinate pairs. Work from left to right when identifying coordinates. Thus, the point on the left is point 1 (0, 1), and the point on the right is point 2 (2, 3). Now we need to just plug those numbers into the equation:

$$slope = \frac{3-1}{2-0}$$

$$slope = \frac{2}{2}$$

$$slope = 1$$

This means that for every increase of 1 for x, y also increased by 1. You can see this in the line. When x equaled 0, y equaled 1, and when x was increased to 1, y equaled 2.

Patterns, Relationships, and Algebraic Reasoning
Solving Real-World Problems with Ratios

Practice Questions

1. A line goes through the point $(-4, 0)$ and the point $(0, 2)$. What is the slope of the line?
   a. 2
   b. 4
   c. $\frac{3}{2}$
   d. $\frac{1}{2}$

2. A line passes through the origin and through the point $(-3, 4)$. What is the slope of the line?
   a. $-\frac{4}{3}$
   b. $-\frac{3}{4}$
   c. $\frac{4}{3}$
   d. $\frac{3}{4}$

3. A line passes through the point $(1, 2)$ and crosses the y-axis at $y = 1$. Which of the following is an equation for this line?
   a. $y = 2x$
   b. $y = x + 1$
   c. $x + y = 1$
   d. $y = \frac{x}{2} - 2$

4. What is an equation for the line passing through the origin and the point $(2, 1)$?
   a. $y = 2x$
   b. $y = \frac{1}{2}x$
   c. $y = x - 2$
   d. $2y = x + 1$

Answer Explanations

Ratios and Unit Rates

1. D: The total faculty is $15 + 20 = 35$. So, the ratio is 35:200. Then, divide both of these numbers by 5, since 5 is a common factor to both, with a result of 7:40.

2. D: Three girls for every two boys can be expressed as a ratio: $3 : 2$. This can be visualized as splitting the school into 5 groups: 3 girl groups and 2 boy groups. The number of students which are in each group can be found by dividing the total number of students by 5:

$$\frac{650 \text{ students}}{5 \text{ groups}} = \frac{130 \text{ students}}{\text{group}}$$

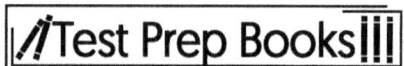

To find the total number of girls, multiply the number of students per group (130) by the number of girl groups in the school (3). This equals 390, Choice D.

3. A: Using the given information of 1 nurse to 25 patients and 325 patients, set up an equation to solve for number of nurses (N):

$$\frac{N}{325} = \frac{1}{25}$$

Multiply both sides by 325 to get N by itself on one side.

$$\frac{N}{1} = \frac{325}{25} = 13 \text{ nurses}$$

Determining the Constant Rate of Proportionality

1. B: In order for the equation $y = 4x$ to hold, each y-value must be equal to 4 times the corresponding x-value in the row. The only option in which this is true for every row is Choice B.

2. C: The equation must be placed in the form $y = kx$ to determine the constant of proportionality k. Dividing both sides by 12 results in the equation $y = \frac{1}{2}x$. Therefore, the constant of proportionality is equal to $\frac{1}{2}$ and Choice C is correct.

3. A: To determine the constant of proportionality, each row must adhere to the equation $y = kx$. Taking the first row and plugging 4 in for x and 10 in for y results in the equation $10 = k \times 4$. Dividing both sides by 4 results in $k = \frac{10}{4} = 2.5$.

Representing the Constant Rate of Change

1. D: The slope is given by the change in y divided by the change in x. The change in y is $2 - 0 = 2$, and the change in x is:

$$0 - (-4) = 4$$

The slope is $\frac{2}{4} = \frac{1}{2}$.

2. A: The slope is given by:

$$m = \frac{y_2 - y_1}{x_2 - x_1} = \frac{0 - 4}{0 - (-3)} = -\frac{4}{3}$$

3. B: From the slope-intercept form, $y = mx + b$, it is known that b is the y-intercept, which is 1. Compute the slope as $\frac{2-1}{1-0} = 1$, so the equation should be $y = x + 1$.

4. B: The slope will be given by $\frac{1-0}{2-0} = \frac{1}{2}$. The y-intercept will be 0 since it passes through the origin. Using slope-intercept form, the equation for this line is $y = \frac{1}{2}x$.

Geometry

Calculating Geometric Quantities

Identifying Lines and Angles

In geometry, a **line** connects two points, has no thickness, and extends indefinitely in both directions beyond each point. If the length is finite, it's known as a **line segment** and has two **endpoints**. A **ray** is the straight portion of a line that has one endpoint and extends indefinitely in the other direction. An **angle** is formed when two rays begin at the same endpoint and extend indefinitely. The endpoint of an angle is called a **vertex**. **Adjacent angles** are two side-by-side angles formed from the same ray that have the same endpoint.

Angles are measured in **degrees** or **radians**, which is a measure of **rotation**. A **full rotation** equals 360 degrees or 2π radians, which represents a circle. Half a rotation equals 180 degrees or π radians and represents a half-circle. Angle measurement is additive. When an angle is broken into two non-overlapping angles, the total measure of the larger angle equals the sum of the two smaller angles. Lines are **coplanar** if they're located in the same plane. Two lines are **parallel** if they are coplanar, extend in the same direction, and never cross. If lines do cross, they're labeled as **intersecting lines** because they "intersect" at one point. If they intersect at more than one point, they're the same line. **Perpendicular lines** are coplanar lines that form a right angle at their point of intersection.

As an example, the figure below shows a set of parallel lines and a set of perpendicular lines.

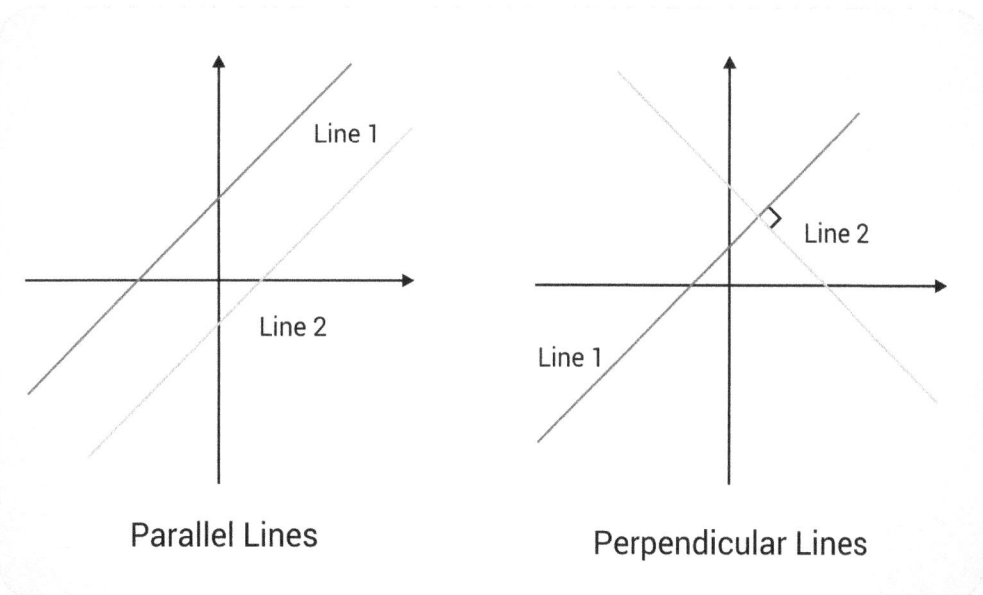

Two lines are parallel if they have the same slope and different intercept. Two lines are perpendicular if the product of their slope equals -1.

153

> **Example**
>
> $y = \frac{1}{4}x + 5$ and $y = \frac{1}{4}x - 2$ are parallel lines because they both have a slope of $\frac{1}{4}$.
>
> $y = -2x - 6$ and $y = \frac{1}{2}x + 1$ are perpendicular because $-2 \times \frac{1}{2} = -1$.

Parallel lines never intersect unless they are the same line, and perpendicular lines intersect at a right angle. If two lines aren't parallel, they must intersect at one point. Determining equations of lines based on properties of parallel and perpendicular lines appears in word problems. To find an equation of a line, both the slope and a point the line goes through are necessary. Therefore, if an equation of a line is needed that's parallel to a given line and runs through a specified point, the slope of the given line and the point are plugged into the point-slope form of an equation of a line. Secondly, if an equation of a line is needed that's perpendicular to a given line running through a specified point, the negative reciprocal of the slope of the given line and the point are plugged into the point-slope form. Also, if the point of intersection of two lines is known, that point will be used to solve the set of equations. Therefore, to solve a system of equations, the point of intersection must be found. If a set of two equations with two unknown variables has no solution, the lines are parallel.

The **Parallel Postulate** states that if two parallel lines are cut by a transversal, then the corresponding angles are equal. Here is a picture that highlights this postulate:

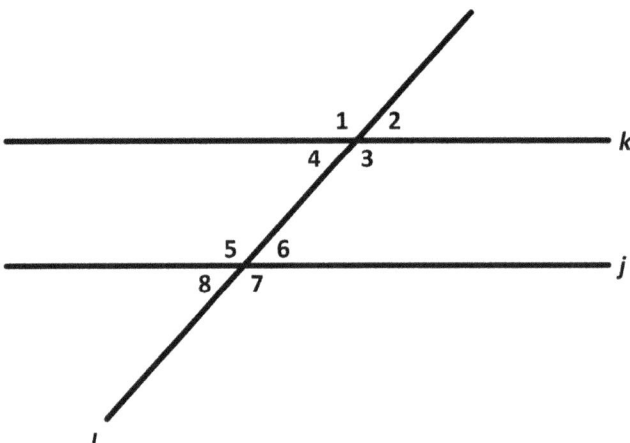

Because lines *k* and *i* are parallel, when cut by transversal *l*, angles 1 and 5 are equal, angles 2 and 6 are equal, angles 4 and 8 are equal, and angles 3 and 7 are equal. Note that angles 1 and 2, 3 and 4, 5 and 6, and 7 and 8 add up to 180 degrees.

This statement is equivalent to the **Alternate Interior Angle Theorem**, which states that when two parallel lines are cut by a transversal, the resultant interior angles are congruent. In the picture above, angles 3 and 5 are congruent, and angles 4 and 6 are congruent.

An equivalent statement to the Parallel Postulate is that the sum of all angles in a triangle is 180 degrees. Therefore, given any triangle, if two angles are known, the third can be found accordingly.

Geometry
Calculating Geometric Quantities

Examples

Example 1: Find the missing angles in the following picture:

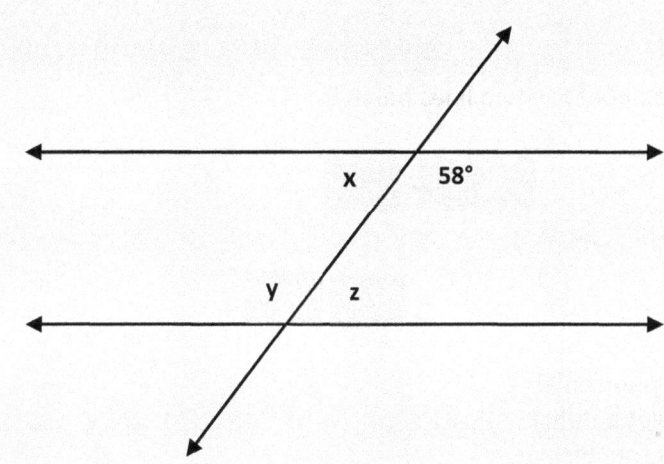

The Parallel Postulate or the Alternate Interior Angle Theorem can be used to find the missing angles. Assuming that the lines are parallel, angle x is found to be 122 degrees. Angle x and the 58-degree angle add up to 180 degrees. The Alternate Interior Angle Theorem states that angle y is equal to 58 degrees. Also, angles y and z add up to 180 degrees, so angle z is 122 degrees. Note that angles x and z are also alternate interior angles, so their equivalence can be used to find angle z as well.

Practice Questions

1. What is the measurement of angle f in the following picture? Assume the lines are parallel.

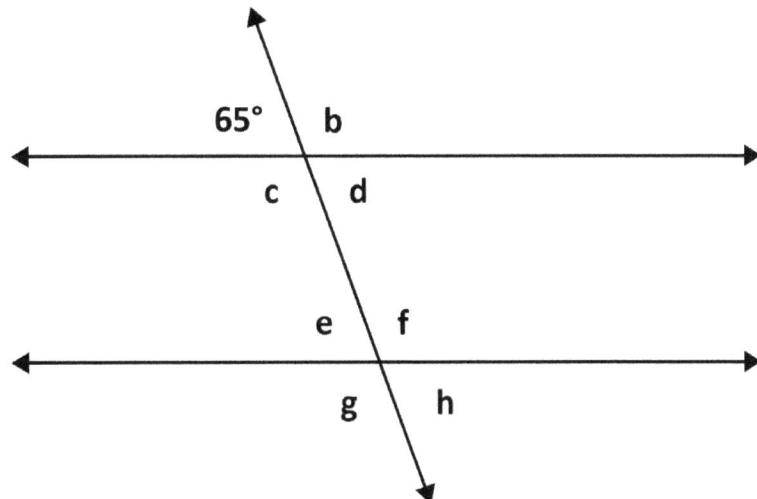

    a. 65 degrees
    b. 115 degrees
    c. 125 degrees
    d. 55 degrees

2. Which graph will be a line parallel to the graph of $y = 3x - 2$?
   a. $2y - 6x = 2$
   b. $y - 4x = 4$
   c. $3y = x - 2$
   d. $2x - 2y = 2$

3. Which of the following statements is true about the two lines below?

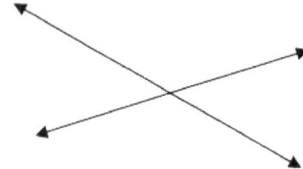

   a. The two lines are parallel but not perpendicular.
   b. The two lines are perpendicular but not parallel.
   c. The two lines are both parallel and perpendicular.
   d. The two lines are neither parallel nor perpendicular.

Classifying Angles

An **angle** consists of two rays that have a common endpoint. This common endpoint is called the **vertex** of the angle. The two rays can be called sides of the angle. The angle below has a vertex at point *B* and the sides consist of ray *BA* and ray *BC*. An angle can be named in three ways:

1. Using the vertex and a point from each side, with the vertex letter in the middle.
2. Using only the vertex. This can only be used if it is the only angle with that vertex.
3. Using a number that is written inside the angle.

For example, the angle below can be written ∠*ABC* (read angle *ABC*), ∠*CBA*, ∠*B*, or ∠1.

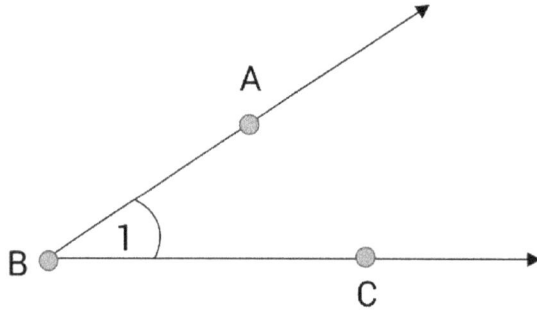

Geometry
Calculating Geometric Quantities

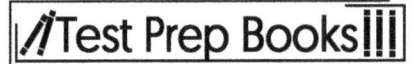

An angle divides a plane, or flat surface, into three parts: the angle itself, the interior (inside) of the angle, and the exterior (outside) of the angle. The figure below shows point M on the interior of the angle and point N on the exterior of the angle.

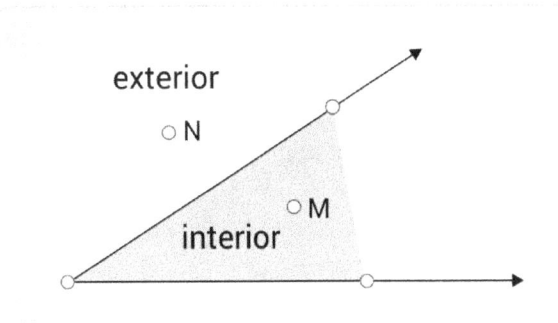

Angles can be measured in units called degrees, with the symbol °. The degree measure of an angle is between 0° and 180° and can be obtained by using a protractor.

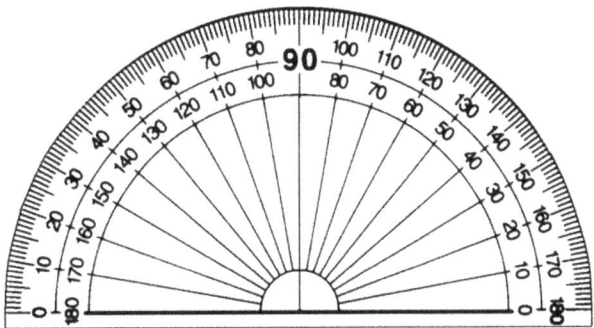

A straight angle (or simply a line) measures exactly 180°. A right angle's sides meet at the vertex to create a square corner. A right angle measures exactly 90° and is typically indicated by a box drawn in the interior of the angle. An acute angle has an interior that is narrower than a right angle. The measure of an acute angle is any value less than 90° and greater than 0°. An obtuse angle has an interior that is wider than a right angle. The measure of an obtuse angle is any value greater than 90° but less than 180°. Acute angles include 89.9°, 47°, 12°, and 1°. Obtuse angles include 90.1°, 110°, 150°, and 179.9°.

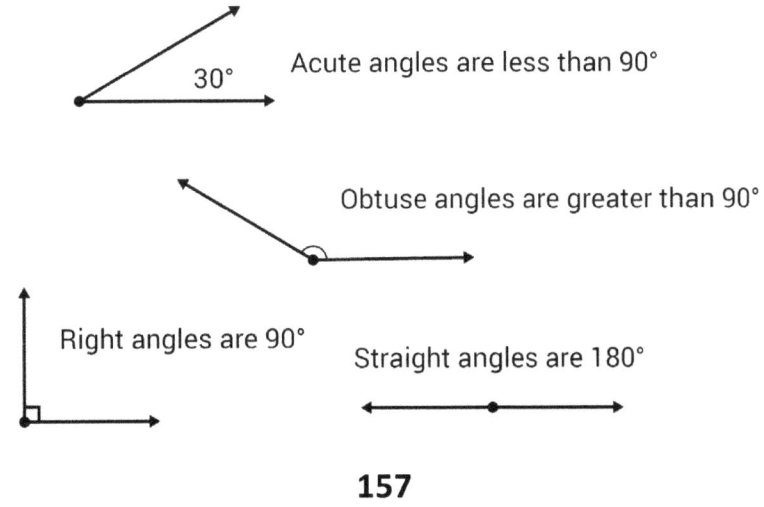

Practice Questions

1. A clock reads 5:00 am. What is the measure of the angle formed by the two hands of that clock?
   a. 300 degrees
   b. 150 degrees
   c. 75 degrees
   d. 210 degrees

2. What is the measure of Angle B to the nearest degree displayed on the following protractor?

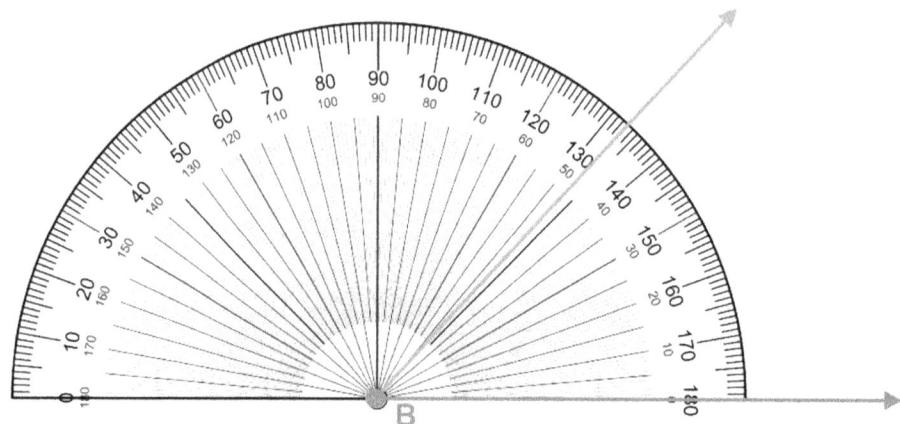

   a. 136°
   b. 133°
   c. 53°
   d. 47°

3. An angle measures 54 degrees. In order to correctly determine the measure of its complementary angle, what concept is necessary?
   a. Two complementary angles sum up to 180 degrees.
   b. Complementary angles are always acute.
   c. Two complementary angles sum up to 90 degrees.
   d. Complementary angles sum up to 360 degrees.

Geometry
Calculating Geometric Quantities

Classifying Two-Dimensional Figures

A **polygon** is a closed two-dimensional figure consisting of three or more sides. Polygons can be either convex or concave. A polygon that has interior angles all measuring less than 180° is **convex**. A **concave** polygon has one or more interior angles measuring greater than 180°.

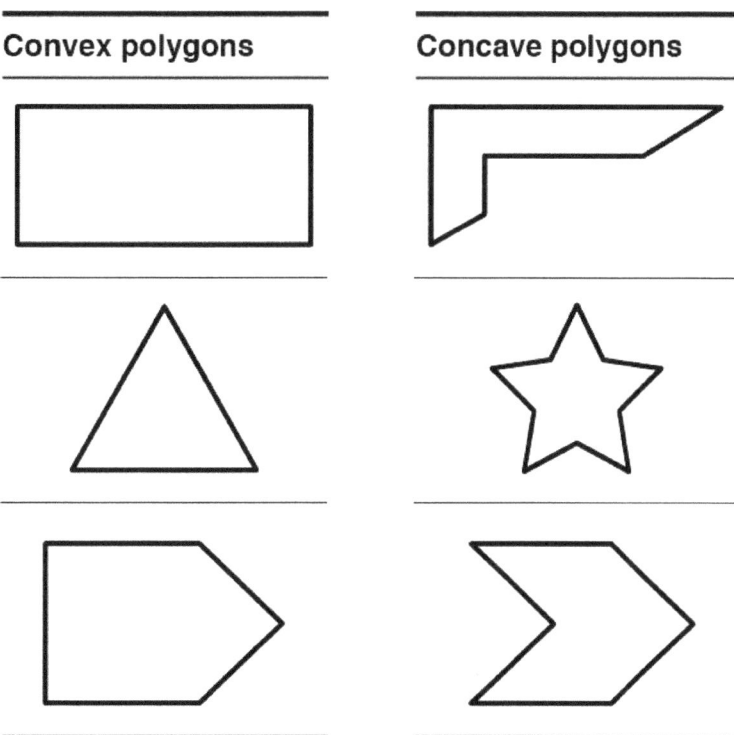

Polygons can be classified by the number of sides (also equal to the number of angles) they have. The following are the names of polygons with a given number of sides or angles:

# of Sides	Name of Polygon
3	Triangle
4	Quadrilateral
5	Pentagon
6	Hexagon
7	Septagon (or heptagon)
8	Octagon
9	Nonagon
10	Decagon

Equiangular polygons are polygons in which the measure of every interior angle is the same. The sides of equilateral polygons are always the same length. If a polygon is both equiangular and equilateral, the polygon is defined as a **regular polygon**.

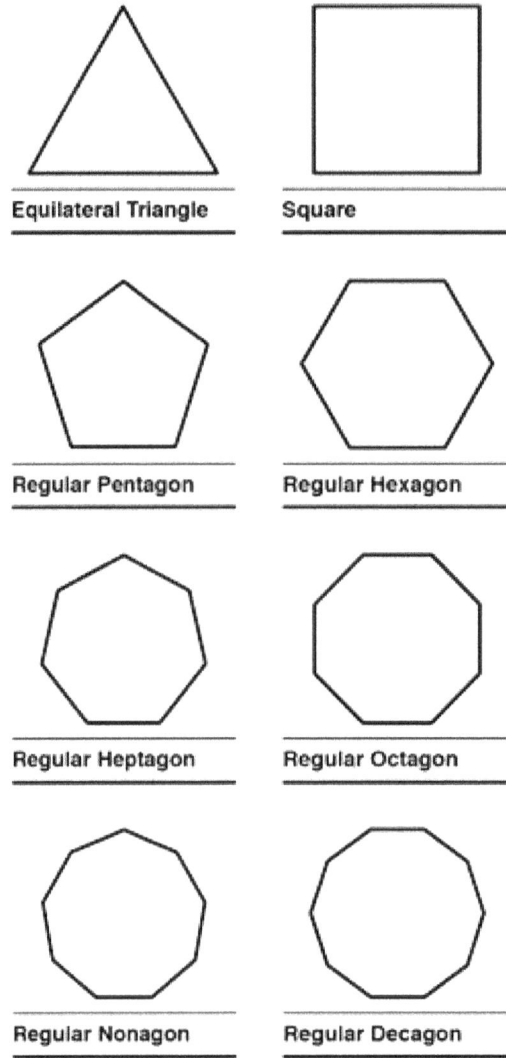

Triangles can be further classified by their sides and angles. A triangle with its largest angle measuring 90° is a **right triangle**.

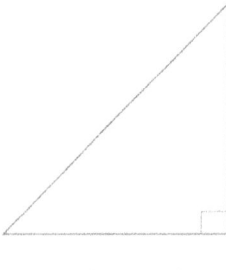

Right triangle

Geometry
Calculating Geometric Quantities

A triangle with the largest angle less than 90° is an **acute triangle**. A triangle with the largest angle greater than 90° is an **obtuse triangle**. A triangle consisting of two equal sides and two equal angles is an **isosceles triangle**. A triangle with three equal sides and three equal angles is an **equilateral triangle**. A triangle with no equal sides or angles is a **scalene triangle**.

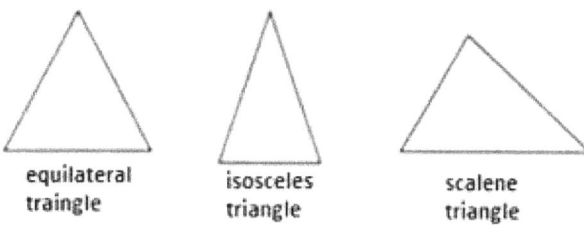

Quadrilaterals can be further classified according to their sides and angles. A quadrilateral with exactly one pair of parallel sides is called a **trapezoid**. A quadrilateral that shows both pairs of opposite sides parallel is a **parallelogram**. Parallelograms include rhombuses, rectangles, and squares. A **rhombus** has four equal sides. A **rectangle** has four equal angles (90° each). A **square** has four 90° angles and four equal sides. Therefore, a square is both a rhombus and a rectangle.

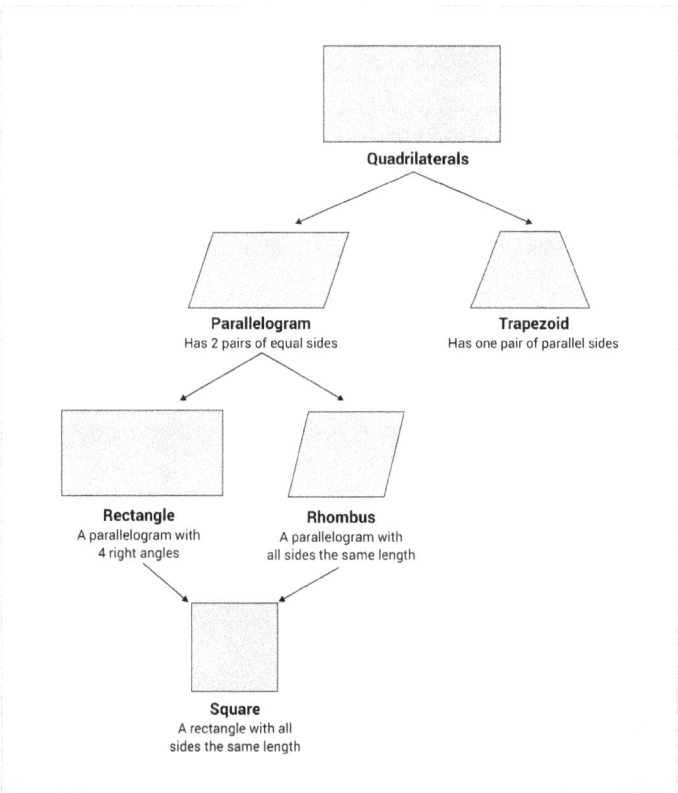

Geometry
Calculating Geometric Quantities

There are many key facts related to geometry that are applicable. The sum of the measures of the angles of a triangle are 180°, and for a quadrilateral, the sum is 360°. Rectangles and squares each have four right angles. A **right angle** has a measure of 90°.

Practice Questions

1. Which four-sided shape is always a rectangle?
   a. Rhombus
   b. Square
   c. Parallelogram
   d. Quadrilateral

2. Which of the following is NOT a parallelogram?

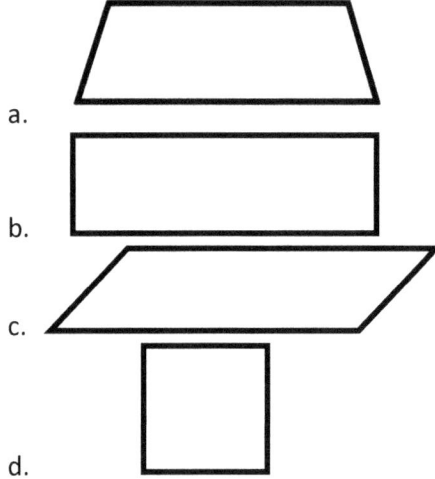

   a.
   b.
   c.
   d.

3. Which of the following figures is not a polygon?
   a. Decagon
   b. Cone
   c. Triangle
   d. Rhombus

Geometry
Calculating Geometric Quantities

Classifying Three-Dimensional Figures

A solid is a three-dimensional figure that encloses a part of space. Common three-dimensional shapes include spheres, prisms, cubes, pyramids, cylinders, and cones.

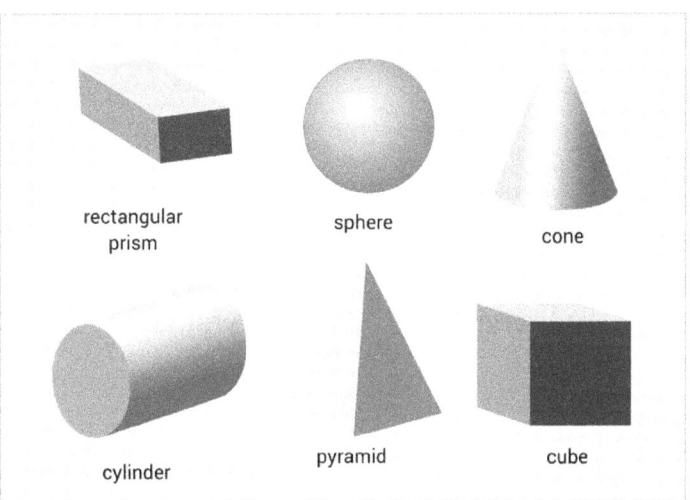

Solids consisting of all flat surfaces that are polygons are called polyhedrons. The two-dimensional surfaces that make up a polyhedron are called faces. Types of polyhedrons include prisms and pyramids. A prism consists of two parallel faces that are congruent (or the same shape and same size), and lateral faces going around (which are parallelograms). A prism is further classified by the shape of its base.

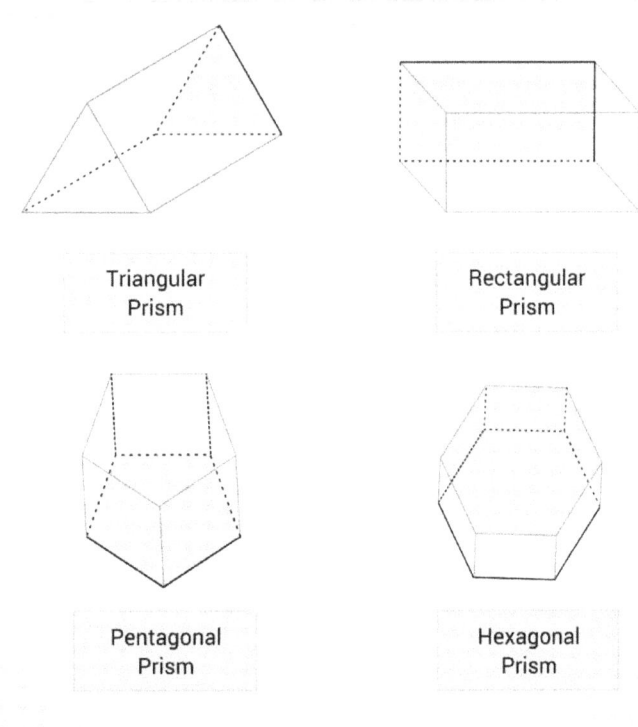

A pyramid consists of lateral faces (triangles) that meet at a common point called the vertex and one other face that is a polygon, called the base. A pyramid can be further classified by the shape of its base.

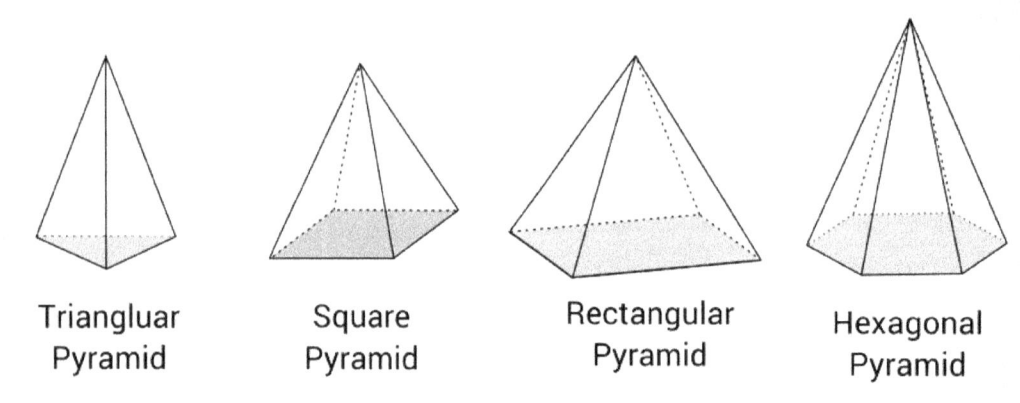

Triangluar Pyramid   Square Pyramid   Rectangular Pyramid   Hexagonal Pyramid

A tetrahedron is another name for a triangular pyramid. All the faces of a tetrahedron are triangles.

Solids that are not polyhedrons include spheres, cylinders, and cones. A sphere is the set of all points a given distance from a given center point. A sphere is commonly thought of as a three-dimensional circle. A cylinder consists of two parallel, congruent (same size) circles and a lateral curved surface. A cone consists of a circle as its base and a lateral curved surface that narrows to a point called the vertex.

Similar polygons are the same shape but different sizes. More specifically, their corresponding angle measures are congruent (or equal) and the length of their sides is proportional. For example, all sides of one polygon may be double the length of the sides of another. Likewise, similar solids are the same shape but different sizes. Any corresponding faces or bases of similar solids are the same polygons that are proportional by a consistent value.

Geometry
Calculating Geometric Quantities

Practice Questions

1. Which of the following three-dimensional shapes is a pyramid?

a.

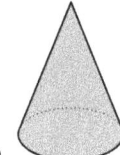
b.

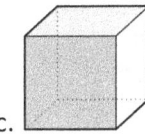
c.

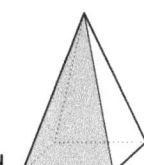
d.

2. How many faces does a rectangular prism have?
   a. 2
   b. 4
   c. 6
   d. 12

3. Which of the following shapes has a circular base?
   a. Pyramid
   b. Cube
   c. Cone
   d. Rectangular prism

The Pythagorean Theorem

The value of a missing side of a right triangle may be determined two ways. The first way is to apply the Pythagorean Theorem, and the second way is to apply Trigonometric Ratios. The Pythagorean Theorem states that for every right triangle, the square of the length of the hypotenuse is equal to the sum of the squares of the lengths of the remaining two sides. The hypotenuse is the longest side of a right triangle, and is also the side opposite the right angle.

According to the diagram, $a^2 + b^2 = c^2$, where c represents the hypotenuse, and a and b represent the lengths of remaining two sides of the right triangle. The Pythagorean Theorem may be applied a multitude of ways.

Geometry
Calculating Geometric Quantities

Examples

Example 1: A person wishes to build a garden in the shape of a rectangle, having the dimensions of 5 feet by 8 feet. The garden's design includes a diagonal board to separate various types of plants. What is the length of the diagonal board?

The Pythagorean Theorem can be used to determine the length of the diagonal board.

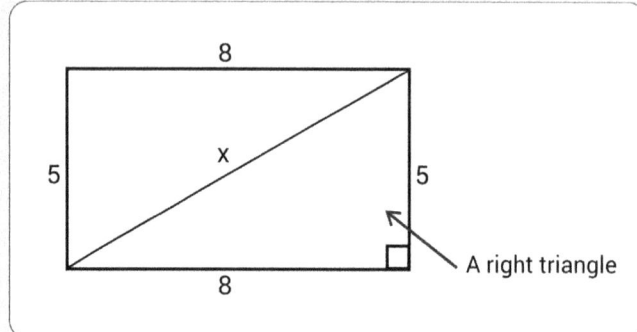

$$a^2 + b^2 = c^2$$
$$5^2 + 8^2 = c^2$$
$$25 + 64 = c^2$$
$$c = \sqrt{89}$$
$$c = 9.43$$

Practice Questions

1. Given the triangle below, find the value of x if $y = 21$.

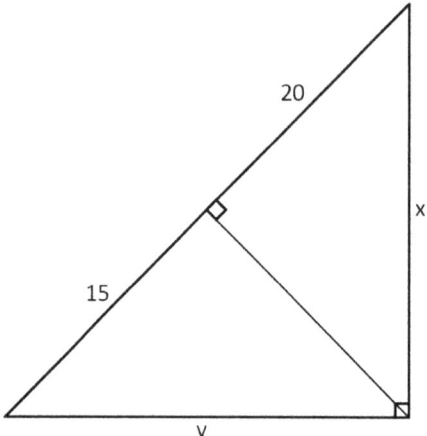

   a. 35
   b. 28
   c. 25
   d. 26

Geometry
Calculating Geometric Quantities

2. What is the value of x in the following triangle?

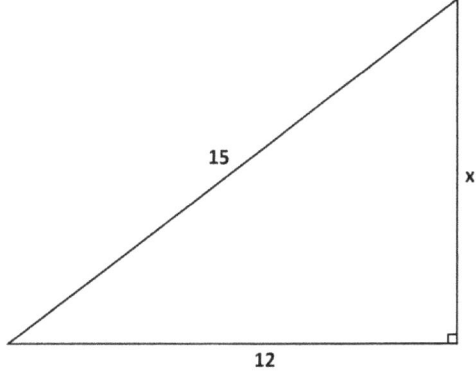

a. 19.2
b. 9
c. 3
d. 7.5

3. What is the length of the hypotenuse of a right triangle with one leg equal to 3 centimeters and the other leg equal to 4 centimeters?
a. 7 cm
b. 5 cm
c. 25 cm
d. 12 cm

Properties of Circles

The **arc of a circle** is the distance between two points on the circle. The length of the arc of a circle in terms of **degrees** is easily determined if the value of the central angle is known. The length of the arc is simply the value of the central angle.

Example

In this example, the length of the arc of the circle in degrees is 75°.

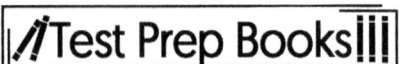

To determine the length of the arc of a circle in **distance**, the student will need to know the values for both the central angle and the radius. This formula is:

$$\frac{\text{central angle}}{360°} = \frac{\text{arc length}}{2\pi r}$$

The equation is simplified by cross-multiplying to solve for the arc length.

Examples

Example 1: Find the arc length in the figure below.

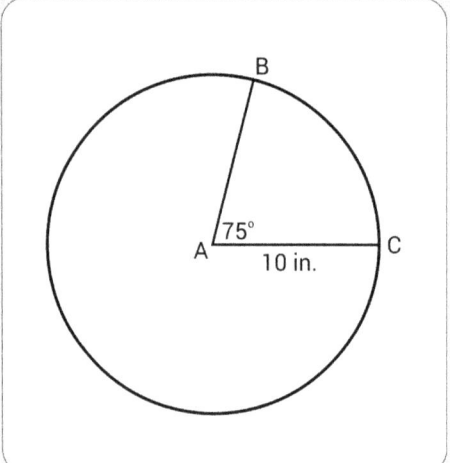

The student should substitute the values of the central angle (75°) and the radius (10 inches) into the formula to solve for the arc length.

$$\frac{75°}{360°} = \frac{\text{arc length}}{2(3.14)(10 \text{in.})}$$

To solve the equation, first cross-multiply: $4710 = 360 \times (arc\ length)$. Next, divide each side of the equation by 360. The result of the formula is that the arc length is 13.1 (rounded).

Practice Questions

1. According to building code regulations, the roof of a house has to be set at a minimum angle of 39° up to a maximum angle of 48° to ensure snow and rain will properly slide off it. What is the maximum incline in terms of radians?

   a. $\frac{\pi}{4}$

   b. $\frac{\pi}{15}$

   c. $\frac{4\pi}{15}$

   d. $\frac{3\pi}{4}$

Geometry
Calculating Geometric Quantities

2. Two chords intersect inside of a circle. The segments of one chord have lengths 3 and $x + 2$. The segments of the other chord have lengths x and $3x + 2$. What are the lengths of these chords?
   a. 1 units
   b. 2 units
   c. 3 units
   d. 6 units

3.

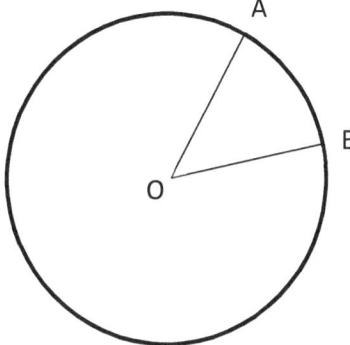

The length of arc $AB = 3\pi$ cm. The length of $\overline{OA} = 12$ cm. What is the degree measure of $\angle AOB$?
   a. 30 degrees
   b. 40 degrees
   c. 45 degrees
   d. 55 degrees

Finding Perimeter and Area

Perimeter is the measurement of a distance around something or the sum of all sides of a polygon. Think of perimeter as the length of the boundary, like a fence. In contrast, **area** is the space occupied by a defined enclosure, like a field enclosed by a fence.

When thinking about perimeter, think about walking around the outside of something. When thinking about area, think about the amount of space or **surface area** something takes up.

Square

The perimeter of a square is measured by adding together all of the sides. Since a square has four equal sides, its perimeter can be calculated by multiplying the length of one side by 4. Thus, the formula is $P = 4 \times s$, where s equals one side.

Example

The following square has side lengths of 5 meters:

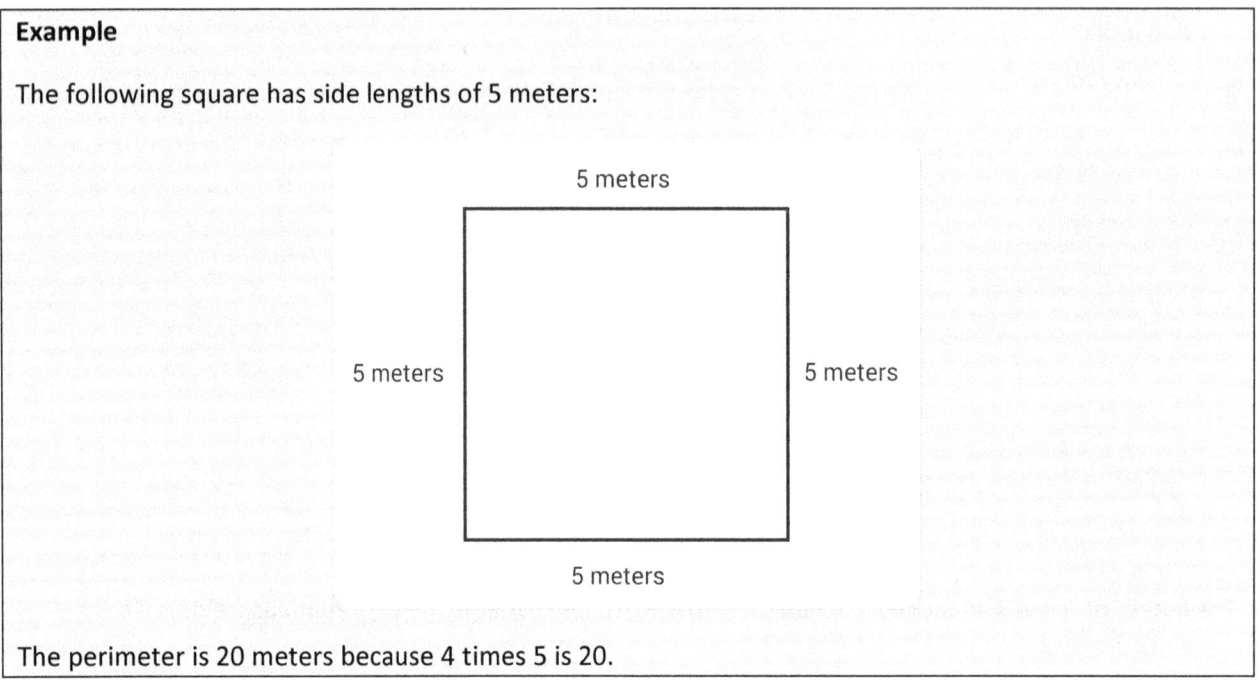

The perimeter is 20 meters because 4 times 5 is 20.

The area of a square is the length of a side squared.

Example

If a side of a square is 7 centimeters, then the area is 49 square centimeters. The formula for this example is:

$$A = s^2 = 7^2 = 49 \text{ square centimeters}$$

Rectangle

Like a square, a rectangle's perimeter is measured by adding together all of the sides. But as the sides are unequal, the formula is different. A rectangle has equal values for its lengths (long sides) and equal values for its widths (short sides), so the perimeter formula for a rectangle is:

$$P = l + l + w + w = 2l + 2w$$

l equals length
w equals width

The area is found by multiplying the length by the width, so the formula is $A = l \times w$.

Geometry
Calculating Geometric Quantities

Example

If the length of a rectangle is 10 inches and the width 8 inches, then the perimeter is 36 inches because:

$$P = 2l + 2w = 2(10) + 2(8) = 20 + 16 = 36 \text{ inches}$$

If a rectangle has a length of 6 inches and a width of 7 inches, then the area is 42 square inches:

$$A = lw = 6(7) = 42 \text{ square inches}$$

Triangle

A triangle's perimeter is measured by adding together the three sides, so the formula is $P = a + b + c$, where $a, b,$ and c are the values of the three sides. The area is the product of one-half the base and height so the formula is:

$$A = \frac{1}{2} \times b \times h$$

It can be simplified to:

$$A = \frac{bh}{2}$$

The base is the bottom of the triangle, and the height is the distance from the base to the peak. If a problem asks to calculate the area of a triangle, it will provide the base and height.

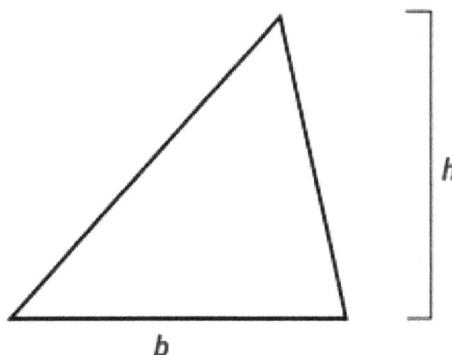

Geometry
Calculating Geometric Quantities

Example

If the base of the triangle is 2 feet and the height 4 feet, then the area is 4 square feet. The following equation shows the formula used to calculate the area of the triangle:

$A = \frac{1}{2}bh = \frac{1}{2}(2)(4) = 4$ square feet

Circle

A circle's perimeter—also known as its circumference—is measured by multiplying the diameter by π.

Diameter is the straight line measured from one end to the direct opposite end of the circle.

π is referred to as pi and is equal to 3.14 (with rounding).

So, the formula is $\pi \times d$.

This is sometimes expressed by the formula $C = 2 \times \pi \times r$, where r is the radius of the circle. These formulas are equivalent, as the radius equals half of the diameter.

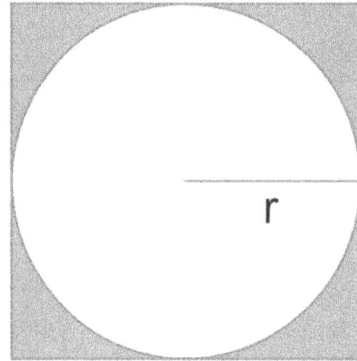

The area of a circle is calculated through the formula $A = \pi \times r^2$. The test will indicate either to leave the answer with π attached or to calculate to the nearest decimal place, which means multiplying by 3.14 for π.

Example

For a circle with a radius of 6, the circumference would be $2 \times \pi \times 6 = 12\pi$. The area would be $\pi \times 6^2 = 36\pi$.

Practice Questions

1. The total perimeter of a rectangle is 36 cm. If the length is 12 cm, what is the width?
   a. 3 cm
   b. 12 cm
   c. 6 cm
   d. 8 cm

2. Using the following diagram, calculate the total circumference, rounding to the nearest decimal place:

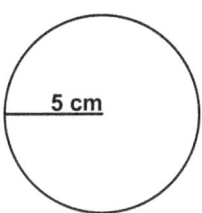

 a. 25.0 cm
 b. 15.7 cm
 c. 78.5 cm
 d. 31.4 cm

3. A rectangle was formed out of pipe cleaner. Its length was $\frac{1}{2}$ foot and its width was $\frac{11}{2}$ inches. What was its area in square inches?
 a. $\frac{11}{4}$ inch²
 b. $\frac{11}{2}$ inch²
 c. 22 inch²
 d. 33 inch²

4. The perimeter of a 6-sided polygon is 56 cm. The length of three of the sides are 9 cm each. The length of two other sides are 8 cm each. What is the length of the missing side?
 a. 11 cm
 b. 12 cm
 c. 13 cm
 d. 10 cm

5. An equilateral triangle has a perimeter of 18 feet. If a square whose sides have the same length as one side of the triangle is built, what will be the area of the square?
 a. 6 square feet
 b. 36 square feet
 c. 256 square feet
 d. 1000 square feet

Decomposing Composite Figures

The perimeter of an irregular polygon is found by adding the lengths of all of the sides. In cases where all of the sides are given, this will be very straightforward, as it will simply involve finding the sum of the provided lengths. Other times, a side length may be missing and must be determined before the perimeter can be calculated.

Example

Consider the figure below:

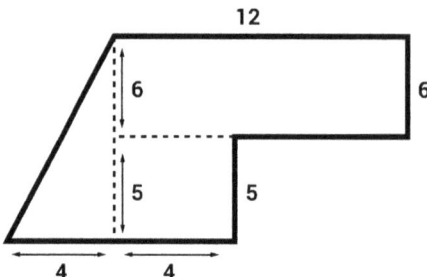

All of the side lengths are provided except for the angled side on the left. Test takers should notice that this is the hypotenuse of a right triangle. The other two sides of the triangle are provided (the base is 4 and the height is $6 + 5 = 11$). The Pythagorean Theorem can be used to find the length of the hypotenuse, remembering that $a^2 + b^2 = c^2$.

Substituting the side values provided yields $(4)2 + (11)2 = c^2$.

Therefore, $c = \sqrt{16 + 121} = 11.7$

Finally, the perimeter can be found by adding this new side length with the other provided lengths to get the total length around the figure:

$$4 + 4 + 5 + 8 + 6 + 12 + 11.7 = 50.7$$

Although units are not provided in this figure, remember that reporting units with a measurement is important.

The area of an irregular polygon is found by decomposing, or breaking apart, the figure into smaller shapes. When the area of the smaller shapes is determined, these areas are added together to produce the total area of the area of the original figure.

Geometry
Calculating Geometric Quantities

Example

Consider the same figure provided before:

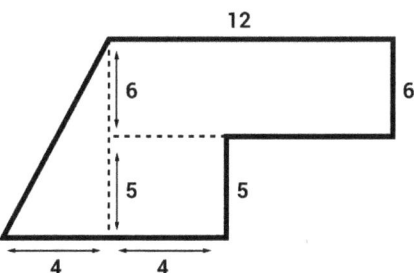

The irregular polygon is decomposed into two rectangles and a triangle. The area of the large rectangles ($A = l \times w \to A = 12 \times 6$) is 72 square units. The area of the small rectangle is 20 square units:

$$(A = 4 \times 5)$$

The area of the triangle ($A = \frac{1}{2} \times b \times h \to A = \frac{1}{2} \times 4 \times 11$) is 22 square units. The sum of the areas of these figures produces the total area of the original polygon:

$$A = 72 + 20 + 22 \to A = 114 \text{ square units}$$

Practice Questions

1. What is the perimeter of the figure below? Note that the solid outer line is the perimeter.

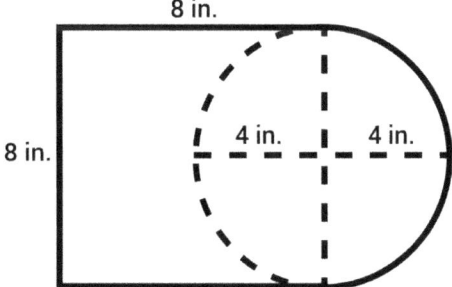

    a. 48.565 in
    b. 36.565 in
    c. 39.78 in
    d. 39.565 in

2. In the figure below, what is the area of the shaded region?

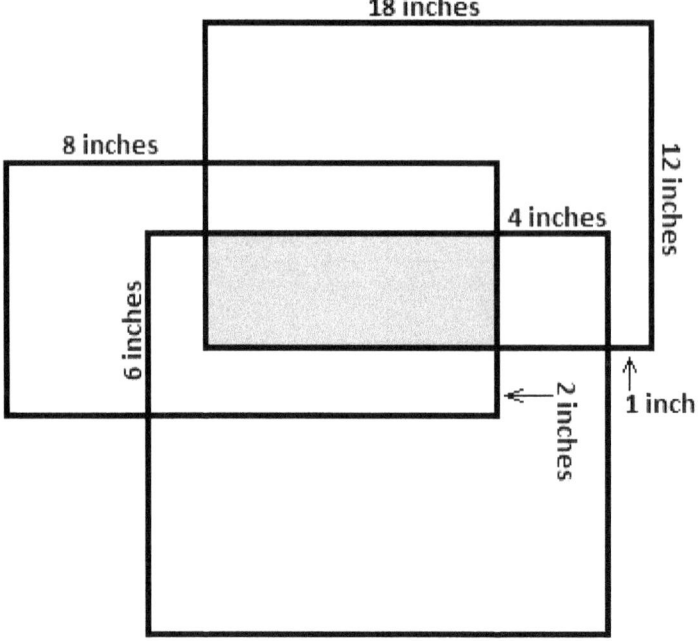

a. 48 sq. inches
b. 52 sq. inches
c. 44 sq. inches
d. 56 sq. inches

3. Determine the missing side length in the following figure:

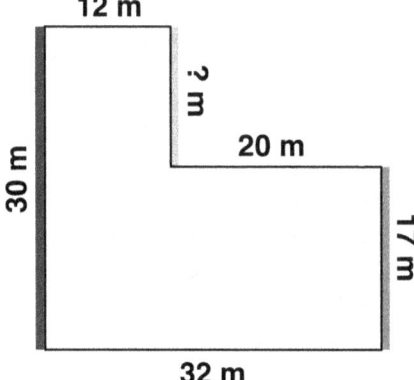

a. 20 m
b. 13 m
c. 12 m
d. 10 m

Geometry
Calculating Geometric Quantities

Finding Volume and Surface Area

Geometry in three dimensions is similar to geometry in two dimensions. The main new feature is that three points now define a unique plane that passes through each of them. Three-dimensional objects can be made by putting together two-dimensional figures in different surfaces. Below, some of the possible three-dimensional figures will be provided, along with formulas for their volumes and surface areas.

Volume is the measurement of how much space an object occupies, like how much space is in the cube. Volume questions will ask how much of something is needed to completely fill the object. The most common surface area and volume questions deal with spheres, cubes, and rectangular prisms.

Surface area of a three-dimensional figure refers to the number of square units needed to cover the entire surface of the figure. This concept is similar to using wrapping paper to completely cover the outside of a box. For example, if a triangular pyramid has a surface area of 17 square inches (written $17in^2$), it will take 17 squares, each with sides one inch in length, to cover the entire surface of the pyramid. Surface area is also measured in square units.

A **rectangular prism** is a box whose sides are all rectangles meeting at 90° angles. Such a box has three dimensions: length, width, and height. If the length is x, the width is y, and the height is z, then the volume is given by $V = xyz$.

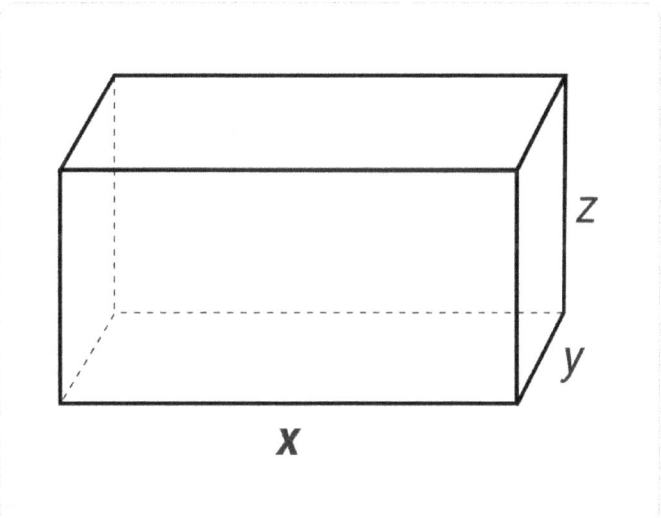

The surface area will be given by computing the surface area of each rectangle and adding them together. There is a total of six rectangles. Two of them have sides of length x and y, two have sides of length y and z, and two have sides of length x and z. Therefore, the total surface area will be given by:

$$SA = 2xy + 2yz + 2xz$$

A **cube** is a special type of rectangular solid in which its length, width, and height are the same. If this length is s, then the formula for the volume of a cube is $V = s \times s \times s$. The surface area of a cube is $SA = 6s^2$.

A **rectangular pyramid** is a figure with a rectangular base and four triangular sides that meet at a single vertex. If the rectangle has sides of length x and y, then the volume will be given by $V = \frac{1}{3}xyh$.

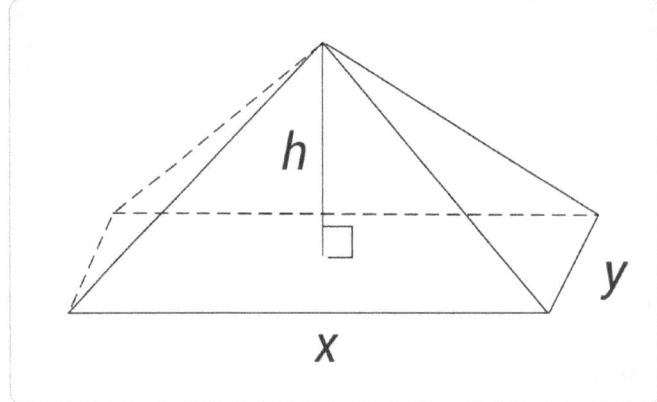

Many three-dimensional figures (solid figures) can be represented by nets consisting of rectangles and triangles. The surface area of such solids can be determined by adding the areas of each of its faces and bases.

Finding the surface area using this method requires calculating the areas of rectangles and triangles. To find the area (A) of a rectangle, the length (l) is multiplied by the width (w) → $A = l \times w$.

To calculate the area (A) of a triangle, the product of $\frac{1}{2}$, the base (b), and the height (h) is found:

$$A = \frac{1}{2} \times b \times h$$

A **sphere** is a set of points all of which are equidistant from some central point. It is like a circle, but in three dimensions. The volume of a sphere of radius r is given by:

$$V = \frac{4}{3}\pi r^3$$

The surface area is given by $A = 4\pi r^2$.

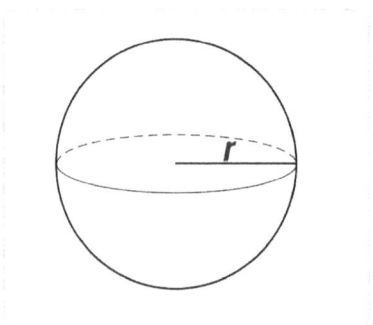

Geometry
Calculating Geometric Quantities

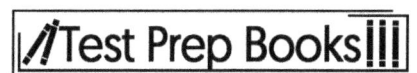

The volume of a **cylinder** is then found by adding a third dimension onto the circle. Volume of a cylinder is calculated by multiplying the area of the base (which is a circle) by the height of the cylinder. Doing so results in the equation $V = \pi r^2 h$.

The volume of a **cone** is $\frac{1}{3}$ of the volume of a cylinder. Therefore, the formula for the volume of a cone is:

$$\frac{1}{3}\pi r^2 h$$

Examples

Example 1: Find the surface area of a rectangle with a length of 8 cm and a width of 4 cm.

The area of a rectangle with a length of 8 cm and a width of 4 cm is calculated: $A = (8 \text{ cm}) \times (4 \text{ cm}) \rightarrow A = 32 \text{ cm}^2$.

Example 2: Find the area of a triangle with a base of 11 cm and a height of 6 cm.

Note that the height of a triangle is measured from the base to the vertex opposite of it forming a right angle with the base. The area of a triangle with a base of 11 cm and a height of 6 cm is calculated:

$$A = \frac{1}{2} \times (11 \text{ cm}) \times (6 \text{ cm})$$

$$A = 33 \text{ cm}^2$$

Example 3: Find the surface area of the triangular prism shown below, which is represented by a net consisting of two triangles and three rectangles.

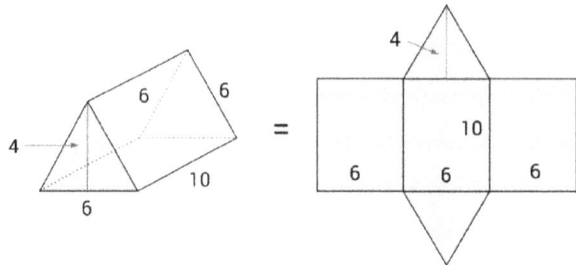

The surface area of the prism can be determined by adding the areas of each of its faces and bases. The surface area (SA) = area of triangle + area of triangle + area of rectangle + area of rectangle + area of rectangle.

$$SA = \left(\frac{1}{2} \times b \times h\right) + \left(\frac{1}{2} \times b \times h\right) + (l \times w) + (l \times w) + (l \times w)$$

$$SA = \left(\frac{1}{2} \times 6 \times 4\right) + \left(\frac{1}{2} \times 6 \times 4\right) + (6 \times 10) + (6 \times 10) + (6 \times 10)$$

$$SA = (12) + (12) + (60) + (60) + (60)$$

$SA = 204$ square units

Example 4: What is the volume of a cylinder with a radius of 5 feet and a height of 10 feet?

If the radius is 5 feet and the height of the cylinder is 10 feet, the cylinder's volume is calculated by using the following equation: $\pi 5^2 \times 10$. Substituting 3.14 for π, the volume is 785 ft³.

Practice Questions

1. What is the volume of a box with rectangular sides 5 feet long, 6 feet wide, and 3 feet high?
    a. 60 cubic feet
    b. 75 cubic feet
    c. 90 cubic feet
    d. 14 cubic feet

2. A truck is carrying three cylindrical barrels. Their bases have a diameter of 2 feet, and they have a height of 3 feet. What is the total volume of the three barrels in cubic feet?
    a. 3π
    b. 9π
    c. 12π
    d. 15π

Geometry
Calculating Geometric Quantities

3. If the volume of a sphere is 288π cubic meters, what are the radius and surface area of the same sphere?
   a. Radius is 6 meters and surface area is 144π square meters
   b. Radius is 36 meters and surface area is 144π square meters
   c. Radius is 6 meters and surface area is 12π square meters
   d. Radius is 36 meters and surface area is 12π square meters

4. What is the volume of a pyramid with a square base, whose side is 6 inches, and whose height is 9 inches?
   a. 324 in³
   b. 72 in³
   c. 108 in³
   d. 18 in³

5. What is the volume of a rectangular prism with the height of 3 centimeters, a width of 5 centimeters, and a depth of 11 centimeters?
   a. 19 cm³
   b. 165 cm³
   c. 225 cm³
   d. 150 cm³

6. What is the volume of a cube with the side equal to 3 inches?
   a. 6 in³
   b. 27 in³
   c. 9 in³
   d. 3 in³

Answer Explanations

Identifying Lines and Angles

1. B: Because the 65-degree angle and angle b sum to 180 degrees, the measurement of angle b is 115 degrees. From the Parallel Postulate, angle b is equal to angle f. Therefore, angle f measures 115 degrees.

2. A: Parallel lines have the same slope. The slope of C can be seen to be $\frac{1}{3}$ by dividing both sides by 3. The others are in standard form $Ax + By = C$, for which the slope is given by $\frac{-A}{B}$. The slope of A is 3, the slope of B is 4. The slope of D is 1.

3. D: The two lines are neither parallel nor perpendicular. Parallel lines will never intersect or meet. Therefore, the lines are not parallel. Perpendicular lines intersect to form a right angle (90°). Although the lines intersect, they do not form a right angle, which is usually indicated with a box at the intersection point. Therefore, the lines are not perpendicular.

Classifying Angles

1. B: Each hour on the clock represents 30 degrees. For example, 3:00 represents a right angle. Therefore, 5:00 represents 150 degrees.

181

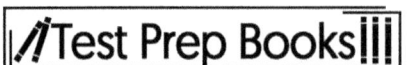

Geometry
Calculating Geometric Quantities

2. D: Angle *B* is an acute angle because it is smaller than a right angle, which is 90°. Therefore, we can immediately eliminate Choices *A* and *B*. To determine the measure of the angle, look at where the ray that is not along the bottom crosses the arc of the protractor. It falls between the 40 and 50; specifically, it is at 47°. If the ray along the bottom was going towards the left and the other ray stayed where it is now, the angle would be obtuse, and the number of degrees would be read as 133°.

3. C: The measure of two complementary angles sums up to 90 degrees. Subtracting one angle from 90 gives the complimentary angle:

$$90 - 54 = 36$$

Therefore, the complementary angle is 36 degrees.

Classifying Two-Dimensional Figures

1. B: A rectangle is a specific type of parallelogram. It has 4 right angles. A square is a rhombus that has 4 right angles. Therefore, a square is always a rectangle because it has two sets of parallel lines and 4 right angles.

2. A: A parallelogram has two sets of parallel sides. Choice *A* is a trapezoid and only has one set of parallel sides. The rest of the answer choices have two sets.

3. B: A polygon is a closed two-dimensional figure consisting of three or more sides. A decagon is a polygon with 10 sides. A triangle is a polygon with three sides. A rhombus is a polygon with 4 sides. A cone is a three-dimensional figure and is classified as a solid.

Classifying Three-Dimensional Figures

1. B: Choice *A* is a cylinder, Choice *B* is a cone, Choice *C* is a cube, and Choice *D* is a pyramid. One difference between a cone and a pyramid is that a cone has a circular base, and a pyramid has a base that is not a circle. Choice *D* is the only answer that meets the definition of a pyramid.

2. C: A rectangular prism is a three dimensional shape that has six faces, twelve edges, and eight vertices. The top and base are rectangles, and the pairs of opposite faces are congruent. Choice *C* is the only answer that lists the correct number of sides. An example can be seen here:

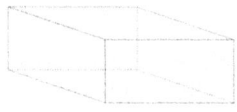

3. C: A cone has a circular base. The other options have bases that are not circular. For instance, a cube has a base that is a square, a rectangular prism has a base that is a rectangle, and a pyramid can have a square base. Only Choice *C* is correct.

The Pythagorean Theorem

1. B: This triangle can be labeled as a right triangle because it has a right-angle measure in the corner. The Pythagorean Theorem can be used here to find the missing side lengths. The Pythagorean Theorem states that $a^2 + b^2 = c^2$, where a and b are side lengths and c is the hypotenuse. The hypotenuse, c, is equal to 35, and 1 side, a, is equal to 21. Plugging these values into the equation forms:

$$21^2 + b^2 = 35^2$$

Geometry
Calculating Geometric Quantities

Squaring both given numbers and subtracting them yields the equation:

$$b^2 = 784$$

Taking the square root of 784 gives a value of 28 for b. In the equation, b is the same as the missing side length x.

2. B: This problem can be solved using the Pythagorean Theorem. The triangle has a hypotenuse of 15 and one leg of 12. These values can be substituted into the Pythagorean formula to yield:

$$12^2 + b^2 = 15^2$$

$$144 + b^2 = 225$$

$$81 = b^2$$

$$b = 9$$

In this problem, b is represented by x so $x = 9$ is the correct answer.

3. B: This answer is correct because $3^2 + 4^2$ is $9 + 16$, which is 25. Taking the square root of 25 is 5. Choice A is not the correct answer because that is $3 + 4$. Choice C is not the correct answer because that is stopping at $3^2 + 4^2$ is $9 + 16$, which is 25. Choice D is not the correct answer because that is 3×4.

Properties of Circles

1. C: To find the angle in radians, multiply by π and divide by 180. When you simplify $\frac{48° \times \pi}{180}$, you get $\frac{4\pi}{15}$. Choice A is not the correct answer because $\frac{\pi}{4}$ is 45°. Choice B is not the correct answer because $\frac{\pi}{15}$ is 12°. Choice D is not the correct answer because $\frac{3\pi}{4} = 135°$.

2. D: The method to equate the two chord lengths is $3 + x + 2 = x + 3x + 2$, add like terms, $5 + x = 4x + 2$, solve for x ($x = 1$), and substitute 1 back into the equation. Choice A is not the correct answer because 1 is the solution for x, not the length of the chord. Choice B is not the correct answer because 2 is one of the terms of the chord length when adding like terms. Choice C is not the correct answer because 3 is only the coefficient of one of the terms when solving.

3. C: The formula to find arc length is $s = \theta r$ where s is the arc length, θ is the radian measure of the central angle, and r is the radius of the circle. Substituting the given information produces 3π cm $= \theta 12$ cm. Solving for θ yields $\theta = \frac{\pi}{4}$. To convert from radian to degrees, multiply the radian measure by

$$\frac{180}{\pi} : \frac{\pi}{4} \times \frac{180}{\pi} = 45°$$

Finding Perimeter and Area

1. C: The formula for the perimeter of a rectangle is $P = 2l + 2w$, where P is the perimeter, l is the length, and w is the width. The first step is to substitute all of the data into the formula:

$$36 = 2(12) + 2w$$

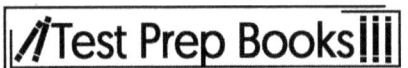

Simplify by multiplying 2×12:

$$36 = 24 + 2w$$

Simplifying this further by subtracting 24 on each side, which gives:

$$36 - 24 = 24 - 24 + 2w$$

$$12 = 2w$$

Divide by 2:

$$6 = w$$

The width is 6 cm. Remember to test this answer by substituting this value into the original formula:

$$36 = 2(12) + 2(6)$$

2. D: To calculate the circumference of a circle, use the formula $2\pi r$, where r equals the radius or half of the diameter of the circle and $\pi = 3.14 \ldots$. Substitute the given information, $2\pi 5 = 31.4 \ldots$, answer D.

3. D: Area $=$ length $\times$ width. The answer must be in square inches, so all values must be converted to inches. $\frac{1}{2}$ ft is equal to 6 inches. Therefore, the area of the rectangle is equal to $6 \times \frac{11}{2} = \frac{66}{2} = 33$ square inches.

4. C: Perimeter is found by calculating the sum of all sides of the polygon.

$9 + 9 + 9 + 8 + 8 + s = 56$, where s is the missing side length. Therefore, 43 plus the missing side length is equal to 56. The missing side length is 13 cm.

5. B: An equilateral triangle has three sides of equal length, so if the total perimeter is 18 feet, each side must be 6 feet long. A square with sides of 6 feet will have an area of $6^2 = 36$ square feet.

Decomposing Composite Figures

1. B: The figure is composed of three sides of a square and a semicircle. The sides of the square are simply added: $8 + 8 + 8 = 24$ inches. The circumference of a circle is found by the equation $C = 2\pi r$. The radius is 4 in, so the circumference of the circle is 25.13 in. Only half of the circle makes up the outer border of the figure (part of the perimeter) so half of 25.13 in is 12.565 in. Therefore, the total perimeter is:

$$24 \text{ in} + 12.565 \text{ in} = 36.565 \text{ in}$$

The other answer choices use the incorrect formula or fail to include all of the necessary sides.

2. B: This can be determined by finding the length and width of the shaded region. The length can be found using the length of the top rectangle, which is 18 inches, then subtracting the extra length of 4 inches and 1 inch. This means the length of the shaded region is 13 inches. Next, the width can be determined using the 6 inch measurement and subtracting the 2 inch measurement. This means that the width is 4 inches. Thus, the area is:

$$13 \times 4 = 52 \text{ sq. in.}$$

Geometry
Calculating Geometric Quantities

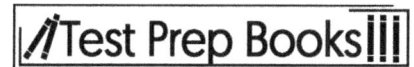

3. B: If this was a rectangle, the length would be 32 meters, and the width would be 30 meters. However, there is a smaller rectangle cut out of this larger rectangle which has a length of 20 meters and a width that needs to be found. The width is equal to 17 m plus the missing value. Therefore, the missing length is $30 - 17 = 13$ m, making Choice *B* the correct answer.

Finding Volume and Surface Area

1. C: The formula for the volume of a box with rectangular sides is the length times width times height, so $5 \times 6 \times 3 = 90$ cubic feet.

2. B: The formula for the volume of a cylinder is $\pi r^2 h$, where r is the radius and h is the height. The diameter is twice the radius, so these barrels have a radius of 1 foot. That means each barrel has a volume of $\pi \times 1^2 \times 3 = 3\pi$ cubic feet. Since there are three of them, the total is $3 \times 3\pi = 9\pi$ cubic feet.

3. A: Because the volume of the given sphere is 288π cubic meters, this means $\frac{4}{3}\pi r^3 = 288\pi$. This equation is solved for r to obtain a radius of 6 meters. The formula for the surface area of a sphere is $4\pi r^2$, so if $r = 6$ in this formula, the surface area is 144π square meters.

4. C: The volume of a pyramid is (length × width × height), divided by 3, and ($6 \times 6 \times 9$), divided by 3 is 108 in³. Choice *A* is incorrect because 324 in³ is (length × width × height) without dividing by 3. Choice *B* is incorrect because 6 is used for height instead of 9 (($6 \times 6 \times 6$) divided by 3) to get 72 in³. Choice *D* is incorrect because 18 in³ is (6×9), divided by 3 and leaving out a 6.

5. B: The volume of a rectangular prism is the length × width × height, and 3 cm × 5 cm × 11 cm is 165 cm³. Choice *A* is not the correct answer because that is 3 cm + 5 cm + 11 cm. Choice *C* is not the correct answer because that is 15^2. Choice *D* is not the correct answer because that is 3 cm × 5 cm × 10 cm.

6. B: The volume of a cube is the length of the side cubed, and 3 inches cubed is 27 in³. Choice *A* is not the correct answer because that is 2×3 inches. Choice *C* is not the correct answer because that is 3×3 inches, and Choice *D* is not the correct answer because there was no operation performed.

Measurement and Data

Interpreting Information from Tables, Graphs, and Charts

Summarizing and Representing Data on Tables

The field of statistics describes relationships between quantities that are related, but not necessarily in a deterministic manner. For example, a graduating student's salary will often be higher when the student graduates with a higher GPA, but this is not always the case. Likewise, people who smoke tobacco are more likely to develop lung cancer, but, in fact, it is possible for non-smokers to develop the disease as well. **Statistics** describes these kinds of situations, where the likelihood of some outcome depends on the starting data.

Descriptive statistics involves analyzing a collection of data to describe its broad properties such average (or mean), what percent of the data falls within a given range, and other such properties. An example of this would be taking all of the test scores from a given class and calculating the average test score. **Inferential statistics** attempts to use data about a subset of some population to make inferences about the rest of the population. An example of this would be taking a collection of students who received tutoring and comparing their results to a collection of students who did not receive tutoring, then using that comparison to try to predict whether the tutoring program in question is beneficial.

Data can be represented in many ways. It is important to be able to organize the data into categories that could be represented using one of these methods. Equally important is the ability to read these types of diagrams and interpret their meaning.

Tables

One of the most common ways to express data is in a table. The primary reason for plugging data into a table is to make interpretation more convenient. It's much easier to look at the table than to analyze results in a narrative paragraph. When analyzing a table, pay close attention to the title, variables, and data.

Measurement and Data
Interpreting Information from Tables, Graphs, and Charts

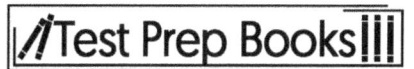

Let's analyze a theoretical antibiotic study. The study has 6 groups, named A through F, and each group receives a different dose of medicine. The results of the study are listed in the table below.

Results of Antibiotic Studies		
Group	Dosage of Antibiotics in milligrams (mg)	Efficacy (% of participants cured)
A	0 mg	20%
B	20 mg	40%
C	40 mg	75%
D	60 mg	95%
E	80 mg	100%
F	100 mg	100%

Tables generally list the title immediately above the data. The title should succinctly explain what is listed below. Here, "Results of Antibiotic Studies" informs the audience that the data pertains to the results of scientific study on antibiotics.

Identifying the variables at play is one of the most important parts of interpreting data. Remember, the independent variable is intentionally altered, and its change is independent of the other variables. Here, the dosage of antibiotics administered to the different groups is the independent variable. The study is intentionally manipulating the strength of the medicine to study the related results. Efficacy is the dependent variable since its results **depend** on a different variable, the dose of antibiotics. Generally, the independent variable will be listed before the dependent variable in tables.

Also play close attention to the variables' labels. Here, the dose is expressed in milligrams (mg) and efficacy in percentages (%). Keep an eye out for questions referencing data in a different unit measurement or questions asking for a raw number when only the percentage is listed.

Now that the nature of the study and variables at play have been identified, the data itself needs be interpreted. Group A did not receive any of the medicine. As discussed earlier, Group A is the control, as it reflects the amount of people cured in the same timeframe without medicine. It's important to see that efficacy positively correlates with the dosage of medicine. A question using this study might ask for the lowest dose of antibiotics to achieve 100% efficacy. Although Group E and Group F both achieve 100% efficacy, it's important to note that Group E reaches 100% with a lower dose.

Practice Questions

The table below shows the number of students in Ms. Jackson' class who play each sport.

Sports Played By Students in Ms. Jackson's Class

Sport	Frequency
Soccer	ⅠⅠⅠⅠ ⅠⅠ
Swimming	Ⅰ
Track	ⅠⅠⅠ
Baseball	ⅠⅠⅠⅠ Ⅰ
Basketball	ⅠⅠⅠⅠ Ⅰ
Tennis	ⅠⅠ

1. Which of the following dot plots correctly represents the data in the table?

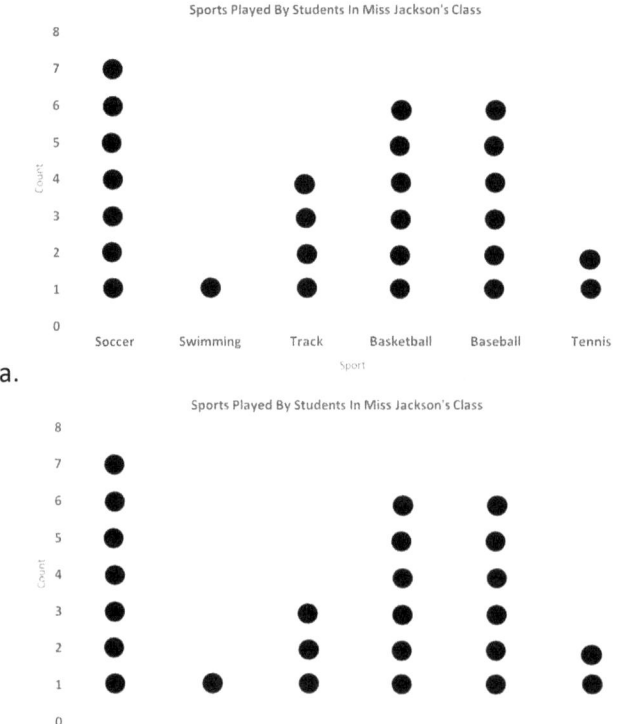

a.

b.

Measurement and Data
Interpreting Information from Tables, Graphs, and Charts

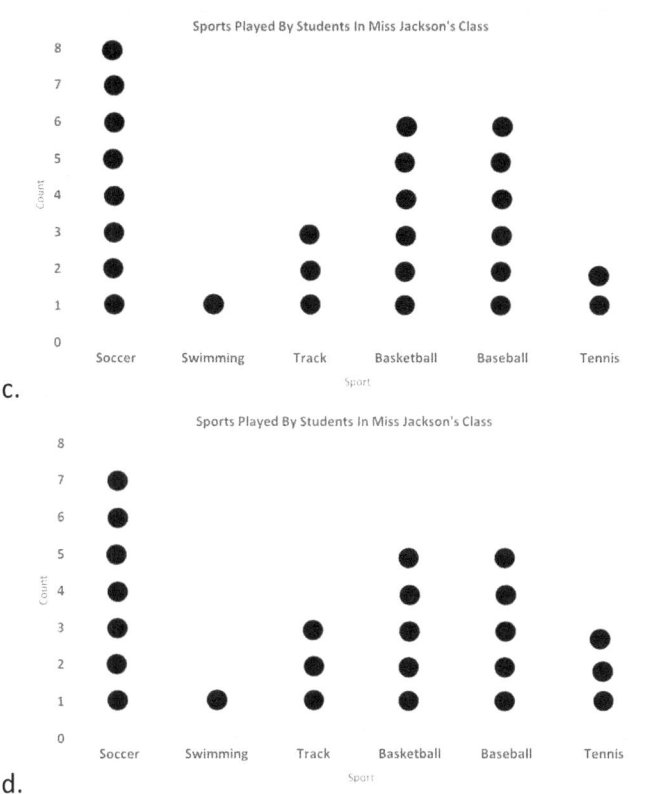

c.

d.

2. The following dot plot represents the number of children in each family from a survey. How many families were surveyed?

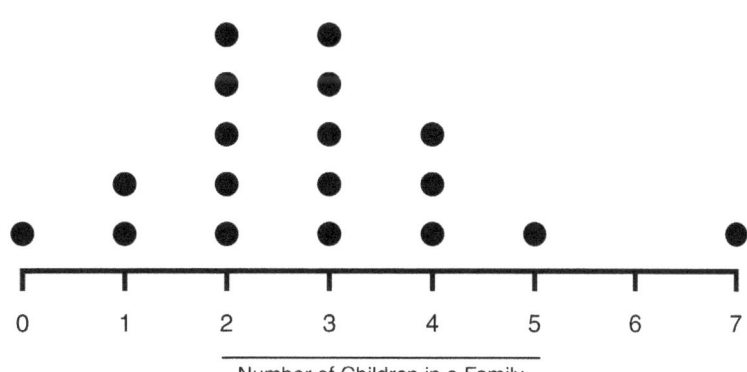

a. 18
b. 7
c. 41
d. 10

Summarizing and Representing Data on Graphs

Graphs provide a visual representation of data. The variables are placed on the two axes. The bottom of the graph is referred to as the horizontal axis or x-axis. The left-hand side of the graph is known as the vertical axis or y-axis. Typically, the independent variable is placed on the x-axis, and the dependent variable is located on the y-axis. Sometimes the x-axis is a timeline, and the dependent variables for different trials or groups have been measured throughout points in time; time is still an independent variable but is not always immediately thought of as the independent variable being studied.

Example

The most common types of graphs are the bar graph and the line graph.

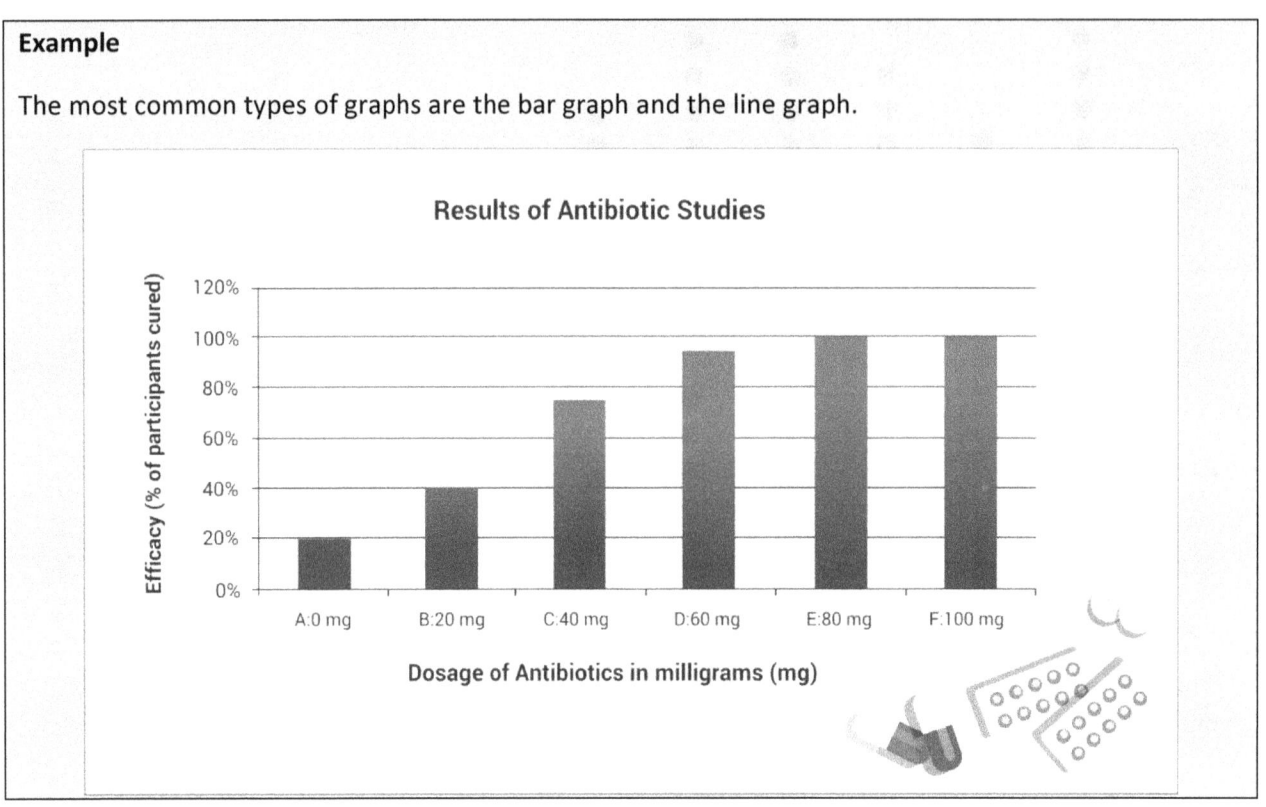

The **bar graph** above expresses the data from the table entitled "Results of Antibiotic Studies." To interpret the data for each group in the study, look at the top of their bars and read the corresponding efficacy on the y-axis.

Measurement and Data
Interpreting Information from Tables, Graphs, and Charts

Example

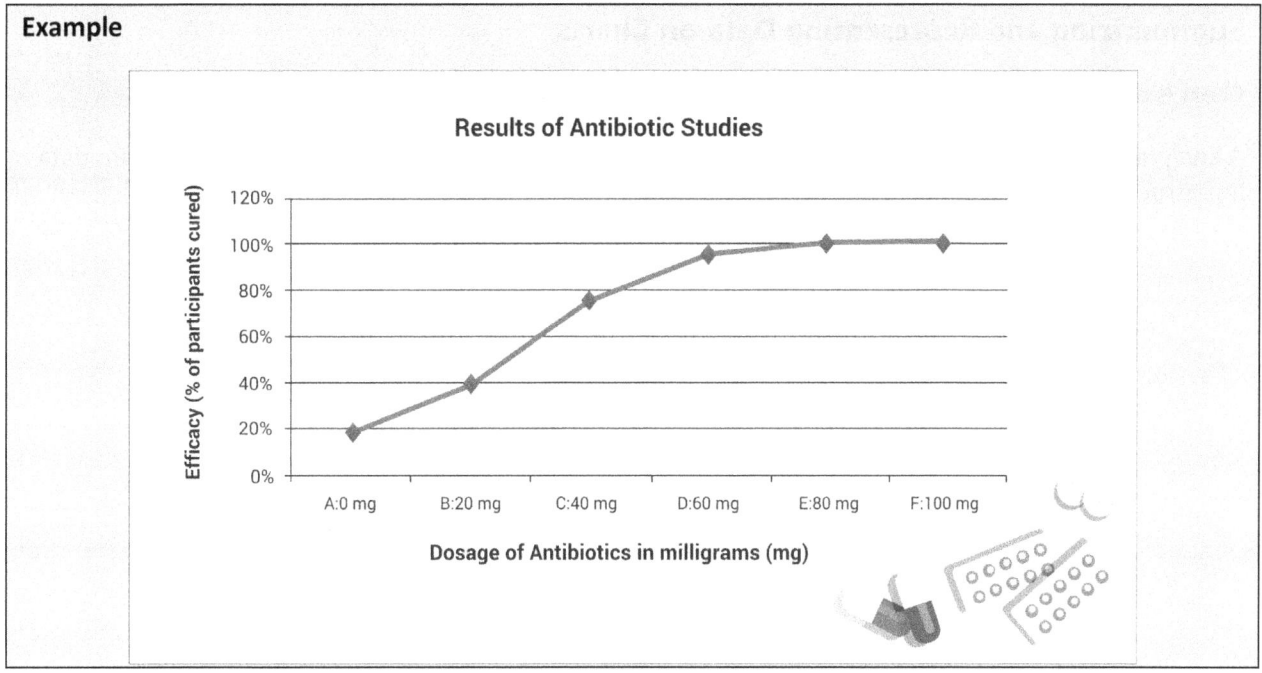

Here, the same data is expressed on a **line graph**. The points on the line correspond with each data entry. Reading the data on the line graph works like the bar graph. The data trend is measured by the slope of the line.

Practice Questions

1. Given the value of a given stock at monthly intervals, which graph should be used to best represent the trend of the stock?
   a. Box plot
   b. Line plot
   c. Line graph
   d. Circle graph

2. Monthly sales data for a company is given over a period of a year. Which of the following graphs would best represent the data?
   a. Circle graph
   b. Box plot
   c. Dot plot
   d. Line graph

Summarizing and Representing Data on Charts

Chart is a broad term that refers to a variety of ways to represent data.

A **line plot** is a diagram that shows quantity of data along a number line. It is a quick way to record data in a structure similar to a bar graph without needing to do the required shading of a bar graph.

A **tally chart** is a diagram in which tally marks are utilized to represent data. Tally marks are a means of showing a quantity of objects within a specific classification.

Number of days with rain	Number of weeks
0	II
1	HHT
2	HHT
3	HHT
4	HHT HHT HHT IIII
5	HHT I
6	HHT I
7	IIII

Data is often recorded using fractions, such as half a mile, and understanding fractions is critical because of their popular use in real-world applications. Also, it is extremely important to label values with their units when using data. For example, regarding length, the number 2 is meaningless unless it is attached to a unit. Writing 2 cm shows that the number refers to the length of an object.

A **picture graph** is a diagram that shows pictorial representation of data being discussed. The symbols used can represent a certain number of objects. Notice how each fruit symbol in the following graph represents a count of two fruits. One drawback of picture graphs is that they can be less accurate if each

Measurement and Data
Interpreting Information from Tables, Graphs, and Charts

symbol represents a large number. For example, if each banana symbol represented ten bananas, and students consumed 22 bananas, it may be challenging to draw and interpret two and one-fifth bananas as a frequency count of 22.

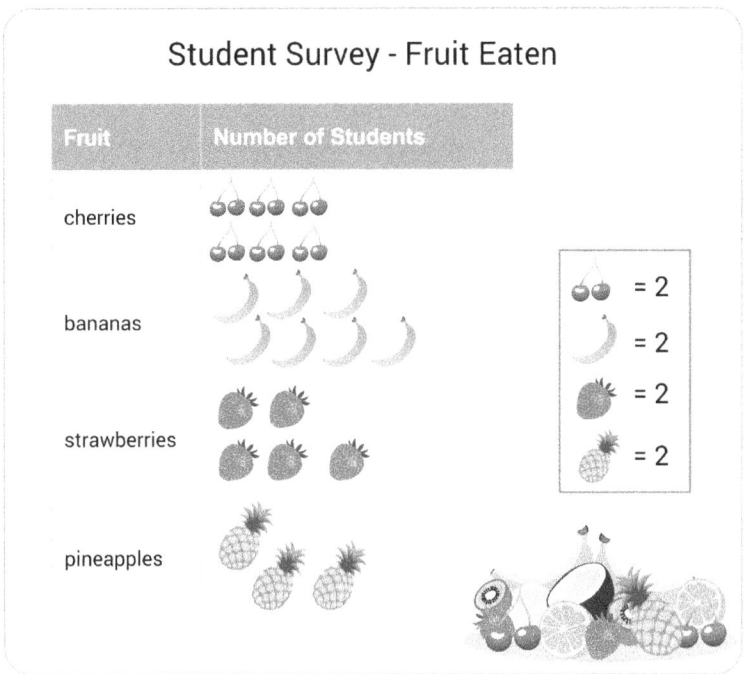

A circle graph, also called a pie chart, shows categorical data with each category representing a percentage of the whole data set. To make a circle graph, the percent of the data set for each category must be determined. To do so, the frequency of the category is divided by the total number of data points and converted to a percent.

As an example, if 80 people were asked what their favorite sport is and 20 responded basketball, basketball makes up 25% of the data ($\frac{20}{80} = 0.25 = 25\%$). Each category in a data set is represented by a **slice** of the circle proportionate to its percentage of the whole.

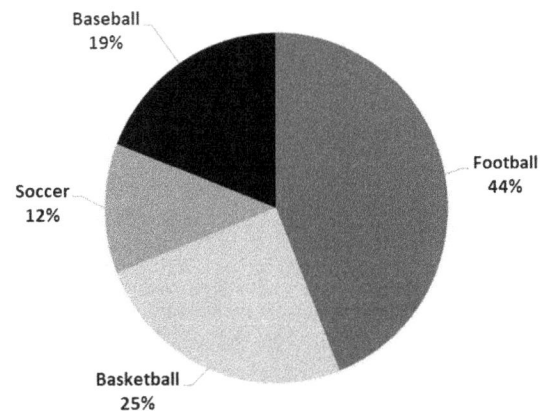

A scatter plot displays the relationship between two variables. Values for the independent variable, typically denoted by x, are paired with values for the dependent variable, typically denoted by y. Each set of corresponding values are written as an ordered pair (x, y). To construct the graph, a coordinate grid is labeled with the x-axis representing the independent variable and the y-axis representing the dependent variable. Each ordered pair is graphed.

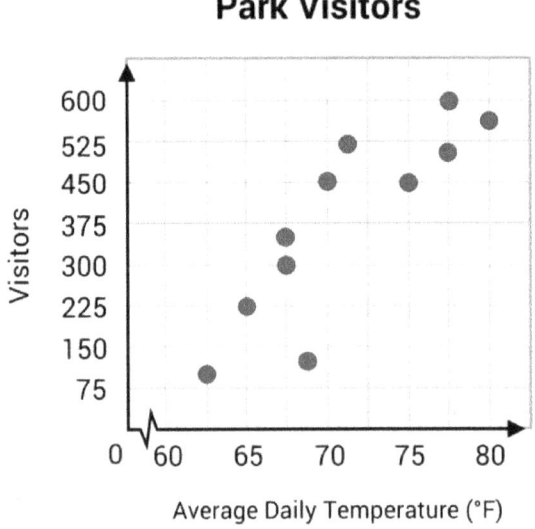

Like a scatter plot, a line graph compares two variables that change continuously, typically over time. Paired data values (ordered pair) are plotted on a coordinate grid with the x- and y-axis representing the two variables. A line is drawn from each point to the next, going from left to right. A double line graph simply displays two sets of data that contain values for the same two variables.

The double line graph below displays the profit for given years (two variables) for Company A and Company B (two data sets).

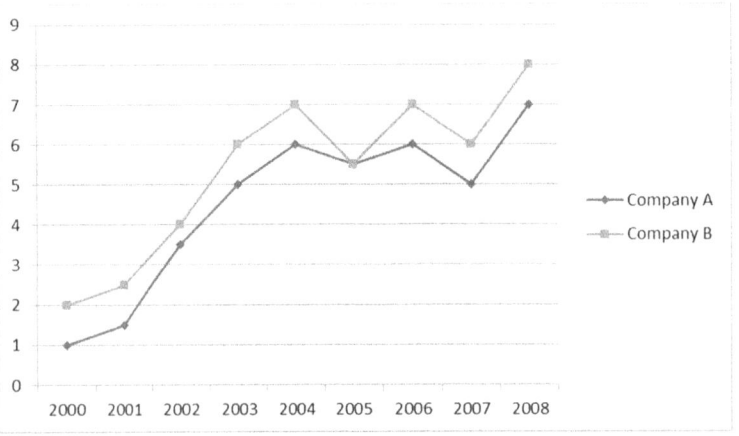

Measurement and Data
Interpreting Information from Tables, Graphs, and Charts

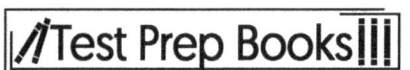

Choosing the appropriate graph to display a data set depends on what type of data is included in the set and what information must be shown.

Scatter plots and line graphs can be used to display data consisting of two variables. Examples include height and weight, or distance and time. A correlation between the variables is determined by examining the points on the graph. Line graphs are used if each value for one variable pairs with a distinct value for the other variable. Line graphs show relationships between variables.

Practice Questions

1. This chart indicates how many sales of CDs, vinyl records, and MP3 downloads occurred over the last year. Approximately what percentage of the total sales was from CDs?

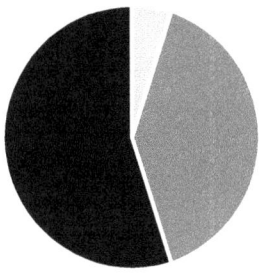

Total Sales of Vinyl Records, CDs, and MP3 Downloads (in millions)

Vinyl ▪ CD ▪ MP3

   a. 55%
   b. 25%
   c. 40%
   d. 5%

2. The following bar graph represents the number of summer camp sign-ups per type. Approximately what percentage of the total sign-ups were cheerleading?

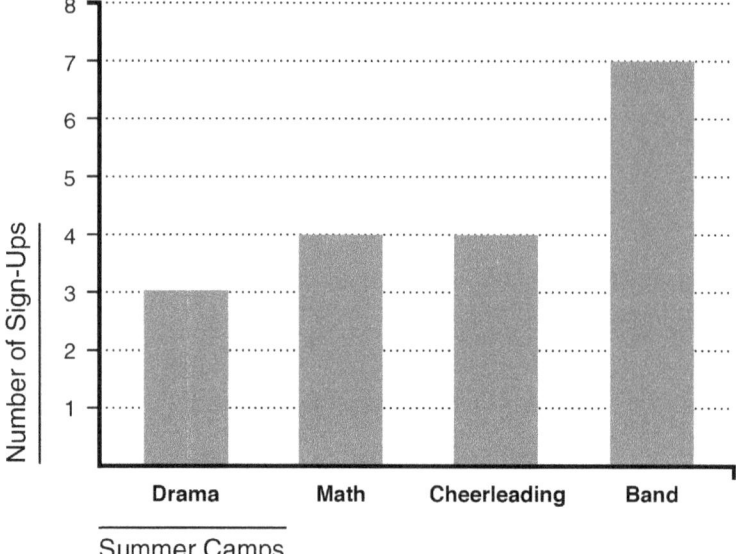

a. 4%
b. 40%
c. 22.2%
d. 16.7%

Solving Problems Using Categorical Data

A **line plot** is a display of data that is plotted along a number line that shows **frequency**, or how often the same data exists. The frequency is drawn using either an x or a dot.

Measurement and Data
Interpreting Information from Tables, Graphs, and Charts

Example

The following is a line plot drawn that represents the data containing the numbers 0, 1, 2, 3, 4, 5. This data could represent the number of siblings students in a class have. Note that because there are 6 x's at the 2 on the plot, there must be 6 occurrences of 2 in the data. That means six students have 2 siblings.

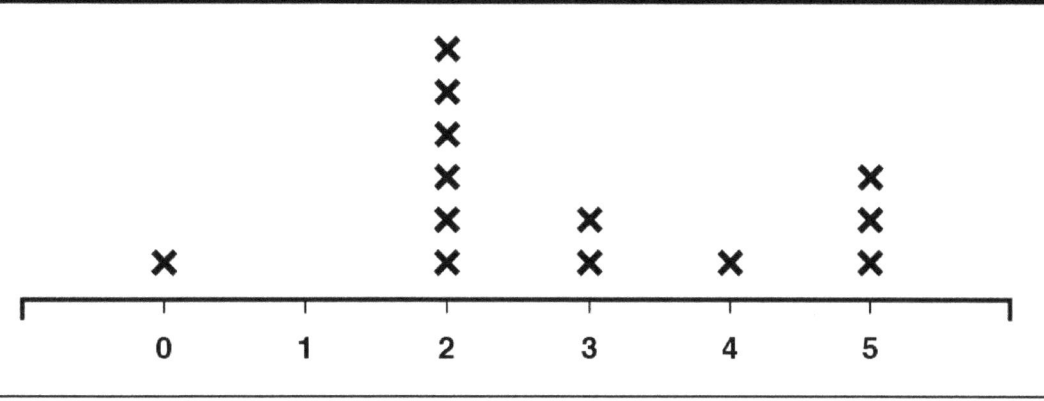

A line plot can be used to display a data set of measurements in fractions of units as well. The reason why this type of plot is necessary would be to organize data of different measurements in a real-world situation. Not every measurement will be a whole number.

Example

Let's say you collected 15 leaves from the backyard and measured them to the nearest quarter inch. Your measurements were 3 quarter-inch leaves, 6 half-inch leaves, 5 three quarter-inch leaves, and 1 one-inch leaves. The line plot that represents this data is shown here:

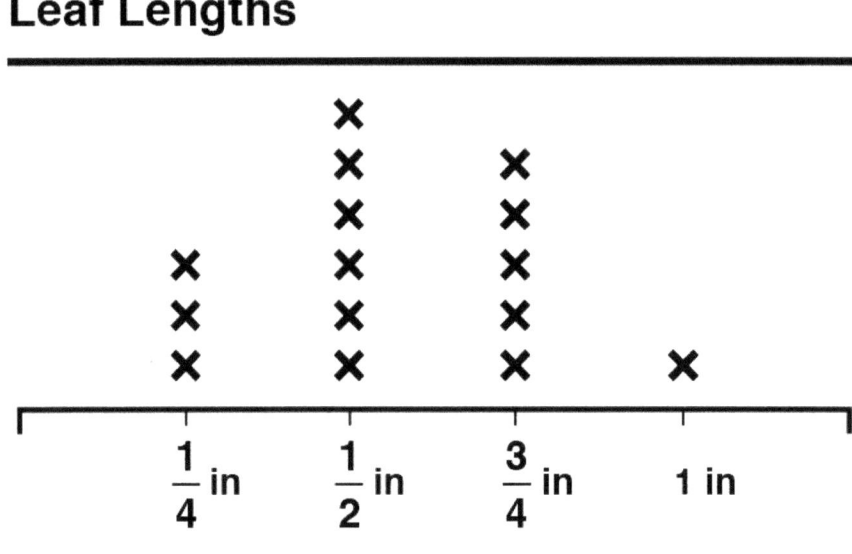

Note that the number line shows the four different measurement possibilities and the x's represent the frequency, or number of times, that each measurement appeared. This line plot can be used to answer questions about the data set. For instance, the tallest height at the half-inch mark shows that this was the most frequent found measurement. Also, the chart could be used to find the difference in lengths between the longest and shortest leaf found, which is called the **range** of the measurements. The longest leaf was 1 inch and the shortest leaf was a quarter-inch, so the difference is found through subtraction, with a result of $\frac{3}{4}$ inch.

Measurement and Data
Interpreting Information from Tables, Graphs, and Charts

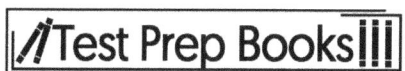

Practice Questions

1. The following graph compares the various test scores of the top three students in each of these teacher's classes. Based on the graph, which teacher's students had the lowest range of test scores?

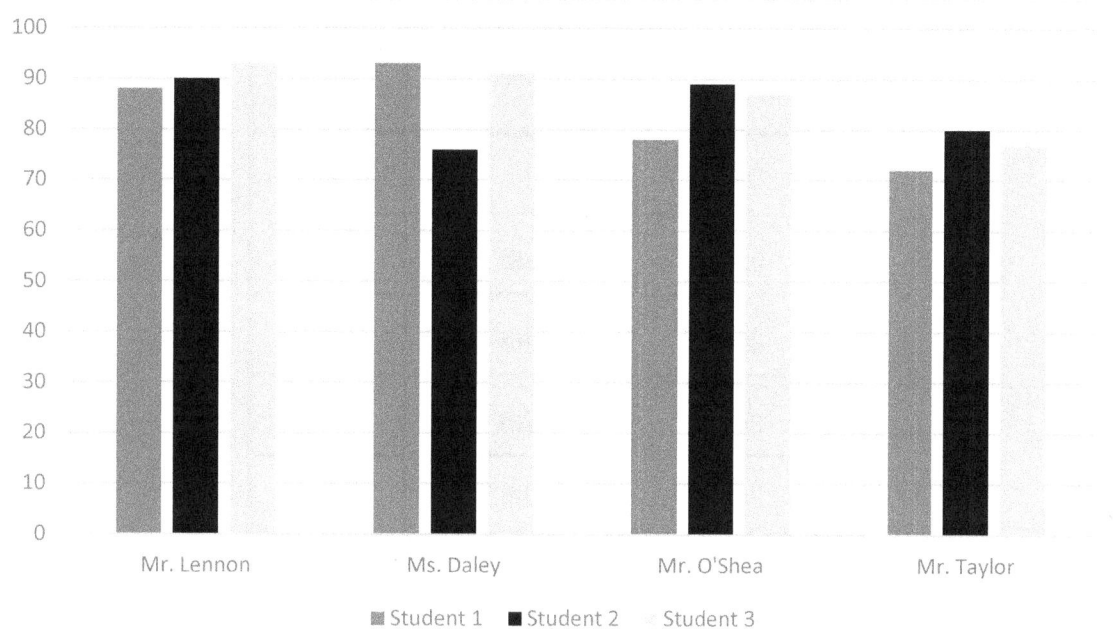

a. Mr. Lennon
b. Mr. O'Shea
c. Mr. Taylor
d. Ms. Daley

2. The following table shows the temperature readings in Ohio during the month of January. How many more times was the temperature between 28-30 degrees than between 20-24 degrees?

Maximum Temperatures in degrees	Tally marks	Frequency
20 - 22	I	1
22 - 24	JHT II	7
24 - 26	JHT	5
26 - 28	JHT IIII	9
28 - 30	JHT JHT	10

a. 3 times
b. 9 times
c. 2 times
d. 10 times

Measurement and Data
Interpreting Information from Tables, Graphs, and Charts

3. How many more votes do blueberries have than bananas on the graph of a Favorite Fruit survey?

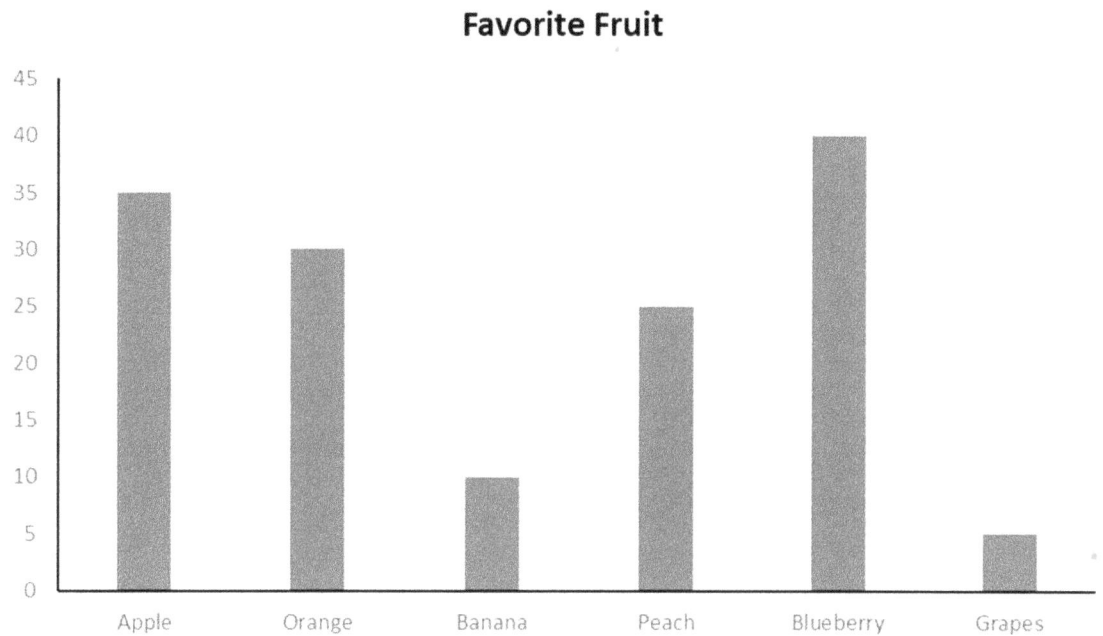

a. 10
b. 15
c. 20
d. 30

4. An accounting firm charted its income on the following pie graph. If the total income for the year was $500,000, how much of the income was received from Audit and Taxation Services?

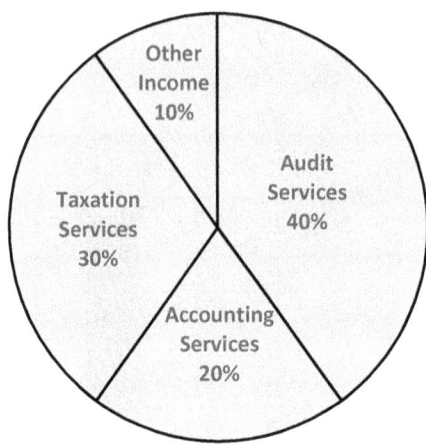

Income

a. $200,000
b. $350,000
c. $150,000
d. $300,000

Comparing Data from Two Data Sets

Be careful of questions with competing studies. These questions will ask the student to interpret which of two studies shows the greater amount or the higher rate of change between two results.

Example
A research facility runs studies on two different antibiotics: Drug A and Drug B. The Drug A study includes 1,000 participants and cures 600 people. The Drug B study includes 200 participants and cures 150 people. Which drug is more successful?
The first step is to determine the percentage of each drug's rate of success. Drug A was successful in curing 60% of participants, while Drug B achieved a 75% success rate. Thus, Drug B is more successful based on these studies, even though it cured fewer people.

Sample size and experiment consistency should also be considered when answering questions based on competing studies. Is one study significantly larger than the other? In the antibiotics example, the Drug A study is five times larger than Drug B. Thus, Drug B's higher efficacy (desired result) could be a result of the smaller sample size, rather than the quality of drug.

Consistency between studies is directly related to sample size.

Measurement and Data
Interpreting Information from Tables, Graphs, and Charts

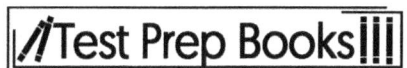

> **Example**
>
> Let's say the research facility elects to conduct more studies on Drug B. In the next study, there are 400 participants, and 200 are cured. The success rate of the second study is 50%.

The results are clearly inconsistent with the first study, which means more testing is needed to determine the drug's efficacy. A hallmark of mathematical or scientific research is repeatability. Studies should be consistent and repeatable, with an appropriately large sample size, before drawing extensive conclusions.

Examples

> Example 1. The following table represents two sets of final exam scores from two different classes. The mean from which class is higher, Class A or Class B?
>
> | Class A | Class B |
> |---------|---------|
> | 50 | 76 |
> | 76 | 55 |
> | 77 | 22 |
> | 78 | 99 |
> | 34 | 76 |
> | 54 | 68 |
> | 44 | 76 |

The mean from each class can be found by adding up the individual scores and dividing by 7, which is the total number of scores for each class. The mean for class A is $\frac{413}{7} = 59$, and the mean for class B is $\frac{472}{7} \approx 67.4$. Therefore, the mean from Class B is higher.

Practice Questions

1. A science class of 50 students had 46% of the students score above a C on the final exam. A math class of 60 students had 35% of the students score above a C on the final exam. Which of the following is true?
    a. The science class had more students score above a C than the math class.
    b. The math class had more students score above a C than the science class.
    c. The science and math class had the same number of students score above a C.
    d. None of these conclusions are guaranteed, based on the provided data.

203

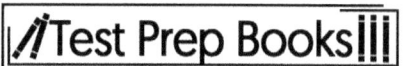

2. The following table represents two sets of race times from two different sets of runners. Which of the following is true?

Set A	Set B
24 min	23 min
25 min	24 min
27 min	25 min
27 min	26 min
28 min	27 min
29 min	28 min
27 min	28 min

a. The mode from Set A is higher.
b. The mode from Set B is higher.
c. The mode from each set is the same.
d. Neither set has a mode.

3. An elementary school has 90 students in third grade, which equals 24% of the total student population. A high school has 126 students that are freshman, which equals 36% of the total student population. Which of the following is true?
a. The elementary school and high school populations are the same size.
b. The elementary school has a larger student population than the high school.
c. The high school has a larger student population than the elementary school.
d. None of these conclusions are guaranteed, based on the provided data.

Answer Explanations

Summarizing and Representing Data on Tables

1. B: The dot plot in Choice *B* is correct because, like the table, it shows that 7 students play soccer, 1 swims, 3 run track, 6 play basketball, 6 play baseball, and 2 play tennis. Each dot represents one student, just like one hash mark in the table represents one student.

2. A: Each dot represents an individual family. The total number of dots is 18, so there were 18 families surveyed and Choice *A* is the correct answer.

Summarizing and Representing Data on Graphs

1. C: The scenario involves data consisting of two variables: month and stock value. Box plots display data consisting of values for one variable. Therefore, a box plot is not an appropriate choice. Both line plots and circle graphs are used to display frequencies within categorical data. Neither can be used for the given scenario. Line graphs display two numerical variables on a coordinate grid and show trends among the variables, so this is the correct choice.

2. D: A circle graph would not be a good choice, since there would be twelve wedges needed to be shown. Therefore, Choice *A* can be eliminated, as the circle would be too crowded. Box plots and dot plots are used for univariate data (having only one variable), so these are not great options as well, eliminating Choices *B* and *C*. Choice *D*, line graph, is the best option, since it is a great way to show data over time.

Measurement and Data
Interpreting Information from Tables, Graphs, and Charts

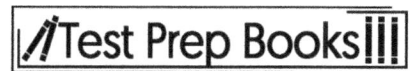

Summarizing and Representing Data on Charts

1. C: The sum total percentage of a pie chart must equal 100%. Since the CD sales take up less than half of the chart and more than a quarter (25%), it can be determined to be 40% overall. This can also be measured with a protractor. The angle of a circle is 360°. Since 25% of 360° would be 90° and 50% would be 180°, the angle percentage of CD sales falls in between; therefore, it would be Choice C.

2. C. The total number of sign-ups is found by adding up each individual category: $3 + 4 + 4 + 7 = 18$. There were 4 cheerleading sign-ups, so the corresponding percentage is $\frac{4}{18}$, which is approximately equal to 22.2%, making Choice C the correct answer.

Solving Problems Using Categorical Data

1. A: To calculate the range in a set of data, subtract the highest value with the lowest value. In this graph, the range of Mr. Lennon's students is 5, which can be seen physically in the graph as having the smallest difference compared with the other teachers between the highest value and the lowest value.

2. C: To calculate this, the following equation is used: $10 - (7 + 1) = 2$. The number of times the temperature was between 28-30 degrees was 10. Finding the total number of times the temperature was between 20-24 degrees requires totaling the categories of 20-22 degrees and 22-24 degrees, which is $7 + 1 = 8$. This total is then subtracted from the other category in order to find the difference. Choice A only subtracts the 28-30 degrees from the 22-24 degrees category. Choice B only subtracts the 28-30 degrees category from the 20-22 degrees category. Choice D is simply the number from the 28-30 degrees category.

3. D: The total number of blueberry votes on the graph is 40, and the total number of banana votes is 10. To find the difference, solve the following equation: $40 - 10 = 30$. The difference in votes is 30. All of the other selections involve misreading or miscalculating the number of votes.

4. B: Since the total income is $500,000, then a percentage of that can be found by multiplying the percent of Audit Services as a decimal, or 0.40, by the total of 500,000. This answer is found from the equation: $500000 \times 0.4 = 200000$. The total income from Audit Services is $200,000.

For the income received from Taxation Services, the following equation can be used: $500000 \times 0.3 = 150000$. The total income from Audit Services and Taxation Services is: $150,000 + 200,000 = 350,000$.

Another way of approaching the problem is to calculate the easy percentage of 10% then multiply it by 7 because the total percentage for Audit and Taxation Services was 70%. 10% of 500,000 is 50,000. Then multiplying this number by 7 yields the same income of $350,000.

Comparing Data from Two Data Sets

1. A: The science class had 46% of 50 students score above a C. This is equal to $0.46 \times 50 = 23$ students. This means that $50 - 23 = 27$ students in that class scored a C or below. The math class had 35% of 60 students score above a C. This is equal to $0.35 \times 60 = 21$ students. This means that $60 - 21 = 39$ students in that class scored a C or below. Therefore, the science class had more students score above a C than the math class, making Choice A the correct answer.

2. B: The mode in each set is the value that appears the greatest number of times. The mode in Set A is 27, and the mode in Set B is 28. Therefore, the mode in Set B is higher and Choice B is the right answer.

3. B: The elementary school has $\frac{90}{0.24} = 375$ students. The high school has $\frac{126}{0.36} = 350$ students. Therefore, the elementary school is larger than the high school, which makes Choice *B* correct.

Explaining the Relationship Between Two Variables

Identifying Independent and Dependent Quantities

Independent variables are also controlled by the scientist, but they are the same only for each group or trial in the experiment. Each group might be composed of students that all have the same color of car or each trial may be run on different soda brands. The independent variable of an experiment is what is being indirectly tested because it causes change in the dependent variables.

Dependent variables experience change caused by the independent variable and are what is being measured or observed.

As an example, college acceptance rates could be a dependent variable of an experiment that sorted a large sample of high school students by an independent variable such as test scores. In this experiment, the scientist groups the high school students by the independent variable (test scores) to see how it affects the dependent variable (their college acceptance rates).

Note that most variables can be held constant in one experiment but independent or dependent in another. For example, when testing how well a fertilizer aids plant growth, its amount of sunlight should be held constant for each group of plants, but if the experiment is being done to determine the proper amount of sunlight a plant should have, the amount of sunlight is an independent variable because it is necessarily changed for each group of plants.

Measurement and Data
Explaining the Relationship Between Two Variables

Correlation

An *X-Y* **diagram**, also known as a scatter diagram, visually displays the relationship between two variables. The independent variable is placed on the *x*-**axis**, or horizontal axis, and the dependent variable is placed on the *y*-**axis**, or vertical axis.

Example

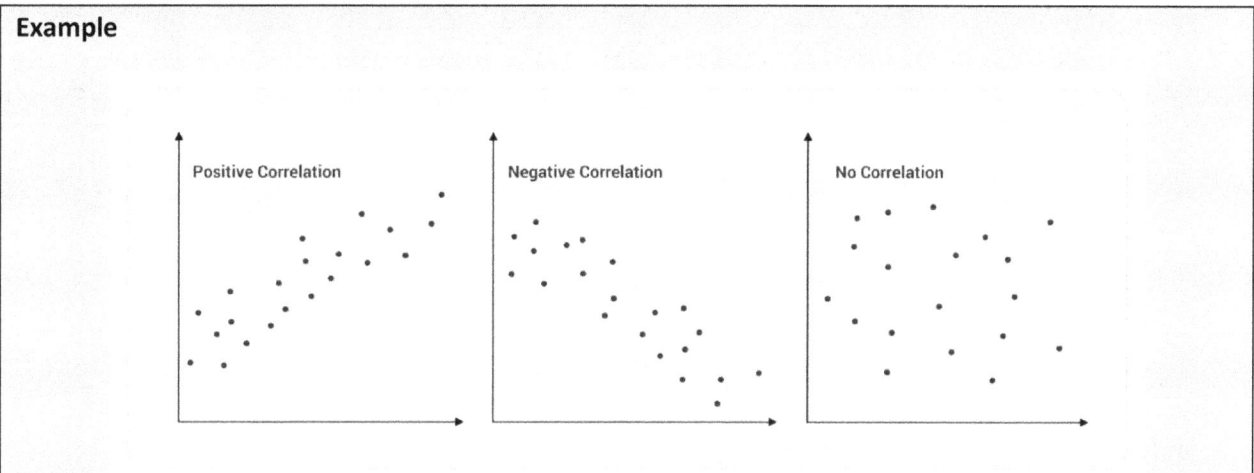

As shown in the figures above, an *X-Y* diagram may result in positive, negative, or no correlation between the two variables.

In the first scatter plot as the *Y* factor increases the *X* factor increases as well. The opposite is true as well: as the *X* factor increases the *Y* factor also increases. Thus, there is a positive correlation because one factor appears to positively affect the other factor.

It's important to note, however, that a positive correlation between two variables doesn't equate to a cause-and-effect relationship. For example, a positive correlation between labor hours and units produced may not equate to a cause and effect relationship between the two. Any instance of correlation only indicates how likely the presence of one variable is in the instance of another. The variables should be further analyzed to determine which, if any, other variables (i.e., quality of employee work) may contribute to the positive correlation.

Practice Questions

1. A line that travels from the bottom-left of a graph to the upper-right of the graph indicates what kind of relationship between a predictor and a dependent variable?
    a. Positive
    b. Negative
    c. Exponential
    d. Logarithmic

2. What is the best description of the relationship between Y and X in the following graph?

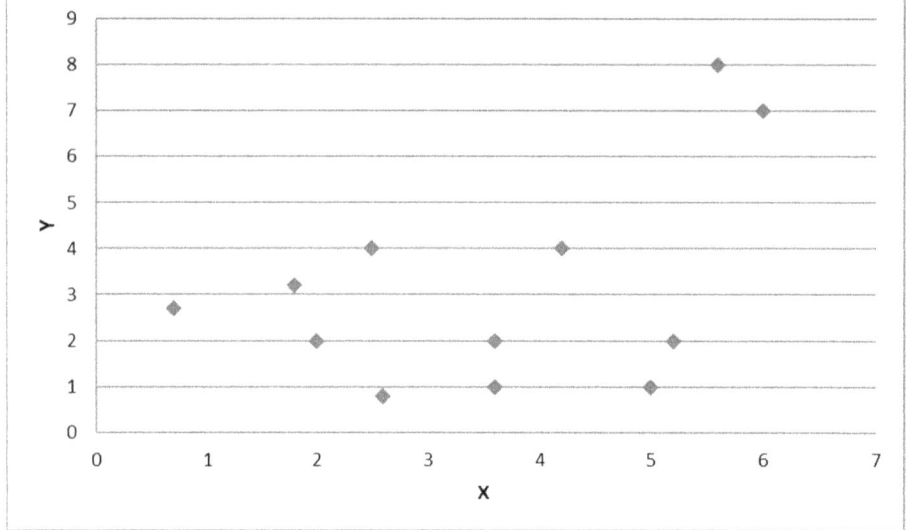

a. The data has normal distribution.
b. X and Y have a negative relationship.
c. There is no relationship.
d. X and Y have a positive relationship.

3. The following scatter plot represents two variables where the predictor variable is plotted along the horizontal axis and the dependent variable is plotted along the vertical axis. Which of the following relationships exists between the predictor and dependent variables?

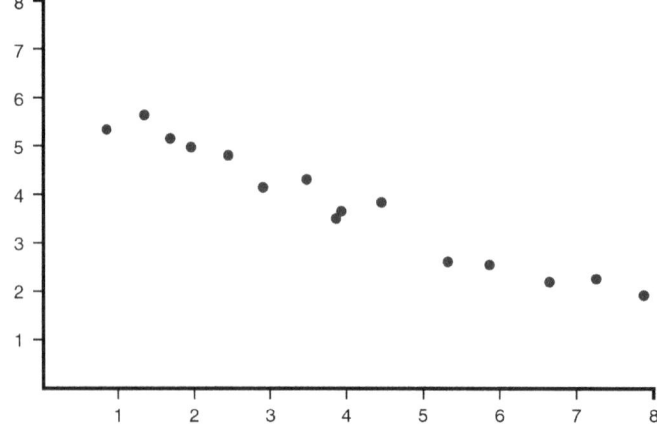

a. Positive linear
b. Negative linear
c. Exponential
d. Logarithmic

Understanding Variability

In an experiment, variables are the key to analyzing data, especially when data is in a graph or table. Variables can represent anything, including objects, conditions, events, and amounts of time.

Measurement and Data
Explaining the Relationship Between Two Variables

Covariance is a general term referring to how two variables move in relation to each other.

For example, take an employee that gets paid by the hour. For them, hours worked and total pay have a positive covariance. As hours worked increases, so does pay.

Constant variables remain unchanged by the scientist across all trials. Because they are held constant for all groups in an experiment, they aren't being measured in the experiment, and they are usually ignored. Constants can either be controlled by the scientist directly like the nutrition, water, and sunlight given to plants, or they can be selected by the scientist specifically for an experiment like using a certain animal species or choosing to investigate only people of a certain age group.

Practice Questions

1. Given the following scatter plot, which of the following is true?

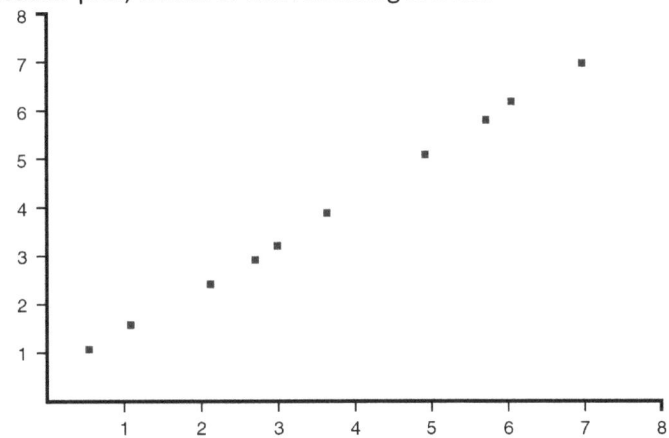

a. There is a large positive covariance between the variables.
b. There is a small positive covariance between the variables.
c. There is a large negative covariance between the variables.
d. There is near zero covariance between the variables.

2. Given the following scatter plot, which of the following is true?

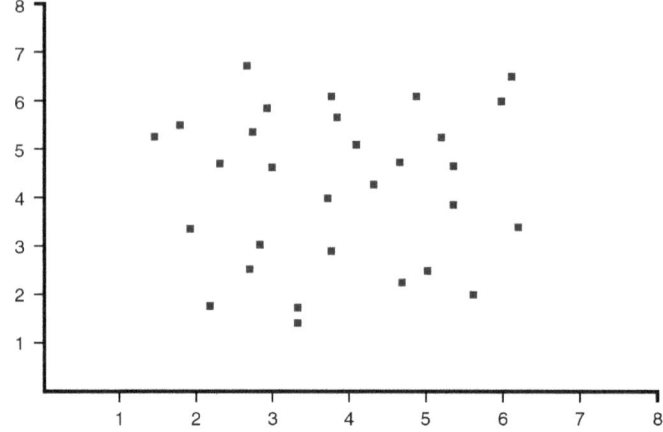

a. There is a large positive covariance between the variables.
b. There is a small positive covariance between the variables.
c. There is a large negative covariance between the variables.
d. There is near zero covariance between the variables.

Answer Explanations

Identifying Independent and Dependent Quantities

1. A: This vector indicates a positive relationship. A negative relationship would show points traveling from the top-left of the graph to the bottom-right. Exponential and logarithmic functions aren't linear (don't create a straight line), so these options could have been immediately eliminated.

2. C: There is no verifiable relationship between the two variables. While it may seem to have somewhat of a positive correlation because of the last two data points: (5.6, 8) and (6, 7), you must also take into account the two data points before those (5, 1) and (5.2, 2) that have low Y values despite high X values. Data with a normal distribution (Choice A) has an arc to it. This data does not.

3. B: A line can be drawn through the points graphed on the plot. The line would decrease from left to right, showing a negative linear relationship between the variables. Therefore, Choice B is the correct answer. If the line increased from left to right instead, a positive linear relationship would exist.

Understanding Variability

1. A: Covariance measures how two variables vary together. In this example, as the variable increases along the horizontal axis, so does the variable along the vertical axis. If a line were to be drawn connecting the points, it would be straight. Therefore, there is a large positive covariance between the variables, making Choice A the correct answer.

2. D: Covariance measures how two variables vary together. In this example, there is no relationship between the variable along the horizontal axis and the variable along the vertical axis. As one changes, the other one does not change in a similar manner. Therefore, there is near zero covariance between the variables, which means Choice D is correct.

Evaluating Information Using Statistics

Describing the Center, Spread, and the Shape of Data

A set of data can be described in terms of its center, spread, shape and any unusual features. The center of a data set can be measured by its mean, median, or mode. The spread of a data set refers to how far the data points are from the center (mean or median). A data set with data points clustered around the center will have a small spread. A data set covering a wide range will have a large spread.

When a data set is displayed as a graph like the one below, the shape indicates if a sample is normally distributed, symmetrical, or has measures of skewness. When graphed, a data set with a normal distribution will resemble a bell curve.

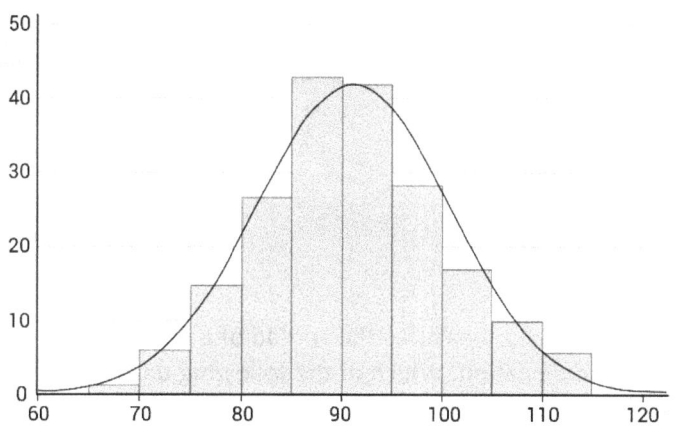

If the data set is symmetrical, each half of the graph when divided at the center is a mirror image of the other. If the graph has fewer data points to the right, the data is skewed right. If it has fewer data points to the left, the data is skewed left.

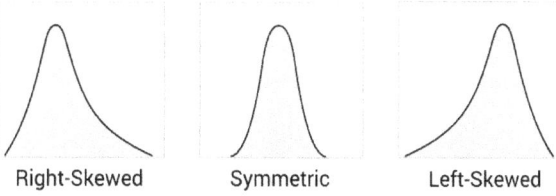

A description of a data set should include any unusual features such as gaps or outliers. A gap is a span within the range of the data set containing no data points. An outlier is a data point with a value either extremely large or extremely small when compared to the other values in the set.

The graphs above can be referred to as **unimodal** since they all have a single peak. This is in contrast to **bimodal** graphs that have multiple peaks.

Practice Questions

1. What is the mean of the following data shown in the distribution?

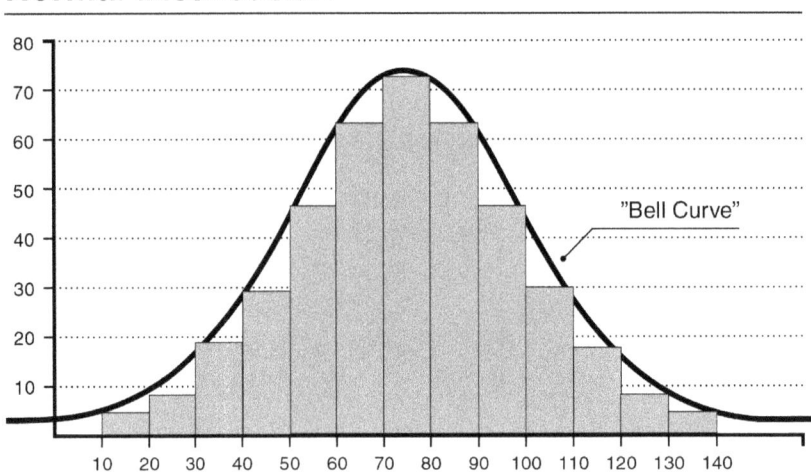

a. 60
b. 72
c. 80
d. 140

2. The standard deviation of a data set measures the spread of a data set. The more spread apart the data set, the larger the standard deviation. Which of the following data sets has the largest standard deviation?

a. 80, 80, 80, 80, 80, 80
b. 76, 77, 78, 79, 80, 81
c. 75, 76, 76, 77, 78, 79
d. 100, 90, 80, 70, 60, 50

Finding Measures of Center

The center of a set of data (statistical values) can be represented by its mean, median, or mode. These are sometimes referred to as measures of central tendency.

Mean

The first property that can be defined for this set of data is the **mean**. This is the same as average. To find the mean, add up all the data points, then divide by the total number of data points.

Example

Suppose that in a class of 10 students, the scores on a test were 50, 60, 65, 65, 75, 80, 85, 85, 90, 100. Therefore, the average test score will be:

$$\frac{50 + 60 + 65 + 65 + 75 + 80 + 85 + 85 + 90 + 100}{10} = 75.5$$

Measurement and Data
Evaluating Information Using Statistics

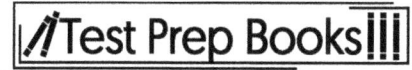

The mean is a useful number if the distribution of data is normal (more on this later), which roughly means that the frequency of different outcomes has a single peak and is roughly equally distributed on both sides of that peak. However, it is less useful in some cases where the data might be split or where there are some **outliers**. Outliers are data points that are far from the rest of the data.

Example

Suppose there are 10 executives and 90 employees at a company. The executives make $1000 per hour, and the employees make $10 per hour.

Therefore, the average pay rate will be:

$$\frac{\$1000 \cdot 11 + \$10 \cdot 90}{100} = \$119 \; per \; hour$$

In this case, this average is not very descriptive since it's not close to the actual pay of the executives *or* the employees.

Median

Another useful measurement is the **median**. In a data set, the median is the point in the middle. The middle refers to the point where half the data comes before it and half comes after, when the data is recorded in numerical order.

Example

For instance, these are the speeds of the fastball of a pitcher during the last inning that he pitched (in order from least to greatest):

$$90, 92, 93, 93, 95, 96, 97, 97, 97$$

There are nine total numbers, so the middle or **median** number is the 5th one, which is 95.

In cases where the number of data points is an even number, then the average of the two middle points is taken. In the previous example of test scores, the two middle points are 75 and 80. Since there is no single point, the average of these two scores needs to be found. The average is:

$$\frac{75 + 80}{2} = 77.5$$

The median is generally a good value to use if there are a few outliers in the data. It prevents those outliers from affecting the "middle" value as much as when using the mean.

Since an outlier is a data point that is far from most of the other data points in a data set, this means an outlier also is any point that is far from the median of the data set. The outliers can have a substantial effect on the mean of a data set, but they usually do not change the median or mode, or do not change them by a large quantity.

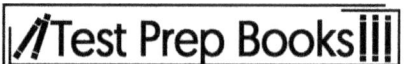

**Measurement and Data
Evaluating Information Using Statistics**

Example

Consider the data set (3, 5, 6, 6, 6, 8). This has a median of 6 and a mode of 6, with a mean of $\frac{34}{6} \approx 5.67$. Now, suppose a new data point of 1000 is added so that the data set is now (3, 5, 6, 6, 6, 8, 1000). The median and mode, which are both still 6, remain unchanged. However, the average is now $\frac{1034}{7}$, which is approximately 147.7.

In this case, the median and mode will be better descriptions for most of the data points.

The reason for outliers in a given data set is a complicated problem. It is sometimes the result of an error by the experimenter, but often they are perfectly valid data points that must be taken into consideration.

Mode

One additional measure to define for X is the **mode**. This is the data point that appears most frequently. If two or more data points all tie for the most frequent appearance, then each of them is considered a mode.

Example

In the case of the test scores, where the numbers were 50, 60, 65, 65, 75, 80, 85, 85, 90, 100, there are two modes: 65 and 85.

Practice Questions

1. The table below shows tickets purchased during the week for entry to the local zoo. What is the mean of adult tickets sold for the week?

Day of the Week	Age	Tickets Sold
Monday	Adult	22
Monday	Child	30
Tuesday	Adult	16
Tuesday	Child	15
Wednesday	Adult	24
Wednesday	Child	23
Thursday	Adult	19
Thursday	Child	26
Friday	Adult	29
Friday	Child	38

a. 24.2
b. 21
c. 22
d. 26.4

Measurement and Data
Evaluating Information Using Statistics

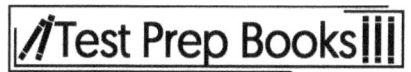

2. A data set is comprised of the following values: 30, 33, 33, 26, 27, 32, 33, 35, 29, 27. Which of the following has the greatest value?
   a. Mean
   b. Median
   c. Mode
   d. Range

3. The first five of six numbers have a sum of 25. The average of all six numbers is 6. What is the sixth number?
   a. 8
   b. 10
   c. 11
   d. 12

4. Five students take a test. The scores of the first four students are 80, 85, 75, and 60. If the median score is 80, which of the following could NOT be the score of the fifth student?
   a. 60
   b. 80
   c. 85
   d. 100

5. Dwayne has received the following scores on his math tests: 78, 92, 83, 97. What is the overall median of Dwayne's current scores?
   a. 89
   b. 98
   c. 95.5
   d. 87.5

6. For a group of 20 men, the median weight is 180 pounds and the range is 30 pounds. If each man gains 10 pounds, which of the following would be true?
   a. The median weight will increase, and the range will remain the same.
   b. The median weight and range will both remain the same.
   c. The median weight will stay the same, and the range will increase.
   d. The median weight and range will both increase.

Answer Explanations

Describing the Center, Spread, and the Shape of Data

1. B: In a normal bell-curve distribution, 50% of the data lies below the mean, and 50% of the data lies above the mean. The middle of the data lies in the 70-80 bucket, which has a height around 72, as shown on the vertical axis. This is the mean, so Choice *B* is correct.

2. D: All the data sets have a similar mean (somewhere around 70 or 80), but only Choice *D* contains data points further from the mean, so that is the correct answer. For instance, 100 and 50 are two data points in that set that are extremely far from the mean. Therefore, this data set has the largest standard deviation. Choice *A* has a standard deviation of 0, since all of the data values are the same.

215

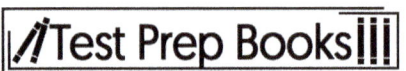

Finding Measures of Center

1. C: To find the mean, or average, of a set of values, add the values together and then divide by the total number of values. Each day of the week has an adult ticket amount sold that must be added together. The equation is as follows:

$$\frac{22 + 16 + 24 + 19 + 29}{5} = 22$$

2. C: Each value can be calculated so that they can be compared to find which one is the greatest. The mean is equal to:

$$\frac{26 + 27 + 27 + 29 + 30 + 32 + 33 + 33 + 33 + 35}{10} = 30.5$$

The median is equal to:

$$\frac{30 + 32}{2} = 31$$

The mode is equal to 33 because that number occurs 3 times in the data set. The range is equal to:

$$35 - 26 = 9$$

Therefore, the mode is the greatest value of the answer choices.

3. C: The average is calculated by adding all six numbers, then dividing by 6. The first five numbers have a sum of 25. If the total divided by 6 is equal to 6, then the total itself must be 36. The sixth number must be $36 - 25 = 11$.

4. A: Lining up the given scores provides the following list: 60, 75, 80, 85, and one unknown. Because the median needs to be 80, it means 80 must be the middle data point out of these five. Therefore, the unknown data point must be the fourth or fifth data point, meaning it must be greater than or equal to 80. The only answer that fails to meet this condition is 60.

5. D: For an even number of total values, the *median* is calculated by finding the *mean* or average of the two middle values once all values have been arranged in ascending order from least to greatest. In this case, $(92 + 83) \div 2$ would equal the median of 87.5, Choice *D*.

6. A: If each man gains 10 pounds, every original data point will increase by 10 pounds. Therefore, the man with the original median will still have the median value, but that value will increase by 10. The smallest value and largest value will also increase by 10 and, therefore, the difference between the two won't change. The range does not change in value and, thus, remains the same.

Converting Between Standard and Metric Systems

Identifying Relative Sizes of Measurement Units

Measurement is how an object's length, width, height, weight, and so on, are quantified. Measurement is related to counting, but it is a more refined process.

Measurement and Data
Converting Between Standard and Metric Systems

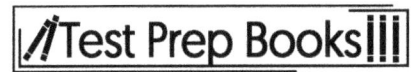

Weight units can vary, based on whether the substance being measured is a liquid or a solid. Standard units of weight to measure liquids include *ounces*, *pints*, *quarts*, and *gallons*. Occasionally, solids can also be measured using pints and quarts. For example, both milk and berries can be measured in pints. Other units of weight are *pounds* and *tons*.

Some units of measure are represented as square or cubic units depending on the solution. For example, perimeter is measured in units, area is measured in square units, and volume is measured in cubic units.

Also be sure to use the most appropriate unit for the thing being measured. A building's height might be measured in feet or meters while the length of a nail might be measured in inches or centimeters. Additionally, for SI units, the prefix should be chosen to provide the most succinct available value. For example, the mass of a bag of fruit would likely be measured in kilograms rather than grams or milligrams, and the length of a bacteria cell would likely be measured in micrometers rather than centimeters or kilometers.

The proper instruments for measurements depend upon the units being measured. The following instruments are used for measuring the listed values, along with the specific units they measure:

- Volume: Measuring cup (fluid ounces, cups), graduated cylinder (cubic centimeters, milliliters), beaker (milliliters)

- Weight: Scale (pounds, Newtons)

Examples

Example 1: With what instrument would Mart measure a cup of sugar he wants to combine with other ingredients to make a pie?

The correct answer is a measuring cup.

If Mart needed to measure large quantities of liquid, he could use a quart, pint, or gallon measuring container. The conversions between cups and quarts is four cups per one quart, and between quarts and gallons, it's four quarts per one gallon.

If Mart needed 2 quarts of liquid for a recipe and only has a measuring cup, how could he measure out 2 quarts? The solution would involve Mart measuring out 2 quarts by filling the cup 8 times.

Practice Questions

1. Which of the following are units that would be taught in a lecture covering the metric system?
   a. Inches, feet, miles, pounds
   b. Millimeters, centimeters, meters, pounds
   c. Kilograms, grams, kilometers, meters
   d. Teaspoons, tablespoons, ounces

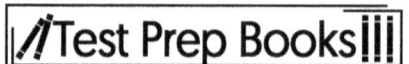

2. Which of the following is the appropriate tool for measuring the amount of water in a bathtub full enough to cover an adult?
    a. Measuring cup
    b. Tablespoon
    c. Liter container
    d. Gallon container

3. Which of the following would be the best unit suited to measure the height of a school building?
    a. Centimeters
    b. Millimeters
    c. Meters
    d. Kilometers

4. Which of the following would be the best unit suited to measure the amount of liquid in a juice glass?
    a. Gallons
    b. Ounces
    c. Liters
    d. Quarts

Solving Measurement Problems Using the Operations

American Measuring System

The measuring system used today in the United States developed from the British units of measurement during colonial times. The most typically used units in this customary system are those used to measure weight, liquid volume, and length, whose common units are found below. In the customary system, the basic unit for measuring weight is the ounce (oz); there are 16 ounces (oz) in 1 pound (lb) and 2000 pounds in 1 ton. The basic unit for measuring liquid volume is the ounce (oz); 1 ounce is equal to 2 tablespoons (tbsp) or 6 teaspoons (tsp), and there are 8 ounces in 1 cup, 2 cups in 1 pint (pt), 2 pints in 1 quart (qt), and 4 quarts in 1 gallon (gal). For measurements of length, the inch (in) is the base unit; 12 inches make up 1 foot (ft), 3 feet make up 1 yard (yd), and 5280 feet make up 1 mile (mi).

However, as there are only a set number of units in the customary system, with extremely large or extremely small amounts of material, the numbers can become awkward and difficult to compare. Here is a conversion chart for common customary measurements:

Common Customary Measurements		
Length	Weight	Capacity
1 foot = 12 inches	1 pound = 16 ounces	1 cup = 8 fluid ounces
1 yard = 3 feet	1 ton = 2,000 pounds	1 pint = 2 cups
1 yard = 36 inches		1 quart = 2 pints
1 mile = 1,760 yards		1 quart = 4 cups
1 mile = 5,280 feet		1 gallon = 4 quarts
		1 gallon = 16 cups

Measurement and Data
Converting Between Standard and Metric Systems

Metric System

Aside from the United States, most countries in the world have adopted the metric system embodied in the International System of Units (SI). The three main SI base units used in the metric system are the meter (m), the kilogram (kg), and the liter (L); meters measure length, kilograms measure mass, and liters measure volume.

These three units can use different prefixes, which indicate larger or smaller versions of the unit by powers of ten. This can be thought of as making a new unit which is sized by multiplying the original unit in size by a factor.

These prefixes and associated factors are:

Metric Prefixes			
Prefix	Symbol	Multiplier	Exponential
kilo	k	1,000	10^3
hecto	h	100	10^2
deca	da	10	10^1
no prefix		1	10^0
deci	d	0.1	10^{-1}
centi	c	0.01	10^{-2}
milli	m	0.001	10^{-3}

The correct prefix is then attached to the base. Some examples:

1 milliliter equals .001 liters.
1 kilogram equals 1,000 grams.

Examples

Example 1: Jana wants to travel to visit Alice, who lives one hundred and fifty miles away. If she can drive at fifty miles per hour, how long will her trip take?

The quantity to find is the *time* of the trip. The time of a trip is given by the distance to travel divided by the speed to be traveled. The problem determines that the distance is one hundred and fifty miles, while the speed is fifty miles per hour. Thus, 150 divided by 50 is $150 \div 50 = 3$. Because *miles* and *miles per hour* are the units being divided, the miles cancel out. The result is 3 hours.

Example 2: Bernard wishes to paint a wall that measures twenty feet wide by eight feet high. It costs ten cents to paint one square foot. How much money will Bernard need for paint?

The final quantity to compute is the *cost* to paint the wall. This will be ten cents ($0.10) for each square foot of area needed to paint. The area to be painted is unknown, but the dimensions of the wall are given; thus, it can be calculated.

The dimensions of the wall are 20 feet wide and 8 feet high. Since the area of a rectangle is length multiplied by width, the area of the wall is $8 \times 20 = 160$ square feet. Multiplying 0.1×160 yields $16 as the cost of the paint.

Practice Questions

1. If a car can travel 300 miles in 4 hours, how far can it go in an hour and a half?
    a. 100 miles
    b. 112.5 miles
    c. 135.5 miles
    d. 150 miles

2. A train traveling 50 miles per hour takes a trip lasting 3 hours. If a map has a scale of 1 inch per 10 miles, how many inches apart are the train's starting point and ending point on the map?
    a. 14
    b. 12
    c. 13
    d. 15

3. A solution needs 5 ml of saline for every 8 ml of medicine given. How much saline is needed for 45 ml of medicine?
    a. $\frac{225}{8}$ ml
    b. 72 ml
    c. 28 ml
    d. $\frac{45}{8}$ ml

4. A piggy bank contains 12 dollars' worth of nickels. A nickel weighs 5 grams, and the empty piggy bank weighs 1,050 grams. What is the total weight of the full piggy bank?
    a. 1,110 grams
    b. 1,200 grams
    c. 2,250 grams
    d. 2,200 grams

5. The Cross family is planning a trip to Florida. They will be taking two cars for the trip. One car gets 18 miles to the gallon of gas. The other car gets 25 miles to the gallon. If the total trip to Florida is 450 miles, and the cost of gas is $2.49/gallon, how much will the gas cost for both cars to complete the trip?
    a. $43.00
    b. $44.82
    c. $107.07
    d. $32.33

Converting Measurements

Converting measurements in different units between the two systems can be difficult because they follow different rules. The best method is to look up an English to Metric system conversion factor and then use a series of equivalent fractions to set up an equation to convert the units of one of the measurements into those of the other.

Measurement and Data
Converting Between Standard and Metric Systems

The table below lists some common conversion values that are useful for problems involving measurements with units in both systems:

English System	Metric System
1 inch	2.54 cm
1 foot	0.3048 m
1 yard	0.914 m
1 mile	1.609 km
1 ounce	28.35 g
1 pound	0.454 kg
1 fluid ounce	29.574 mL
1 quart	0.946 L
1 gallon	3.785 L

Example

A scientist wants to convert 6.8 inches to centimeters. The table above is used to find that there are 2.54 centimeters in every inch, so the following equation should be set up and solved:

$$\frac{6.8 \text{ in}}{1} \times \frac{2.54 \text{ cm}}{1 \text{ in}} = 17.272 \text{ cm}$$

Notice how the inches in the numerator of the initial figure and the denominator of the conversion factor cancel out. (This equation could have been written simply as $6.8 \text{ in} \times 2.54 \text{ cm} = 17.272 \text{ cm}$, but it was shown in detail to illustrate the steps).

The goal in any conversion equation is to set up the fractions so that the units you are trying to convert from cancel out and the units you desire remain.

Examples

Example 1: Convert 2.15 kilograms into ounces.

The first step is to convert kilograms into grams and then grams into ounces. Note that the measurement you begin with does not have to be put in a fraction.

So, in this case, 2.15 kg is by itself although it's technically the numerator of a fraction:

$$2.15 \text{ kg} \times \frac{1{,}000 \text{ g}}{\text{kg}} = 2{,}150 \text{ g}$$

Then, use the conversion factor from the table to convert grams to ounces:

$$2{,}150 \text{ g} \times \frac{1 \text{ oz}}{28.35 \text{ g}} = 75.8 \text{ oz}$$

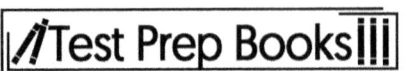

> Example 2: Convert 9 ft³ to yd³.
>
> Because 3 ft is equal to 1 yd, $3^3 = 27$ cubic feet is equal to 1 cubic yard. Therefore, divide 9 by 27 to obtain $\frac{1}{3}$ yd³. In other words,
>
> $$\frac{9 \text{ ft}^3}{1} \times \frac{1 \text{ yd}^3}{27 \text{ ft}^3} = \frac{1}{3} \text{ yd}^3$$
>
> So, 9 ft³ converts to $\frac{1}{3}$ yd³.

Practice Questions

1. Mom's car drove 72 miles in 90 minutes. How fast did she drive in feet per second?

   a. 0.8 feet per second
   b. 48.9 feet per second
   c. 0.009 feet per second
   d. 70.4 feet per second

2. Which of the following is an equivalent measurement for 1.3 cm?
   a. 0.13 m
   b. 13 m
   c. 0.13 mm
   d. 0.013 m

3. Alan currently weighs 200 pounds, but he wants to lose weight to get down to 175 pounds. What is this difference in kilograms? (1 pound is approximately equal to 0.45 kilograms.)
   a. 9.00 kg
   b. 11.25 kg
   c. 78.75 kg
   d. 18.55 kg

4. A grocery store is selling individual bottles of water, and each bottle contains 750 milliliters of water. If 12 bottles are purchased, what conversion will correctly determine how many liters that customer will take home?
   a. 100 milliliters equals 1 liter
   b. 1,000 milliliters equals 1 liter
   c. 1,000 liters equals 1 milliliter
   d. 10 liters equals 1 milliliter

5. How many kilometers is 4,382 feet if 1 foot is equal to 0.3048 meters

**Measurement and Data
Converting Between Standard and Metric Systems**

?
   a. 1.336 kilometers
   b. 14,376 kilometers
   c. 1.437 kilometers
   d. 13,336 kilometers

Answer Explanations

Identifying Relative Sizes of Measurement Units

1. C: Kilograms, grams, kilometers, and meters are all metric units and part of the metric system. Inches, pounds, and baking measurements, such as tablespoons, are not part of the metric system.

2. D: The gallon container would measure the largest capacity of water and therefore be the correct choice. Choices A and B would take a long time to measure the amount of water contained in a bathtub, and Choice C, while slightly faster, is still an impractical selection.

3. C: Centimeters or millimeters could be used to measure a height of a building, but they are not the best choice since they are very small units of measurement. A kilometer is too large of a length to be used, so the best option is a meter, Choice C. A one-story building is typically around four meters high.

4. B: Gallons, liters, and quarts are all too large to determine the amount of liquid in a small juice glass. Consider how big a gallon of milk, a quart of ice cream, and a liter of soda are. Therefore, the best option is to measure in ounces, making Choice B the correct answer. A serving of juice is around six ounces.

Solving Measurement Problems Using the Operations

1. B: 300 miles in 4 hours is $\frac{300}{4} = 75$ miles per hour. In 1.5 hours, the car will go 1.5×75 miles, or 112.5 miles.

2. D: First, the train's journey in the real world is $3 \times 50 = 150$ miles. On the map, 1 inch corresponds to 10 miles, so there are $\frac{150}{10} = 15$ inches on the map between the train's starting point and ending point.

3. A: Every 8 ml of medicine requires 5 ml. The 45 ml first needs to be split into portions of 8 ml. This results in $\frac{45}{8}$ portions. Each portion requires 5 ml. Therefore:

$$\frac{45}{8} \times 5 = 45 \times \frac{5}{8} = \frac{225}{8} \text{ ml}$$

4. C: A dollar contains 20 nickels. Therefore, if there are 12 dollars' worth of nickels, there are $12 \times 20 = 240$ nickels. Each nickel weighs 5 grams. Therefore, the weight of the nickels is $240 \times 5 = 1,200$ grams. Adding in the weight of the empty piggy bank, the filled bank weighs 2,250 grams.

5. C: For the first car, the trip will be 450 miles at 18 miles to the gallon. The total gallons needed for this car will be:

$$450 \div 18 = 25 \text{ gallons}$$

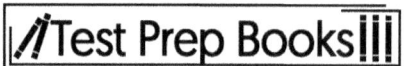

For the second car, the trip will be 450 miles at 25 miles to the gallon, or $450 \div 25 = 18$, which will require 18 gallons of gas. Adding these two amounts of gas gives a total of 43 gallons of gas. If the gas costs $2.49 per gallon, the cost of the trip for both cars is:

$$43 \times \$2.49 = \$107.07$$

Converting Measurements

1. D: This problem can be solved by using unit conversions. The initial units are miles per minute. The final units need to be feet per second. Converting miles to feet uses the equivalence statement 1 mile = 5,280 feet. Converting minutes to seconds uses the equivalence statement 1 minute = 60 seconds. Setting up the ratios to convert the units is shown in the following equation:

$$\frac{72 \text{ miles}}{90 \text{ minutes}} \times \frac{1 \text{ minute}}{60 \text{ seconds}} \times \frac{5{,}280 \text{ feet}}{1 \text{ mile}} = 70.4 \text{ feet per second}$$

The initial units cancel out, and the new, desired units are left.

2. D: 100 cm is equal to 1 m. 1.3 divided by 100 is 0.013. Therefore, 1.3 cm is equal to 0.013 m. Because 1 cm is equal to 10 mm, 1.3 cm is equal to 13 mm.

3. B: Using the conversion rate, multiply the projected weight loss of 25 lb by $0.45 \frac{\text{kg}}{\text{lb}}$ to get the amount in kilograms (11.25 kg).

4. B: $12 \times 750 = 9{,}000$. Therefore, there are 9,000 milliliters of water, which must be converted to liters. 1,000 milliliters equals 1 liter; therefore, 9 liters of water are purchased.

5. A: The conversion can be obtained by setting up and solving the following equation:

$$4{,}382 \text{ ft} \times \frac{0.3048 \text{ m}}{1 \text{ ft}} \times \frac{1 \text{ km}}{1{,}000 \text{ m}} = 1.336 \text{ km}$$

Index

Acute Triangle, 161
Adjacent Angles, 153
Algebraic Expressions, 121, 123
Angle, 153, 154, 155, 156, 157, 158, 160, 161, 162, 164, 167, 168, 181, 182, 183, 205
Arc of a Circle, 167, 168
Area, 33, 34, 38, 45, 71, 72, 78, 93, 169, 170, 171, 172, 173, 174, 175, 176, 177, 178, 179, 180, 181, 183, 184, 185, 217, 219
Area Model, 33, 34, 71, 72, 78
Bar Graph, 190, 191, 192, 196
Base, 17, 24, 25, 26, 51, 114, 115, 132, 163, 164, 165, 171, 172, 174, 178, 179, 181, 182, 218, 219
Base-10, 17, 25, 26, 51
Bimodal, 211
Cartesian Coordinate Plane, 138, 140
Chart, 21, 138, 192, 193, 195, 198, 205, 218
Concave, 159
Cone, 119, 162, 164, 165, 179, 182
Constant Function, 126
Constant Variables, 209
Conversion Factor, 144, 220, 221
Convex, 159
Coplanar, 153
Covariance, 209, 210
Cube, 117, 131, 165, 177, 181, 182, 185
Cube Root, 117
Cubic, 123, 180, 181, 185, 217, 222
Cylinder, 164, 179, 180, 182, 185, 217
Decimal Number, 19, 52, 53
Decimal Place, 19, 54, 55, 56, 58, 59, 80, 90, 105, 172, 173
Decimal Point, 18, 19, 23, 24, 25, 26, 28, 51, 52, 53, 54, 55, 56, 57, 58, 59, 62, 63, 90, 92, 105, 107
Decimals, 13, 14, 17, 19, 26, 51, 53, 54, 55, 56, 57, 58, 59, 62, 66, 90, 92, 104, 105, 107
Decimals and Percentages, 62
Definitions, 13
Degrees, 126, 153, 154, 155, 157, 158, 167, 169, 181, 182, 183, 200, 205

Denominator, 13, 29, 31, 35, 39, 41, 42, 44, 46, 47, 48, 49, 51, 55, 56, 57, 59, 62, 63, 65, 66, 74, 79, 81, 107, 144, 221
Depend, 187, 217
Dependent Variable, 126, 132, 187, 190, 194, 206, 207, 208
  Dependent Variables, 190, 206, 208
Distance, 14, 24, 27, 98, 106, 107, 141, 143, 149, 164, 167, 168, 169, 171, 195, 219
Domain, 125, 126, 129, 130
Endpoints, 153
Equiangular, 160
Equilateral Triangle, 161, 173, 184
Equivalent Fractions, 38, 41, 42, 49, 220
Estimation, 88, 89, 90, 91, 92
Even Function, 127
Even Numbers, 13
Exponent, 24, 25, 28, 108, 112, 114, 115, 116, 123, 134
Fraction, 13, 19, 28, 29, 30, 31, 32, 33, 34, 36, 37, 38, 39, 40, 41, 42, 43, 44, 45, 46, 47, 48, 49, 50, 51, 52, 53, 57, 62, 63, 64, 65, 66, 74, 80, 81, 82, 87, 88, 97, 98, 113, 115, 131, 144, 221
Fractions and Decimals, 63
Fractions and Percentages, 62
Full Rotation, 153
Function, 120, 125, 126, 127, 128, 129, 130, 134, 148
Greatest Common Factor (GCF), 15
Horizontal, 118, 126, 129, 149, 189, 207, 208, 210
Identity Function, 126
Improper Fractions, 31, 47, 49
Independent Variable, 126, 132, 187, 190, 194, 206, 207
  Independent Variables, 206
Integers, 13, 14, 15, 17, 23, 57, 125
Intercept Form, 118
Intersecting Lines, 153
Inverse Operations, 67, 74, 94, 95, 96, 120, 133
Isosceles Triangle, 161
Least Common Denominator, 41, 107
Least Common Multiple (LCM), 15, 16, 17, 41

Like Fractions, 38
Like Terms, 120, 123, 124, 133, 134, 183
Line, 19, 20, 23, 26, 27, 38, 51, 54, 58, 75, 76, 77, 85, 86, 104, 118, 121, 126, 134, 148, 149, 150, 151, 152, 153, 154, 156, 157, 172, 175, 190, 191, 192, 194, 195, 196, 197, 198, 204, 207, 210
Line Graph, 190, 191, 194, 195, 204
Line Plot, 191, 192, 196, 197, 198, 204
Line Segment, 153
Linear, 93, 117, 118, 119, 120, 121, 122, 123, 132, 133, 145, 148, 149, 208, 210
Mean, 92, 141, 144, 186, 203, 211, 212, 213, 214, 215, 216
Median, 211, 212, 213, 214, 215, 216
Mixed Numbers, 19, 31, 43, 47
Mode, 204, 205, 211, 212, 213, 214, 215, 216
Monotone, 126
Multiplicative Identity, 71
Negative, 13, 14, 17, 24, 28, 58, 82, 83, 88, 115, 116, 118, 122, 123, 133, 134, 139, 140, 143, 154, 207, 208, 209, 210
Number Line, 14, 19, 20, 23, 24, 26, 27, 35, 38, 40, 41, 48, 104, 105, 121, 122, 133, 140, 192, 196, 198
Numerator, 29, 31, 36, 39, 43, 44, 46, 47, 48, 49, 51, 57, 62, 63, 65, 66, 74, 79, 81, 92, 107, 221
Obtuse Triangle, 161
Odd Function, 127
Odd Numbers, 13
Origin, 138, 140, 141, 143, 151, 152
Outliers, 211, 213, 214
Parallel, 153, 154, 155, 156, 161, 163, 164, 181, 182
Parallelogram, 161, 162, 182
Perimeter, 169, 170, 171, 172, 173, 174, 175, 183, 184, 217
Perpendicular Lines, 153, 154, 181
Picture Graph, 192
Place Value, 17, 18, 19, 21, 23, 26, 27, 51, 58, 59, 71, 85, 87, 89, 90, 92, 104, 106
Place Value System, 23
Plus/Minus, 116
Point-Slope Form, 118, 154
Polygon, 159, 160, 162, 164, 169, 173, 174, 175, 182, 184
Positive, 13, 14, 15, 17, 24, 27, 28, 29, 58, 82, 83, 88, 116, 118, 122, 124, 131, 134, 139, 140, 143, 207, 208, 209, 210
Power Rule, 115
Prime Numbers, 13, 15, 16, 17
Product, 15, 24, 31, 41, 55, 71, 80, 83, 89, 92, 95, 96, 113, 114, 115, 123, 130, 153, 171, 178
Product Rule, 115
Proper Fractions, 31
Quadrants, 139
Quadratic, 123
Quotient Rule, 115
Radians, 153, 168, 183
Range, 125, 126, 186, 198, 199, 205, 211, 215, 216
Rate of Change, 148, 202
Rational Numbers, 13, 14, 105, 106, 113
Ratios, 61, 135, 143, 144, 151, 165, 224
Ray, 153, 156, 182
Real Numbers, 13, 14, 105, 130
Rectangle, 71, 72, 161, 162, 166, 170, 171, 172, 173, 175, 177, 178, 179, 180, 182, 183, 184, 185, 219
Rectangular Prism, 165, 177, 181, 182, 185
Rectangular Pyramid, 178
Regular Polygon, 160
Relationship, 60, 66, 74, 84, 85, 99, 101, 102, 103, 104, 119, 122, 125, 128, 132, 133, 135, 144, 145, 149, 194, 206, 207, 208, 210
Repeating, 13, 19, 57, 99, 113
Rhombus, 161, 162, 182
Right Angle, 153, 154, 157, 162, 165, 179, 181, 182
Right Triangle, 160, 165, 167, 174, 182
Rotation, 153
Round, 20, 26, 89, 90, 92
Scale Factor, 135, 144, 145
Scalene Triangle, 161
Scientific Notation, 24, 25, 28
Significand, 24
Slice, 30, 193
Slope-Intercept Form, 118, 148, 152
Sphere, 164, 178, 181, 185
Square, 105, 108, 116, 117, 131, 157, 161, 162, 165, 170, 171, 172, 173, 175, 177, 180, 181, 182, 183, 184, 185, 217, 219
Square Root, 105, 116, 117, 131, 183

Index

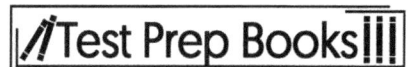

Standard Form, 21, 25, 118, 181
Surface Area, 169, 177, 178, 179, 180, 181, 185
System, 17, 23, 25, 26, 51, 91, 154, 217, 218, 219, 220, 221, 223
Tally Chart, 192
Term, 24, 100, 103, 123, 192, 209
Terminating, 19
Trapezoid, 161, 182
Two-Point Form, 118
Unimodal, 211
Unit Fraction, 29, 31, 36, 41, 43
Unit Rates, 144, 151
Unlike Fractions, 38
Variable, 93, 102, 107, 109, 110, 113, 117, 119, 120, 121, 122, 123, 124, 126, 130, 133, 134, 136, 138, 143, 187, 190, 194, 195, 204, 206, 207, 208, 210
Vertex, 140, 141, 153, 156, 157, 164, 178, 179
Vertical, 53, 118, 126, 128, 129, 134, 149, 190, 207, 208, 210, 215
Vertical Line Test, 126, 134
Volume, 177, 178, 179, 180, 181, 185, 217, 218, 219
Whole Numbers, 13, 14, 17, 31, 43, 44, 50, 56, 59, 71, 74, 103, 104, 105, 130
x-Axis, 118, 140, 142, 143, 144
x-Intercept, 118
y-Axis, 118, 127, 140, 141, 143, 190
y-Intercept, 118, 126
Zero Power Rule, 114
Zeros, 18, 19, 22, 25, 28, 53, 56, 76, 90, 92, 126

Dear ATI TEAS Test Taker,

We would like to start by thanking you for purchasing this practice test book for your ATI TEAS exam. We hope that we exceeded your expectations.

We strive to make our practice questions as similar as possible to what you will encounter on test day. With that being said, if you found something that you feel was not up to your standards, please send us an email and let us know.

We would also like to let you know about other books in our catalog that may interest you.

HESI

This can be found on Amazon: amazon.com/dp/1637756372

CEN

amazon.com/dp/1637752229

ATI TEAS 7

amazon.com/dp/1637759886

We have study guides in a wide variety of fields. If the one you are looking for isn't listed above, then try searching for it on Amazon or send us an email.

Thanks Again and Happy Testing!
Product Development Team
info@studyguideteam.com

FREE Test Taking Tips Video/DVD Offer

To better serve you, we created videos covering test taking tips that we want to give you for FREE. **These videos cover world-class tips that will help you succeed on your test.**

We just ask that you send us feedback about this product. Please let us know what you thought about it—whether good, bad, or indifferent.

To get your **FREE videos**, you can use the QR code below or email freevideos@studyguideteam.com with "Free Videos" in the subject line and the following information in the body of the email:

a. The title of your product

b. Your product rating on a scale of 1-5, with 5 being the highest

c. Your feedback about the product

If you have any questions or concerns, please don't hesitate to contact us at info@studyguideteam.com.

Thank you!

www.ingramcontent.com/pod-product-compliance
Lightning Source LLC
Chambersburg PA
CBHW062128160426
43191CB00013B/2226